D0360290

TRANS-SIBERIAN
RAIL GUIDE

Trans-Siberian RAIL GUIDE

ROBERT STRAUSS

BRADT PUBLICATIONS, UK
HUNTER PUBLISHING, USA

First published in 1987 by Bradt Publications, 41 Nortoft Road, Chalfont St Peter, Bucks SL9 0LA, England.
  Distributed in the USA by Hunter Publishing Inc., 300 Raritan Center Parkway, CN94, Edison, NJ 08818.

British Library Cataloguing in Publication Data

Strauss, Robert
  Trans-Siberian rail guide.
  1. Transsibirskaia magistral' 2.Siberia
  (R.S.F.S.R.) —Description and travel —
  1981-
I.Title
915.7'04854 DK756.2

ISBN 0-946983-06-2

Line drawings by Libby Evans
Maps by Hans van Well

Photographs: page 28, Robert Strauss; pages 32, 99, 132, Simon Palmour; pages ii, 107, 119, 128, Philip Robinson; pages 94, 143 Janet Cross.

Manufactured in the United States of America.

This book is dedicated to Thomas, Alexis and Sammy for whom travel lies in store, to Joyce and Herbert who helped out and to Anne, who would have surely encouraged such a venture.

Transcription

A book which skips between languages such as Russian, Chinese and Japanese is bound to create problems with transcription. Since most readers will be interested in the practical rather than the academic aspects of transcription, I have decided to adhere to modern, standard usage as much as possible. Alternative spellings or historical names are generally included in brackets after the first appearance of a place name in the text.

Acknowledgements

My thanks to all who helped (knowingly or not!) in Europe, Hong Kong, Japan and the Soviet Union with the complicated process of researching, writing and publishing this book.

To the following persons, who all answered the request for information in the Times with contributions large and small, I am especially grateful: Julian Bowden; John Fleming; Mrs de Rehren; Mrs Wikner; Barbara Taylor; James Stratford; Dorothy Abel Smith; Nancy Webber & Lucy Lomax; Joan Smith; Rossana Tich; J.D.Macrae; D.Hudson; Hilary Costa Sanseverino; Catherine Treasure; Janet & Brian Cross; Simon Palmour; Roger Musgrave for Baedeker material; Sylvia Crotty for fascinating extracts from her father's diary; Philip Robinson (expert on Siberian philately and Siberia 'nut') for advice, assistance and painstaking proof-reading.

Thanks also to Bruce Bell for providing the fascinating journals (rescued from the stables) of his explorer relative, John Bell of Antermony; to Adi Tomani for slides and info; to Jonny Morland for technical bakup; to Laurie Fullerton for patient support; to Hilary Bradt, the publisher, who gave steady encouragement.

The publisher wishes to thank Jonathan Cape Ltd., on behalf of the Estate of Peter Fleming, for permission to use extracts from *One's Company*.

The Author

Robert Strauss studied European and Oriental languages before heading off into teaching and writing. Since 1971 he has travelled around Asia and the Far East by various means of transport and has completed a series of journeys on the Trans-Siberian Railway. He has contributed to several travel guides on China and recently co-authored a travel guide to Tibet.

Table of contents

MAPS

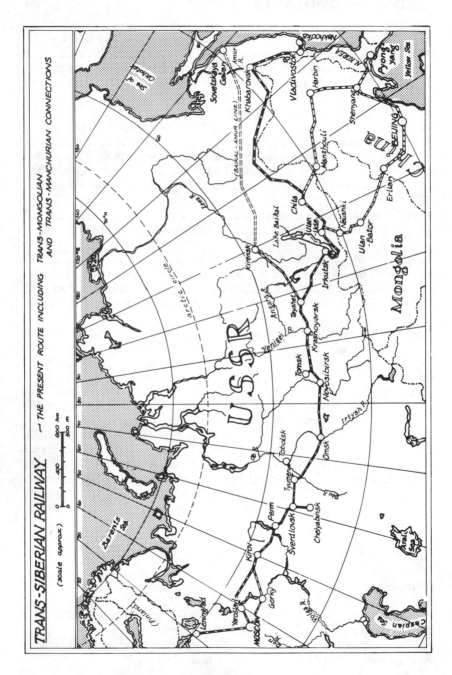

TRANS-SIBERIAN RAILWAY — THE PRESENT ROUTE INCLUDING TRANS-MONGOLIAN AND TRANS-MANCHURIAN CONNECTIONS

(scale approx.)

The beginning...

In June 1985, the publisher placed a tiny advertisement in the Times:

**BEEN ON THE TRANS SIBERIAN
RAILWAY?** Publisher seeks tips.
anecdotes etc. For further information write to Box No. 1994 T
The Times.

Within a short space of time, over forty replies had arrived from England, Europe and beyond. Trans-Siberian travellers young and old, ecstatic and disgruntled, made their views known.

Hilary Costa Sanseverino was mildly baffled: "My cousin has just sent me a cutting from the Times which I am afraid is undated. I have to confess that I was rather at a loss at first glance, as she had also included the adjacent notices on 'loved one's drinking habits' (which I thought was rather cheeky), broomsticks against cancer and news of what I took to be an old friend. It was only at the bottom that I see you ask about the Trans-Siberian Railway..."

Nancy Webber and Lucy Lomax wondered what fired the interest: "My aunt and I are the only people I know who have been hard class on the Trans-Siberian Railway from Moscow to Khabarovsk without a break. So far, no one has seemed unduly interested in this fact. Indeed, the man on the London to Manchester train, whom I couldn't resist telling that the last train I had taken was the 10.10 to Vladivostok, failed even to respond to what I thought was not exactly a run-of-the-mill remark..."

Amongst the piles of anecdotes, tips, illustrations, articles, extracts from diaries, and photocopies from old travel guides were offers of home movies and help to write the book.

The generosity and interest of these contributors is greatly appreciated and, hopefully, our readers will continue this tradition since a guidebook of this kind can only really spark if it reflects the experience of a wide cross-section of those who have taken the Trans-Siberian.

If you have useful background information, news of changes, helpful travel tips or perhaps a choice anecdote you'd like to share, please write. A free copy of the next edition goes to contributors of the most useful material. In addition, the best anecdote/contribution for each edition receives a prize of £25, which in this first edition, was awarded to Hilary Costa Sanseverino.

Part 1

THE STUFF OF DREAMS

The dream

Travellers often describe a journey on the Trans-Siberian railway as the fulfilment of a dream. Perhaps it is a dream fired by the urge to escape, to answer the call of the Orient, to take the longest possible train ride — after which everything just *has* to be greener on the other side.

In *To the Back of Beyond*, a description of his travels in Central Asia, Fitzroy Maclean refers to the attraction of the Trans-Siberian:

> My journeys, as often as not, have been by train. Trains, even in these days of champagne suppers served to soft music by trim air-hostesses at a height of 30,000 feet, still have an appeal, for me at any rate: not so much the branch lines of British Railways as the great transcontinental expresses, thundering through the night with their precious load of diplomats, multi-millionaires, blonde countesses, confidence men and secret agents.
>
> But for the ultimate in railway travel you must, to my mind, go to Russia, and on through Russia to Central Asia and Siberia, where you can travel by train for days on end until your fellow passengers and the conductor and the waitresses in the dining car have all become old friends. ... Trains provide the perfect background for so many things the Russians value: warmth, and human contacts and gregariousness, and eating and drinking and long, long conversations. I hope they will continue to do so. You can cross Siberia by jet in a few hours, where a train takes as many days. But it is not at all the same thing.

There is still a mystique to the journey, and some de luxe carriages still run true to their name, but, unless you join a specially arranged tour, the ingredients are unlikely to include the gas lamps, polished mahogany panelling, red velvet curtains, plush sofas, sumptuous dining-car and gleaming steam locomotives in regular use just a decade or two ago.

So why go? One reason might be that travelling in many parts of the globe has now become so fast, so soft, clean and undemanding that some travellers welcome a challenge. Whether they choose this route to start a journey between Europe and Asia or to conclude it, they will have the advantages of a gradual transition which helps gently to blunt the edges of culture shock. Also, the Trans-Siberian railway is not just a bridge to Japan, China or Europe, but an increasingly popular component of travel — group or independent — for visitors concentrating on the Soviet Union.

It is not a trip for those intent on soft options or perfectionists, such as an elderly German, who was known to specialise several years ago in joining tours to the Soviet Union with the sole purpose of collecting, with the aid of a stopwatch and a complaints notebook, a mountain of evidence to prove that the tour company had failed to adhere exactly to the tour specifications. Once he had returned home, the pensioner took the tour company to court and demanded another free trip in compensation ... to the Soviet Union!

The stock response of people meeting a Trans-Siberian rail traveller is "Of course I've always wanted to go, it's been my dream for years ... but it must be boring ... what do you do all the time?" The Trans-Siberian travellers who replied to the advertisement in *The Times* were almost all full of enthusiasm for the trip and only one mentioned boredom as a problem because he had travelled alone. Catherine Treasure wrote: "I was never bored — in six days I read only 100 pages of *War and Peace* and spent the rest of the time talking, writing, drinking tea, eating, playing tag on platforms, watching scenery and searching for delicious spiced gingerbread available at some of the stations."

Rossana Tich also found entertainment: "I spent a lot of time playing cards with a group of Chinese sportsmen. We'd sit in the dining car, often joined by two diplomatic wives and a Chinese man with long fingernails who said he was going to join his rich father in Paris whom he hadn't seen for years. Sometimes I'd go to the sportsmen's compartment where the conversation invariably got round to Western morals and 'yellow pictures'.

"Once I invited the interpreter for the group to my compartment to borrow a book. He was rather nervous because he had been forbidden to visit the diplomatic wives by the Fuwuren (train attendants) in the first class section. He was also very surprised to see that I was sharing a compartment with two German men, one of whom was tall, bearded, and spent a lot of time embroidering a picture of the Stone Forest in China's Yunnan province."

Lucy Lomax enjoyed a simple rest on the move: "My main memory of the holiday is of the beauty of the birch trees. It was the last week in May and the snow and the mud had gone. The grass was green and countless birch trees were just coming into leaf. I rolled up my jacket to serve as a cushion, leaned back against the window dividing the compartment from the corridor, stretched my legs out on my bunk and just gazed out for hours as we rolled along."

In *The Big Red Train Ride*, an amusing account of a Trans--Siberian train journey, Eric Newby puts the trip in a nutshell: "There is no railway journey of comparable length anywhere in the world ... The Trans-Siberian is THE big train ride. All the rest are peanuts."

And he's right.

Train corridors are wider than their European counterpart, and carpeted. Pull-down seats are provided, and passengers gather here to look at the view or exchange views.

Siberia: a brief history

Siberia, the vast backyard and economic El Dorado of the Soviet Union, occupies an area of more than 10 million square kilometres, which stretches over 7000km from the Urals in the west to the Pacific in the east, and over 3500km from the Arctic Ocean in the north to the frontiers of Mongolia and the steppes of Kazakhstan in the south. Siberia includes arctic tundra and permafrost (ground perennially frozen as deep as 1000 metres), 'taiga' (mostly coniferous forest covering almost 40% of the USSR), the southern steppes (through which runs the Trans-Siberian railway) and even arid deserts on the fringes of Central Asia. Population is focused around large cities and vast regions are uninhabited. Russians, Ukrainians and Belorussians constitute over 96% of the population. The remaining 4% includes native Siberian peoples, such as Buryats (of Mongol stock), Yakuts, Tuvans, Khakass and Evenks, many of whom have left a nomadic life of trapping, fishing and reindeer herding and settled in cities.

Officially, Siberia is administered as part of the Russian Soviet Federative Socialist Republic (RSFSR), and comprises three geographical and economic regions: Western Siberia, Eastern Siberia and the Soviet Far East.

Western Siberia (2.4 million square kilometres and a population of 12.9 million) extends from the Urals to the Yenisei river. The coalfields in the Kuzbass region, the oilfields in the Tyumen region and the northern gas fields are amongst the largest reserves of mineral resources in the world.

Eastern Siberia (4.1 million square kilometres and a population of 8.1 million) stretches from the Yenisei to the mountain ranges of the Pacific Ocean watershed. Major economic resources include rich reserves of lignite, huge timber stands (one half of the Soviet total) and hydro-electric power produced from the Yenisei and its tributaries on an enormous scale.

The Soviet Far East (6.2 million square kilometres and a population of 6.8 million) ranges from the Bering Sea in the north to the Amur region in the south. Large reserves of oil, coal and gas are still being discovered and the fishing industry is amongst the largest in the world.

Settlement of Siberia can be traced back to Paleolithic tribes in 40,000 B.C. Towards the beginning of our era, Mongoloid tribes began moving in from the south and the influence of Chinese culture increased. Several centuries later, Central Asian tribes such as the Turki and Kirghiz had moved up to dominate southern and central Siberia, but were themselves swept aside by the Mongol-Tartar invasion led by Ghenghis Khan in the thirteenth century. Tartar domination of Siberia lasted over 300 years, first under Ghenghis Khan and later under the 'Golden Horde' state which was succeeded by the Siberian Khanate.

In 1555, two years after the Tartar stronghold of Kazan had fallen to Ivan the Terrible's troops, the Siberian Khan, Yadiger, realised that an invasion was imminent and offered to place the Khanate under the nominal authority of Russia, in return for protection against his enemies. The offer was accepted, but Yadiger was ousted by Kuchum who moved the capital away from the Russians' reach to Kashlyk (close to present-day Tobolsk). Kuchum withheld the traditional tribute paid in furs, murdered a Russian emissary, and prepared for battle.

Ivan the Terrible granted a merchant clan, headed by Jacob and Gregory Stroganov (reputedly the originator of Beef Stroganov), the rights to lands east of their already vast estates along the Kama river and encouraged them to strike back at Kuchum. The Stroganovs took several years to organise an expedition and enlisted the aid of 840 Cossacks under a man later referred to in Russian history as the 'Conqueror of Siberia' — Yermak Timofeyevich, a former Volga pirate with a price on his head.

Yermak, and his small force armed with arquebuses and muskets, used rafts and boats to launch a series of successful attacks against superior numbers armed with swords, bows and arrows. As the support of local tribes and followers dwindled, Kuchum retreated to his capital at Kashlyk — also known as Sib-ir, 'the sleeping land', from which Siberia takes its name — where he was defeated in October 1582, but managed to escape. Yermak continued his campaigns along the Ob and Irtysh rivers and was rewarded by Ivan the Terrible with a golden suit of armour, reinforcements, and a pardon for the misdeeds of himself and his men. But in 1584, the same year in which Ivan the Terrible died, Kuchum returned with a small band of Tartars and surprised Yermak with a night attack on an island in the Irtysh. According to legend, Yermak, dressed in his suit of armour, attempted to swim the Irtysh but was dragged under by the weight. Local lore recounts a myth that, on the shortest night of the year, "an arm, resplendent in golden armour, emerges from the waters but disappears at once if an attempt is made to grasp it".

The Russians soon recovered from this setback and continued to push into northern and eastern Siberia, where they were either voluntarily accepted as less ruthless rulers than the Tartars or, by using superior firepower, easily overcame hostile tribes. Ostrogs (forts) were built and settlements, such as Tobolsk, Tomsk, Tyumen, Yakutsk and Irkutsk, founded in the 16th and 17th centuries, have become large, industrial cities today.

Much of the exploration and discovery of Siberia was achieved through immense hardship by individuals and small groups. The Cossack leader, Yerofei P. Khabarov (from whom Khabarovsk derives its name), led a small expedition in 1649 to claim possession of the Amur river region. However, Russians and Cossacks meted out such barbarous treatment to the natives that they appealed for help from the Manchu government in China. The Emperor Kang Hsi sent large armies and a fleet of armed junks which eventually convinced the Russians to restore this region to China in 1689 by the Treaty of Nerchinsk.

Between 1719 and 1721, John Bell of Antermony completed a journey from Moscow to Peking via Siberia and back. He travelled as a physician with the Russian Embassy sent by Peter the First to the court of the Emperor Kang Hsi in Peking and became one of the first Englishmen to cross Siberia. His detailed and entertaining account of the journey, from which I have quoted extracts in parts of this guide, was published in 1763 under the title *Travels from St Petersburg in Russia to Diverse Parts of Asia*. His general assessment of Siberia at the end of his journey was optimistic:

> Before I leave this new world, as it may be called, of SIBERIA, I think it well deserves a few general remarks, besides the particulars mentioned in my journal.
>
> This vast extent of eastern continent is bounded by RUSSIA to the west; by GREAT TARTARY to the south; on the east and north by the respective oceans; its circumference is not easy to ascertain. Foreigners commonly are terrified at the very name of SIBERIA, or SIBIR as it is sometimes called; but, from what I have said concerning it, I presume it will be granted that it is by no means so bad as is generally imagined. On the contrary, the country is really excellent, and abounds with all things necessary for the use of man and beast. There is no want of any thing, but people to cultivate a fruitful soil, well watered by many of the noblest rivers in the world; and these stored with variety of such fine fish as are seldom found in other countries. As to fine woods, furnished with all sorts of game and wild fowl, no country can exceed it.
>
> SIBERIA is generally plain, sometimes varied with rising grounds; but contains no high mountains and few hills, except towards the borders of CHINA, where you find many pleasant hills and fruitful valleys.
>
> Considering the extent of this country and the many advantages it possesses, I cannot help being of the opinion that it is sufficient to contain all the nations in EUROPE; where they might enjoy a more comfortable life than many of them do at present. For my part, I think that, had a person his liberty and a few friends, there are few places where he could spend life more agreeably than in some parts of SIBERIA.
>
> Towards the north, indeed, the winter is long and extremely cold. There are also many dreary wastes, and deep woods, terminated only by great rivers or the ocean; but these I would leave the present inhabitants, the honest OSTEAKS, and TONGUSES, and others like them; where, free from ambition and avarice, they spend their lives in peace and tranquility. I am even persuaded that these poor people would not change their situation and manner of life for the finest climate, and all the riches of the east; for I have often heard them say that God, who had placed them in this country, knew what was best for them, and they were satisfied with their lot.

In their search for furs and skins the Russians covered vast distances; the merchants Shelekhov and Baranov set up base in Alaska, and Russian ships traded with Hawaii and California. However, the Tsarist government saw little advantage in these regions and eventually Tsar Alexander II sold Alaska to the United States in 1867 for over seven million dollars in gold. Successive waves of slave labour, voluntary immigrants and exiles colonised Siberia, whilst scientific exploration continued under men such as Bering and Wrangell.

The construction of the Trans-Siberian railway provided a long overdue improvement in communications and stimulated settlement of Siberia. Full-scale development of Siberia's resources is now considered of vital importance to the Soviet economy and projects such as the Baikal-Amur Mainline (BAM) are intended to attract population from the western part of the Soviet Union and create industrial growth.

Travelling across the Soviet Union by train for some 7000km leaves one with the conviction that Russian heavy engineering in essentials is daringly conceived and well executed. The main Trans-Siberian railway system is trule a heroic achievement. Friends are inclined to believe that you will have survived a tedious journey on a single track line with aged steam locomotives cautiously edging their way over perilously fragile bridges with frequent delays due to poor maintenance. The truth is the opposite. The entire system is double track and electrified with colour light signalling, and is enhanced by a liberal amount of welded track. The viaducts across the huge Siberian rivers, to be compared with the Mississipi, are major feats of engineering. Puctuality is exemplary; the Moscow-Beijing through train arrived three minutes late. (Brian Cross)

Building the Trans-Siberian Railway

Before the railway, the only route across Siberia was a trail through mud, dust or snow, trudged for months on end by convicts and exiles. The Trakt, or Great Siberian Post Road as it was sometimes unfittingly known, was also travelled by sledges and sleighs (kibitka) in the winter and tarantasses and telegas in the summer. Baedeker's guidebook to Russia gave a blunt choice: "The *Telega*, or mail cart, is a four-wheeled conveyance without springs and somewhat resembling a rude edition of the American buckboard. As a rule no seats are provided except for the driver, the passengers sitting on their trunks or on the hay or straw with which the bottom of the cart is littered. As the roads are bad, travelling is very rough and often painful ... Where procurable, as it is in most towns, the *Tarantass* is to be preferred. It is somewhat like a hooded Victoria, the body swung by leathers on the wooden frame, or furnished with springs."

Drivers (*yamschchiki*) were invariably drunk, furiously whipping along their horses, and often crashing off the trail. Frequent changes of conveyance made progress painfully slow. Imperial couriers travelling between Irkutsk and Peking were an exception: they could cover this distance of nearly 6,000km in 16 days, travelling constantly at 16km per hour, a speed only possible because they took precedence over other travellers and used over two hundred changes of horses and drivers.

The man credited in 1857 with the first proposal for a steam railway through Siberia was an American, Perry McDonough Collins. This banker and gold-dust broker with a fascination for the business potential of steamship travel in Siberia, sailed down the Amur river and then submitted a detailed proposal to the Russian government for his 'Amoor Railroad Company'.

The American proposal was rejected as was the first Russian one, presented by Count Muravyev-Amurski who was also responsible in 1858 for negotiating the Treaty of Aigun and thereby claiming vast areas in the Amur and Ussuri regions which are still disputed by the Chinese.

Then came an English engineer, named Dull, who fielded the idea of building a tramway between Nizhni Novgorod (present-day Gorki) and Perm, with trams drawn by horses until finance was available for steam locomotives. This was turned down, as was a variation on the tramway theme supplied by another Russian, which envisaged horses galloping down nearly three thousand kilometres of wooden tunnel. The next to try their luck, were a trio of Englishmen: Morison, Sleigh and Horn who were, respectively, a banker, a bankrupt and a lawyer — they too met with rejection.

It took nearly thirty years before prevaricating engineers, provincial governors, Treasury officials and ministers could agree on tentative construction and another three years before complete agreement was given to full-scale construction of the Trans-Siberian Railway. On February 24, 1891, ministerial agreement was reached. Tsar Alexander III, who had been exasperated by the passionately obstructive Finance Minister, Ivan Vyshnegradski and indecisive committees, felt so relieved and buoyant that he issued an Imperial rescript to his Imperial Highness the Tsarevich Nicholas:

YOUR IMPERIAL HIGHNESS!

Having given the order to begin the construction of a continuous railroad line across the whole of Siberia, destined to unite the Siberian lands, so rich in natural endowments, with the railway network of the interior, I entrust You to proclaim My will on this matter upon Your return to the Russian land after Your inspection of the foreign countries of the East. Furthermore, I charge You with the duty of laying the foundation stone, in Vladivostok, of the Ussuri section of the Great Siberian Railway, which is to be built at State expense and under direction of the Government.

Your significant role in the commencement of this truly national task which I have undertaken will give fresh evidence of My sincere desire to facilitate communications between Siberia and the other parts of the Empire and thus will demonstrate to this region, which is so dear to My heart, My very keen interest in its peaceful prosperity.

Beseeching the Lord's blessing upon the long journey through Russia which lies ahead of You.

I remain Your sincerely affectionate

ALEXANDER

The Tsarevich dutifully arrived in Vladivostok ('Mistress of the East') after completing a state visit to Japan where the Lord's blessing may have worked in advance to help him escape an assassination attempt. On May 31, 1891, he dug the first turf and ceremoniously filled a wheelbarrow as a symbolic start on the Ussuri line.

The Committee of Ministers agreed to a construction plan which divided the route into six sections: West Siberian; Mid-Siberian; Ussuri; Circum-Baikal; Trans-Baikal; Amur.

With the promotion of Sergius Witte to Minister of Finance in 1892, the railway received sound financial support and a special 'Committee of the Trans-Siberian', comprising the Heir Apparent and all noted personages of the government, was created to oversee the entire project. The following historical details outline in brief the construction of the Trans-Siberian and also the Chinese Eastern Railways.

The West Siberian Line (1892—1896)*

The connection between Perm and Sverdlovsk in 1878 was followed seven years later by a line to Tyumen. However, the connection between the original starting point of the Trans-Siberian, Chelyabinsk, and the present-day starting point, Sverdlovsk, dates back to 1896. The line was constructed in two sections, the first from Chelyabinsk to Omsk; the second from Omsk to the Ob. In spite of the lack of skilled workers, suitable timber, building stone and drinking water, over two miles of track were laid daily during the summer season and the first section was completed in September 1894. The second section was completed in 1895, although several bridges were completed later with blessing ceremonies — a necessary precaution in view of the frequent accidents.

The Ussuri Line (1891—1897)

Although Tsarevich Nicholas had dug the first spadefuls of earth at Vladivostok in 1891, it took nearly six years to complete the 767km of line to Khabarovsk. Here too, the shortage of labour was acute and an attempt to relieve the situation by importing convict labour from Sakhalin led to an unprecedented rise in Vladivostok's homicide rate. Construction materials took months to be shipped from Russia.

Track-laying was slowed by atrocious conditions as swarms of mosquitoes spread fever, horses were wiped out by Siberian anthrax, rivers rose to unheard of heights and flooded the tracks and Manchurian tigers attacked the camps, striking terror into the Chinese coolies. In 1897, the first official train thundered down the line to Vladivostok at 16km per hour.

The Mid-Siberian Line (1893—1899)

The section of railway from Novonikolayevsk (present-day Novosibirsk) to Irkutsk was started in 1893 and built in two stages. The first stage, completed in 1898, ran from the River Ob to Krasnoyarsk on the west bank of the River Yenisei. The second, completed in 1899, ran from Krasnoyarsk to the outskirts of Irkutsk. The labour gangs had to hack through the thick taiga forest whilst makeshift roads were driven through swamp areas. At one stage, 6,000 rails were bought in England and shipped by Captain Joseph Wiggins via the Kara Sea — above the Arctic Circle — to the Yenisei estuary where they were offloaded. At the same time, the line from Irkutsk to Port Baikal on Lake Baikal was completed against tremendous technical odds which required dynamiting of a trackbed and construction of fifty wooden bridges along about 67km of track.

* dates in brackets indicate the respective years of commencement and completion.

The arrival of the first train in Irkutsk (the Baikal connection only opened in 1900) was celebrated with fanfares on August 16, 1898.

The Lake Baikal Connection

Between 1898 and 1905 the railway line only extended as far as Port Baikal which was at the exit-point of the River Angara from Lake Baikal. The railway committee was thwarted in its plans to push a route round to the south of the lake by the mountains rising sharply from the lake shore.

In 1895, as a provisional measure, the committee then approved the acquisition of a train ferry from the English firm of Armstrong, Mitchell and Co. This ferry, later named *Baikal*, was built at their shipyard in Newcastle on Tyne, dismantled and shipped in meticulously numbered batches to St Petersburg (present-day Leningrad) where it was divided again into 7,000 units which were hauled immense distances by train, barge and sled to Lake Baikal — all in the space of twelve months.

At the lake, British technicians supervised rebuilding of the ferry from the jumbled consignments of thousands of parts which had amazingly, arrived with all important parts intact.

In July 1899 the ship was finally launched without her fifteen boilers, but in April 1900 these had been installed and a regular ferry service started.

The *Baikal*, with a top speed of 22km per hour, could carry 28 goods waggons or an entire express train on three pairs of rails on the main deck; passenger facilites included a chapel (popular with the locals as a marriage venue), a luxury lounge, a buffet, deck space for 650 third-class passengers and cabins for 150 first or second-class passengers. Models of the *Baikal* are usually exhibited in the Local History Museum at Irkutsk and at the Limnological Institute in Listvyanka.

In 1898 an order was placed with the same British firm for a smaller ferry, the *Angara*, which could carry 150 passengers and several hundred tons of cargo. Although the *Angara* had also been built as an ice-breaker, the ice in the winter and spring was often too thick for the ferries. One method which sometimes succeeded was for the *Baikal* to batter a path through the ice for the *Angara*. When the ferries became ice-bound, travellers were wrapped in sheepskins, bundled into huge baskets on the back of horse sleighs and ferried across the lake. At one stage over 2,000 sleighs continuously jingled from one side to the other, covering nearly 50km in under five hours.

When the Japanese attacked the Russian fleet in the Far East in February 1904, Lake Baikal was frozen and threatened to block the rapid movement of military reinforcements. Prince Khilkov, then Minister of Ways and Communications, decided to run rails across the ice from Port Baikal to Tankhoi, on the Circumbaikal Loop line. Although this method had already been used successfully on the Ob and Yenisei rivers, this attempt ended in disaster when a test locomotive crossed ice which had been thinned by warm springs. The train plunged thousands of feet through the water to the lake bed, leaving a gigantic gash in the ice over 20km in length. Another account of the same disaster notes that the location of this plunge was a shallow part of the lake and the locomotive was, in fact, salvaged and spent the rest of its working life on safe rails, between St. Petersburg and Helsinki.

Subsequent attempts, using horses and men to haul dismantled engines and equipment over longer ties (for wider weight distribution) were more successful. Several thousand freight cars, over sixty locomotives and thousands of soldiers crossed the lake in five weeks.

In 1918, members of the Czech Legion set light to the *Baikal* and destroyed it. The *Angara* is still afloat and, reportedly, she was used for a fortnight as a ferry again during the 70s when the Circum-Baikal Loop line was flooded.

Today, the hordes of winter sleighs have disappeared but, as is the case on frozen waterways elsewhere in Siberia, large numbers of heavy lorries and even motor-bikes can be seen criss-crossing Lake Baikal, sometimes using it as a giant skid-pan.

The Circum-Baikal Loop (1899-1904)

This line ran from Port Baikal to Mysovsk, along the shoreline of Lake Baikal through some of the most mountainous terrain of the entire railway. Boats were often the only means of access to construction sites where the labour gangs, confronted with cliffs that fell sheer into the water, blasted cuttings, bored thirty-three tunnels and built over two hundred bridges.

This section also boasts the highest point on the Trans-Siberian line (1025m).

The Trans-Baikal Line (1895-1900)

This section of the line was started on the eastern shore of Lake Baikal, at Mysovsk (now named Babushkin, in honour of an Irkutsk revolutionist of 1905) and continued through Verkhneudinsk (now known as Ulan-Ude) and Chita to Sretensk. Until completion of the Amur line in 1916, passengers took ship at Sretensk to travel down the Shilka and Amur rivers to Khabarovsk, where the Ussuri line with Vladivostok on the Pacific coast had been completed in 1897. Stretches of the route between Ulan-Ude and Sretensk consisted of permafrost, which was either dynamited or thawed with wood fires since pickaxes were useless.

It was in the Yablonovy mountains on this section that perhaps the most spectacular catastrophe occurred, one which added years to the construction time: "A colossal wall of water about four metres high destroyed the construction works in twenty-four hours and swept away hundreds of villages and tens of thousands of cattle along the Ingoda, Onon, Shilka and Amur rivers causing losses worth millions. The rivers changed their channels in places, villages had to be reconstructed and the railway was laid in a totally different location."

The Chinese Eastern Railway (1897-1903)

The railway committee decided against running a line beside the River Amur which was prone to flooding, and instead, negotiated with the Chinese to run a shorter, and thus cheaper line through Manchuria to Vladivostok. The major concern of the Russians, which was not highlighted, was to dominate Manchuria and Korea and gain control of ice-free ports. Since Japan shared similar aims, conflict was inevitable.

Construction started in 1897 on two branches to connect the Chinese Eastern Railway with the Ussuri line in the east and the Transbaikal line in the west. The eastern section, opened in 1899, ran from Ussuriysk to the Manchurian border at Pogranichny; the western section, opened in 1901, started close to Kaidolovo (now Tarskaya), approximately 100km south of Chita, and continued to Manchuria station (now Manzhouli).

Construction of the actual Chinese Eastern Railway commenced along two routes. From the Ussuri region teams of labourers worked towards Harbin, whilst from Harbin itself, other teams split up to work westward to Manzhouli and eastward to the Ussuri region.

As soon as Dalni (now Dalian) and Port Arthur (now Lushun) on the Liaotung peninsular had been handed over by the enfeebled Chinese government to the Russians in 1898, work started on the South Manchurian line which ran between these two cities and Harbin, with a spur line to Yingkou.

Apart from the problems of interpreting and the need to train a work force of over two hundred thousand coolies, the project was hampered by outbreaks of bubonic plague and Asiatic cholera. The small force of Railway Police was rapidly turned into a small army of 5,000 men in order to combat hundreds of *Hunghutze* (Redbeards) who were well-organised bandits specialising in robbery, kidnapping for ransom and pillaging, all across Manchuria. Decapitation of offenders and a subsequent display of heads failed to deter the criminals.

Political upheavals in Peking erupted into the Boxer rebellion in 1900, which eventually led to the destruction of much of the railway facilities and track. Russian troops swarmed in to restore order and on November 3, 1901, the entire Chinese Eastern Railway opened to provisional traffic running from Manzhouli to Vladivostok via Harbin and from Harbin to Port Arthur. Regular traffic started in 1903.

The Japanese considered the railway to be a threat to their interest in Manchuria and the railway proved to be a spark that set off the Russo-

Japanese war between 1904 and 1905. After this war, the Russians surrendered Port Arthur and Dalni and the part of the south Manchurian line running as far as Changchun. The Soviets continued to dominate northern Manchuria and support the Communist movement in the area of the Chinese Eastern Railway until 1929, when Marshal Chang Tso-Lin, a vehement anti-Communist, was blown up in a train. The Marshal's son confiscated the railway, but was soon forced by Stalin to back down and accept Soviet 'management'. The Japanese invasion of Manchuria in 1931 eventually created such chaos on the railway that the Soviets were forced to choose between another war with Japan or outright sale. In 1933 the Japanese government bought the railway from the Soviet Union for 170 million Yen (approx. US$48 million). At the end of World War II, the Soviets again marched into Manchuria, confiscated vast quantities of Japanese equipment and material and set up with the Chinese, yet again, spurious 'joint' administration of the Chinese Changchun Railway (as the Chinese Eastern Railway had been renamed). It was not until 1952, after the Soviet Union had agreed to renounce, without compensation, all rights to Dalni, Port Arthur and the Changchun Railway, that the Chinese finally gained outright possession.

The Amur Line (1908-1916)
When the Japanese emerged victorious in 1904, the Manchurian route was obviously vulnerable to a Japanese attack and the long-suffering railway committee returned to the idea of a line following the River Amur.

In 1908, construction of the Amur Railway was started at Kuenga (close to Sretensk) and continued, out of artillery range of the Manchurian bank of the Amur, in a wide loop via Skovorodino to Khabarovsk. Construction workers battled with the taiga, permafrost, scurvy and vicious insects in stupendous numbers. With the opening of the Amur railway in 1916, the Trans-Siberian Railway had reached its full length.

THE WORKERS
Initially, migrant farmers or peasant settlers were used for construction, but their numbers were not sufficient and eventually an extraordinary mixture of Turks, Persians, Italians, Chinese, Koreans and Russians took over. Stonemasons, riveters and bridgebuilders were hired winter and summer; the rest departed during the winter. Bridgebuilders working in the bitter cold of winter often lost their grip and plunged to their deaths on the frozen river surface. Almost all the masons were Italians whose pay averaged 100 roubles a month (approximately US$50), but other labourers received two roubles a day (approximately US$1) or, in the

case of convicts, 45 kopecks (approximately 25 cents). On the Ussuri Line, Imperial troops considered the work below their dignity and 15,000 coolies were imported each year from Manchuria for the short work season. On the Trans-Baikal Line, labour was so scarce that 1,700 convicts from the mines and 2,500 exiles were pressed into service. On the Chinese Eastern Railway, over 200,000 coolies were employed and when bubonic plague struck, the Russian directors of the railway managed to avert wholesale desertion by offering a 'golden handshake' to the relatives of any employee who died.

Exile

Deportation to Siberia became a common punishment from the end of the 16th century onwards. It proved an efficient and incredibly brutal means of banishing convicts, social misfits and complete innocents. As the demand for labourers in Imperial mines in Siberia increased, even the most trivial of crimes were punished with exile wherever possible and a flood of prisoners trudged into Siberia, destined for slave labour under atrocious conditions. Exiles were graded into four classes: hard-labour convicts; penal colonists; non-criminal deportees and voluntary followers.

Hard-labour convicts and penal colonists had their heads half-shaven, wore heavy fetters and were often branded with a mark to indicate their crime. They were also exiled for life, lost all civil rights and property and, if they survived their penal term, might be permitted to settle.

Deportees had been punished for everything from indolence and drinking to political activity (or even suspicions of such activity). They were usually restricted to a particular district and required to report to the police for a specified period of time, after which they could return home.

Between 1800 and 1914 at least one million people were exiled to Siberia.

For the Railway Committee, the exiles and convicts became a vital source of labour and a large portion of the Trans-Siberian Railway was constructed with their efforts.

As an inducement and in consideration of the work conditions, the committee allowed hard labour convicts (*katorzhniki*) to work without chains and, for eight months of work, their sentences were reduced by a year. For non-criminal exiles, each year of work reduced the sentence by two years. Furthermore, a daily wage of 25 kopecks (approximately 12½ cents) was also provided. Figures are vague but, for example, during the peak period of construction on the Mid Siberian section of the railway, it is estimated that about 12,000 out of an estimated 29,000 workers were deported convicts and 1000 were deportees.

THE COST*

In 1875 the Communication Minister, Constantine Posyet, tendered the figure of US$125 million for a railway from the Volga to the Amur. In 1891, Posyet's successor, Adolf von Hubbenet, estimated construction costs for the railway at US$175 million.

The term 'costs' covered a multitude of items which, to name a few, included preliminary surveys; immigrant, foreign, convict and military labour; railway employees, railway quarters, railway police; carts, horses, sleds, steamers; stone, cement, sand, ballast, bridge girders, timber, rails, tools, provisions; locomotives and rolling–stock.

In 1904, official statistics revealed that the Trans-Siberian had already cost over US$250 million. In addition, the Chinese Eastern, completed in 1903, had cost a minimum of US$173 million whilst the Amur Railway, completed in 1916, consumed at least another US$160 million.

*Figures given here are not definitive and, for ease of reference, all sums are given in approximate US$ equivalents.

The Trans-Siberian today

ROUTINGS

Although there is only one Trans-Siberian Railway, three routings make use of it for considerable distances. For the sake of simplicity, this book emphasises travel from west to east. It is, however, quite possible to arrange the trip in the opposite direction (further details are provided later in the book in separate sections for Japan, Hong Kong and China).

The Trans-Siberian Route: Moscow — Khabarovsk — Nakhodka (Boat/Plane) — Yokohama (Japan) — (Hong Kong).
This is the standard run which immediately springs to mind on mention of the words 'Siberia' and 'Railway' and is an obvious choice for travellers heading to Japan from Europe or vice-versa. If you are pressed for time or don't love trains enough to go the whole hog, part of this route can be covered by air (for example, Moscow to Irkutsk or Irkutsk to Khabarovsk). The full rail trip from Moscow to Nakhodka (including compulsory overnight in Khabarovsk) takes about 8 days and the trip by boat from Nakhodka to Yokohama (Japan) another 2 days. Approximately twice a year, boats travel between Yokohama and Hong Kong*. When you book with Intourist on this route, your rail journey will be timed to connect with a sailing (weekly from April to September) or a flight from Khabarovsk to Niigata (Japan). There are plenty of trains on this route, but tourists can only travel on those trains for which Intourist hold an allocation of berths. The best known train is *Rossya*, which leaves daily.

The following two routes both run to Beijing (Peking) but depart from the Trans-Siberian line at different points after passing Lake Baikal.

The Trans-Manchurian Route: Moscow — Chita — Manzhouli (China) — Harbin — Shenyang — Beijing
Trains on this route are run by SZD (USSR Railways) and do not enter Mongolia, but follow the original Trans-Siberian line across Manchuria before breaking off for Beijing. Weekly departures take 6 days to cover precisely 9,001km.

The Trans-Mongolian Route: Moscow — Ulan-Ude — Naushki — Ulan Bator (Mongolia) — Erlian (China) — Beijing
Trains on this routing are operated by Chinese Railways and run across Mongolia. Weekly departures serve this shorter route (7,865km) which is covered in 5½ days.

---

* These are the INTOURIST boat connections. There are, of course, other boats.

CARRIAGE PLANS

2-berth compartments

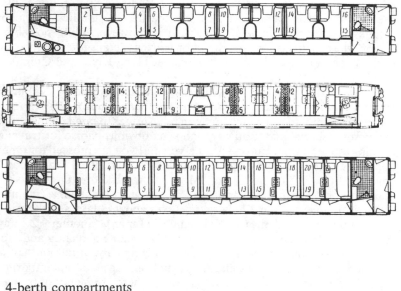

4-berth compartments

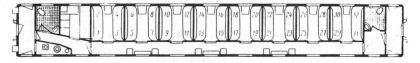

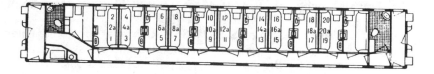

ROLLING-STOCK
Locomotives
Production of steam locomotives in the Soviet Union ceased in 1956, and now that diesel and electric locomotives have taken over, the remaining steam models are either rusting in sad, steam-loco graveyards all along the Trans-Siberian line, or kept for occasional freight switching. Electrification of the line has now mostly been completed but there are still gaps in the eastern section where diesel locomotives are used, and China uses only diesel. The commonest electric locomotives are those of the 'VL' (Vladimir Lenin) class, such as the VL60, VL80 and VL80A.

Carriages
At the Paris Universal Exposition of 1900, the Belgian 'International Sleeping Car Company' displayed sumptuous carriages which were, supposedly, to be used on the Trans-Siberian Railway. The carriages were fitted with the ultimate in good taste and included a smoking room, a lounge with piano, plate-glass mirrors and frescoed ceiling; a hairdressing salon, and a bathroom with a non-slop tub. The Russians also promoted their own 'State Express' which, it was said, would include a restaurant car complete with library and reading–room, a travelling chapel complete with church bells and priest, a gymnasium and a darkroom for photographers. In fact the carriages which finally ran on the Trans-Siberian line fell decidedly short of the vaunted standards, and most of those in use on the Trans-Siberian today are rigidly functional and date back to the early 70s when massive orders were placed with the VEB in Ammendorf (German Democratic Republic).

First class/luxury class These have room for 18 or 36 persons in a combination of two-berth and four-berth compartments. The two–berth versions (which are rare) have the full luxury treatment which includes a comfortable chair, wash basin, a gilded mirror and matching curtains. For group travel the four-berth compartments are often used for only two people. They are roomy, but lack a washbasin. There is a toilet and washbasin at one end of each carriage, and a 220v socket for shavers, but it is almost impossible to have a good wash, owing to the smallness of the cubicle ('designed for a dwarf') and the constant movement of the train.

Each carriage is heated by a solid-fuel boiler (new supplies of coal or coal are taken on at each stop) which is very effective in raising the temperature, but dirty. This, coupled with poor washing facilities, is one of the main complaints of first class passengers.

Second class/tourist class These have room for 38 persons in nine four-berth compartments and one two-berth compartment for the train

attendants. There are toilets at either end of the carriage.
In both first and second class you must make up your own bunks.

Lounge class/'hard' class Usually off-limits to foreign tourists, these
carriages have berths for 81 local passengers.

The true face of Siberia is experienced between the carriages where the
temperature plunges and if you don't miss your grip on slippery handles,
then the bucking train will make sure you lose your balance. Even in
summer it is hazardous because the 'floor' between the carriages is so
uneven and coal dust blows in your face.

During the winter the windows on the train are locked with a special
triangular railway socket wrench and the inner windows are screwed up
tight. Those who travel during the spring may find attempts to let in the
relevant air thwarted by these inner windows. Reportedly, there is a day in
May, decided upon by the authorities and radioed direct to all train crews,
when all inner windows in the trains are unscrewed.

There is a samover for hot water in both first and second class carriages.
Attendants (*provodniks*) supply tea free to first class passengers, and for 8
kopecks to others, in glasses complete with startling holders. These depict
what looks like ICBM's, dancing round the earth in celestial frenzy with
sputniks and shooting stars beneath a crescent moon.

Opposite the samovar is a tap for drinking water.

In the winter, perishable items can be suspended near the carriage door
to keep cool, but a safer alternative is to ask if the provodnik has room in a
'fridge' under the floor.

Tapes and radio programmes are played through the train from a small
studio. The selection ranges from 'St. John's Infirmary', 'La Bamba',
electronic synthesiser and jazz music to news and information about
places en route in Swedish and Japanese. If you feel the music needs a
rest, there is a volume control above the window — those who have
travelled hard sleeper in China may appreciate this.

It is worth remembering that the lavatories are locked shortly before
stops and unlocked shortly afterwards. One surly matron of an attendant
became enraged, several minutes before a stop, with a Swede who was still
in the toilet blithely going about his business and unaware of her fury.
With a flick of her key, she burst in to surprise him in his underwear and
made it clear with sign language that he was to stop relieving himself.
Relevant paper (*toiletnaya bumaga*) is scarce, so do not be surprised to
find neat squares of Pravda — the truth also serves.

PROVODNIKS AND FUWUREN — THE ATTENDANTS

Drivers, dining-car staff and provodniks on the Trans-Siberian express make up a crew of about forty which is under the leadership of a brigadier.

Provodniks have various duties, including making sure passengers are not lost at stops, guarding the samovar, keeping the heating fired with coal and ensuring their carriage is clean and in good technical order. In the winter, they brush ice off the steps and use an ice axe to chop ice from water outlets.

Although some Russian attendants can be rather formidable, there are many exceptions: "The stereotype of the conductress is of plump and fearsome women brandishing power with relish; as usual our reality was different. There were two young girls on our coach and at each station stop, when not having snowball fights, they flirted with a young conductor from another carriage who kept finding some reason to come our way." (Simon Palmour).

The Chinese attendants (*fuwuren*) are meticulous in their attention to thermos flasks and bedding in the carriages and religiously scrub the windows with a bucket and mop at each stop. Their lives are spent on a massive pendulum between Beijing and Moscow with just a few days rest. One of these attendants asked me for help with his English which was being absorbed by reading aloud a book entitled *Topography of the Rockies*. Clearly, successive waves of foreign passengers had all done their duty, but all had started at page 1 and gone no further than page 44 which appeared to be the limit for reading aloud on a Trans-Siberian journey.

Catherine Treasure found someone with specialist knowledge: "The attendant in carriage 9 is a very learned, interesting man who travels on the second Wednesday of every month from Beijing to Moscow and back. If you can find an interpreter, he is well worth a visit because he knows a great deal about Tai Chi Chuan, acupuncture, body pressure points, and, above all, reading of the hand, head and face."

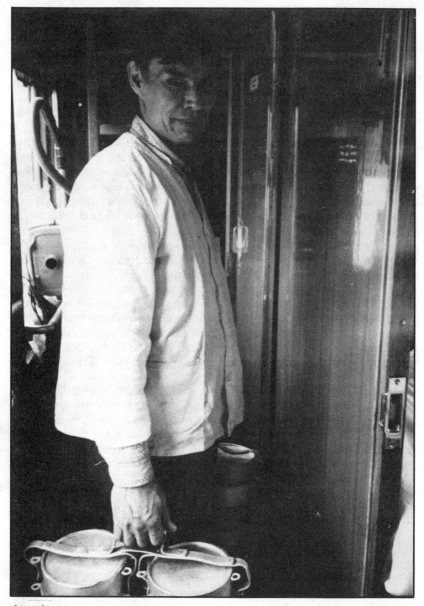

Attendant en route to the Hard Class passengers, with metal containers full of stew.

THE DINING-CAR

Opinions vary on the quality of the Chinese, Mongolian and Russian dining-cars. If considered on the basis of the menu alone, then the Chinese one would certainly rate highest, but the other two make up for their failings with a strange and sometimes fascinating cast of staff and diners.

Russian dining-car

With space for 48 and divided by a partition, the car makes a dowdy impression. Waitresses use a venerable cash register and an abacus. A glass-fronted cabinet contains stocks of wrapped sweets, jams, pickles and cigarettes. Common brands are Phoenix, Kosmos and Belomoskva. Belomoskva is the archetypal 'papiros', which hardly qualifies as a cigarette since ⅞ of it is a paper-and-cardboard filter and only ⅛ tobacco.

The tossing motion of the train at high speed has its most dramatic effect on the dining car. On one of my journeys, the strain of the swaying induced the sudden collapse of a chair together with one very stout diner who went down in a shower of borscht. On another journey, the waitress appeared juggling two plates of goulash, but as the train moved violently into a curve, she was thrown off course between the two opposite tables. As she sank out of sight in majestic slow motion, bravely holding aloft both plates of goulash, I rescued her.

An imposing tourist menu running to many pages in length, in no way reflects the limited choice available. Prices are moderate, so even if you had no personal stocks of food with you on the train, it is hard to imagine spending more than 6 roubles a day and at that generous rate you would have worn out the menu within about 48 hours. Group tourists are sometimes still provided with meal coupons (breakfast, lunch and dinner) although it is just as simple to use roubles providing you remember that there is no official way to change money once on board the train.

Although the train timetable follows Moscow Time, the dining car sets its opening times according to local time. Since the time difference can be as much as 7 hours, this could mean that you sit down to what your stomach, still running on Moscow Time, thinks is lunch, whilst in the real world speeding past the windows outside, the sun is busy setting.

Main dishes vary according to the season, but should include 'bifstek' (Rb0.78), beef Stroganov (Rb0.62) and fried eggs with ham (Rb0.53); soups and starters will possibly include caviar (Rb1.62), pickled cucumber (Rb0.07), soup with chicken (Rb0.40) and borscht soup (Rb0.44). Dual stacks of brown and white bread are always served.

More exciting are the occasional moose steaks and sturgeon (*asyotr*) sometimes served on the train. The latter is generally served schnitzel-style, fried in breadcrumbs, and tastes rather like chicken.

Drinks include mineral water, tasting like a liquid chemistry lab, tea (Rb0.08), coffee and an expensive, acidly vitamin-rich juice (Rb1.45), probably buckthorn. One intrepid menu reader discovered 'berry tea', but when he asked for the drink, the waitress assumed a look of utter astonishment, as if she would have to leap out and pick berries. Quenching your thirst on the Russian train can be a problem: "We found all the bottled drinks much too sweet. Tea was refreshing, but I wish we'd brought some sort of powdered or concentrated drink to add to water" (Janet Cross).

Alcohol, sadly, has been progressively ousted from the dining-car, but for good reasons, not the least being safety. At first, beer and vodka were excluded because of mass inebriation and, reportedly, drunken driving. Then for several years it was possible to buy Crimean champagne, Georgian brandy and wine. An official drive against alcoholism was started in 1984 and none whatsoever is sold now in the dining-car. This explains the mad rush of passengers toting plastic bags at large stations, such as Novosibirsk, who have as long as the train stops to find their *pivo* (beer).

The dining-car staff are approachable and were commended by Catherine Treasure: "Choice of food was a bit limited, but what there was, was very good and warming, as was the waitress. There was plenty of her and she wrapped it all round us as we whiled away the hours, talking in sign language and broken German. 'What do you think of Reagan?' we asked. Hands formed into guns, she cried 'Boom, boom!'. 'And Thatcher?'. With a squawking bird's head gesture, she indicated 'All talk'. 'Are the Russians afraid of the Americans?'. She stiffened proudly, chin thrust into the air, to show that the Russians are fearless, proud and brave.

Perhaps the same waitress served Janet Cross, travelling in 1986: 'She looked like a real battle axe but she turned out to have a warm heart and a marvellous sense of humour (lack of a common language was no barrier). She often winked at us as she strode by, and when I presented her with a *Beautiful Britain* calender, she gave me a smacking kiss, then later linked arms to share our bottle of wine in the traditional Russian fashion' (Janet Cross).

The Mongolian dining-car

This has quite a stylish, 1930s feel to it with cut glass decanters, a waitress in national costume and an elaborate menu, similar in its type and scarcity of dishes to the Russian dining-car. Beef Stroganov, bifstek with egg, soup with egg, pancakes, milk, yoghurt, tea, coffee etc. are available on payment of US dollars which are converted to Tugriks, the Mongolian currency, about three of which are equal to one US dollar. Various souvenir items are on sale too. The comments book is worth a glance.

The Chinese dining-car

This compares favourably with the other two, not just because of the different food, but also for the attention travellers receive from the staff in the Chinese dining-car. Another asset is the large stock of alcohol: Beijing or Qingdao beer at Y1.20 a bottle; Chinese brandy (not exactly subtle) at Y5 a bottle and Chinese liqueurs, which are definitely a wild item for the digestive system of the uninitiated. The menu has a wide selection at reasonable prices — from Y1.90 for pork and vegetable dishes to Y23 for some seafood dishes. A European breakfast is available (omelette, milk and coffee) for about Y2.10.

Sweets, cigarettes, tea, etc. are available too. Those heading into Siberia should stock up on beer — as early as possible — since stocks can run out if everyone else has the same idea.

Not surprisingly, the comments book is full of ecstatic reactions: 'Amazing, real food does exist!' or 'Three guys from Sweden thinks this was heaven'. Others are clearly weary and stick to matter-of- fact comments like: 'A welcome change from the Russian food which I found to be practically inedible' or 'Heaven is relative, food is foremost'. Somebody else has supplied advice to prevent culture shock: 'Don't eat the chopsticks'.

A real breakfast, Russian-style, as enjoyed in 1975 before the disappearance of vodka, clearly proved to be quite an event for J.D.Macrae:

The half dozen Westerners travelling from Nachodka to Moscow used to congregate in the restaurant-car in the evenings and any Russians who wanted to talk English would come and join us. Boris was a Muscovite, about 30, and he suggested that we had breakfast at 9am the next day as he was getting off at Novosibirsk at 10am.

At 9am, except for a figure in uniform, the restaurant-car appeared deserted. Closer inspection revealed that the uniformed figure was Boris — in the full regalia of a Red Army Major. Still his affable self, he had already organised a real Russian breakfast. This consisted of a plate of baked eggs each, a loaf of black bread, two shot glasses and a large block of ice. The block of ice was attacked to expose a bottle of Moskovskaya vodka, which emerged from the bottle like cod liver oil.

Traditionally, one person pours the vodka, a toast is proposed with 'Nasdrovia!', the glasses are drained and then immediately refilled by the other person. This gives the minimum of time to cram down eggs and bread to create a lining to the stomach as a protection against the onslaught of ice-cold vodka early in the morning.

The first bottle was demolished in twenty minutes, but even Boris slowed down on the second, which we completed just as the train was pulling into Novosibirsk. By this time, Boris and I were totally plastered and full of East-West bonhomie and détente. The train stopped. Boris and I staggered to the door with his suitcase and he descended carefully to the platform. As he peered hazily towards the station, his face fell and, turning to me, he said, 'Oh no, shit, my Colonel's come to meet me!'

To his credit, it must be said that Boris looked sober as a judge when he strode up the platform, came to a halt in front of a small, rotund man flanked by two vast sergeants, put down his suitcase and snapped to attention. Unfortunately, he ruined it all by tearing off a crisp salute which neatly removed his cap. The Colonel frowned, the sergeants moved in, the train pulled out and, for all I know, Boris is still mining salt. I can hardly imagine getting roaring drunk with a capitalist is considered de rigeur for Army Majors. I missed a lot of Siberia that day, and didn't lose the hangover until the Urals.

TRAIN TIME

On a trip of this length, the problem with having all the time in the world is that the passage through time zones becomes so confusing that eating and sleeping appear the best refuge. In effect, the train timetable runs according to Moscow Time but Local Time often applies to the stations along the route and to the dining-car opening hours.

The difference between Moscow Time and Local Time is given in the following list which moves eastwards and provides — as approximate orientation only — the names of significant stations and kilometre markings near the limits of each zone:

Moscow to Aleksandrov (km112)	Moscow Time
Aleksandrov to Balesino (km1194)	Moscow Time + 1 hour
Balesino to Tyumen (km2144)	Moscow Time + 2 hours
Tyumen to Tartarskaya (km2889)	Moscow Time + 3 hours
Tartarskaya to Nizhni Poima (km4458)	Moscow Time + 4 hours
Nizhni Poima to P. Zabaikalsk (km5789)	Moscow Time + 5 hours
P. Zabaikalsk to Kundur (km8161)	Moscow Time + 6 hours
Kundur onwards	Moscow Time + 7 hours

Clearly, if you are proceeding westwards across the Soviet Union, you can read the above list backwards and subtract. Greenwich Mean Time (GMT) is Moscow Time £ 3 hours.

To further complicate matters, there is Moscow Summer time, when clocks go forward an hour between March 30 and September 28. Beijing Time is the same as Ulan Bator Time but four hours ahead of Moscow Summer Time or five ahead of Moscow Winter Time. Have a good time!

Breaking the ice

Much of the fun of the trip lies in chance meetings and chatting to fellow passengers. Even if language skills are in short supply, there are plenty of ways to break the ice, such as musical intruments, photos of home, card games, chess, mime, sketches, phrasebooks (there are some 'breaking the ice' phrases in the *Appendix*) and maps. Most of the people who wrote sharing their trans-Siberian experiences described their pleasure in being able to meet Russians and other fellow-passengers.

My most precious personal memories are probably peculiar to a student of Russian: I just love talking to Russians and, even more, singing with them some of their own lovely folksongs, of which I know a great many. Music is a great ice-breaker in personal relationships, and Russians, as a musical race, love to sing. Knowing this, I had prepared and taken along some sheets with the words of songs, hoping to encourage some of my party to start up a sing-song. Since the corridor of the train is the social centre, this was obviously the place, especially as people stand for hours chatting or looking out of the window. So I collected some of our group and, along with the old favourites, we sang some Siberian songs. Gradually the compartment doors opened and, one by one, like rabbits from their warrens, the Russian travellers emerged, shyly at first, then smiling in delight as they joined in. They were so moved that foreigners travelling across Siberia should want to sing of the 'Glorious sea, sacred Baikal'. (Joan Smith)

If you are a woman and have reached the age where wolf whistles are directed at your daughter and not at you, try to get on a train where there are soldiers travelling. They may look an uncouth mob, but the obvious relish with which they will squeeze past you in the corridor is good for your morale. By standing in the corridor, you will also encourage people to come out and talk to you. Much of the conversation with Intourist guides can become very tiresome if it follows an endless party line. If you get into conversation with ordinary people (who probably aren't, if they speak English and are on the train), it's easier to reach those aspects of life common to all — marriage, contraception, etc. are fruitful fields. (Barbara Taylor)

As the 'engleski' girl I was looked at with extreme curiosity and other passengers came by to stare. I did not speak a word of Russian, but with the help of a phrasebook and my fingers made reasonable conversation. What was my job? How much did I earn? Could I give them english money and stamps? Why was I travelling? I taught them to play the card game 'Pelmanism' which went down through the train and they took it very seriously!   I stitched at some embroidery, and my gold thimble intrigued them, likewise my teeth: were they my own because there was no gold? ... A friend had kindly lent me a map of the country, which I showed to my first companions, who looked at it very curiously and with dismay, and I thought them very dim, as they shook their heads, but I suddenly realised 'By appointment to His Imperial Majesty, the Czar of All the Russias' was printed on the cover, and of course so many of the names had altered since the Revolution. No wonder they didn't know! (D. Abel Smith)

I brought a chess-set and only had to walk down the corridor with it to be challenged to a match. I spent many hours playing chess with the kitchen staff, and found it a marvellous way of meeting Russians, even when we had no word of common language. (Roger Crisp)

Most of our fellow passengers, especially the younger ones, appeared to be interested and friendly. Once when the train stopped in the country and people got out to pick flowers, we were each given a little bunch of wild lilies-of-the-valley. (Lucy Lomax).

I went on the Trans-Siberian with a Scotsman dressed in a kilt, whilst I wore cricket whites and took with me stumps, bat and ball, etc. We played cricket on the intermediate stations and involved fellow passengers in our games. (Doug Hudson).

Not everyone welcomes the attentions of their fellow passengers. In a short story entitled *A Chance Acquaintance*, Somerset Maugham described the relationship between two passengers travelling on the Trans-Siberian in 1916:

When you are shut up with a man for ten days in a railway carriage you can hardly fail to learn most of what there is to know about him, and for ten days (for eleven to be exact) Ashenden spent twenty-four hours a day with Mr Harrington. It is true that they went into the dining-room three times a day for their meals, but they sat opposite to one another; it is true that the train stopped for an hour, morning and afternoon, so that they were able to have a tramp up and down the platform, but they walked side by side. Ashenden made acquaintance with some of his fellow-travellers and sometimes they came into the compartment to have a chat, but if they only spoke French or German Mr Harrington would watch them with acidulous disapproval and if they spoke English he would never let them get a word in.

For Mr Harrington was a talker ... It took eleven days at that time to get from Vladivostok to Petrograd and Ashenden felt that he could not have borne another day. If it had been twelve he would have killed Mr Harrington.

Three travellers' tales: 1909 — 1985

The following tales, spanning many decades of Siberian rail travel, are accounts of journeys by three different travellers on the Trans-Manchurian, Trans-Mongolian and Trans-Siberian routes.

1909

Captain O.T.Tuck R.N. was a naval officer who spent most of his career in the Far East. Having learnt Japanese, he became a naval interpreter and assistant naval attache in Tokyo. When, at the age of 33, he was posted back to the Admiralty in 1909, he chose the quickest route via Vladivostok, Manchuria (on The Chinese Eastern Railway) and the Trans-Siberian Railway, rather than the more usual sea passage. He left Japan on March 24, 1909 and arrived punctually in Moscow on April 8. After sightseeing in Moscow, he travelled via St. Petersburg (now Leningrad), Finland, Stockholm, Berlin, Amsterdam, and Hook of Holland to England (Harwich) where he arrived on April 23. Throughout the trip, Captain Tuck kept a diary from which the following extracts have been taken with the kind permission of his daughter, Mrs Sylvia Crotty.

March 24.
Left Tokyo by the 6.30pm Kobe Express. I had quite a send-off and was introduced to Viscount Kaneko who was also on his way to Kobe. He told me that Prince Khilkov, President of the Siberian Railway, worked for five years on American railways incognito, starting with brakesman and ending as Section Manager.

March 25.
Slept rather poorly in the train; it was rather cold. Arrived at Kobe at 10 and went to the Oriental Hotel. Kobe is an uninteresting sort of town after Tokyo; narrow dirty streets and poor shops.

March 26.
Started from Sansomiya by the 8.18am train which went straight to Tsuruga. We passed through two snowstorms before reaching Tsuruga where it began to snow heavily also. Bought my steamer ticket for 37 Japanese Yen. The ship is the *Mongolia* from the Russian Volunteer Fleet. Met Heponstall [a naval colleague] on board and got a cabin to myself. We left soon after the soup, feeling seasick and unhappy. Everyone on the ship is Russian and

the only person who understands English seems to be the Chinese headboy.

March 27.
Brilliantly fine weather, but still rough. I am distinctly seasick and cannot face the meals which I hear from Heponstall are excellent.

March 28.
Arrived at Vladivostock at 11am. Magnificent weather, cold but not bitter; clear air and bright sun. The ice had been broken for us but we had to crash through large pieces between fifty and a hundred feet square. They broke quite easily, though they seemed to be at least a foot thick. After the passports and baggage had been examined, we drove up to the Grand Hotel and got rooms. I was feeling so bad that I went to see a doctor. He jeered at me gently for not knowing French or German, sounded my stomach and gave me some powders which certainly made me feel better. I am to eat fish and egg and no meat but veal.

Walked around the town with Heponstall. The snow is gone from the paths but remains in thawing masses in the streets. We went down and walked on the ice in the harbour. In the evening went with Heponstall, a German big-game hunter and another man who looks like a Viking, to a restaurant. We asked for hors d'oeuvres and they produced crab legs, a foot long, and several kinds of caviar. I ate both; they were delicious but in a short while made me feel so ill that I returned to the hotel and went to bed.

March 29.
Left at 3.15 in the Trans-Siberian Express.

The Grand Hotel are appalling robbers. I bought in Tokyo, a coupon for 8 Yen which I was assured would pay for everything. We had to have breakfast in addition to the two meals included in the ticket and altogether with tips I spent about 5 Yen more than the coupon — 13 Yen in all.

The hotel was very inferior and only one man understood any English. Other passengers in the train are a German Consul and a few others. Perhaps more will board at Kharbin [Harbin]. The bay, skirted by the train after Vladivostock, is all frozen. We saw many sledges crossing it.

March 30.
Did not get up till 2; my inside was very unruly all last night and

gave me a good deal of exercise. The bed is most comfortable, and I have a compartment to myself. Spoke of my stomach trouble to a little Japanese doctor named Fujinami who, very kindly, gave me some of his own private store of medicine — a powder which he guaranteed would cure it. The powder seemed to have the desired effect and I feel much better.

March 31.

A day of bright sunshine, snow-clad plains and occasional stops at stations where one walks up and down without realising the temperature till one faces the wind. My travelling companion turns out to be Dr Sanders of Hong Kong, an excellent fellow and we have many acquaintances in common. My inside is better, thanks to the powerful medicine of Dr Fujinami. This morning at 9 we came round the big spiral that leads up to a tunnel through the hills. The country beyond is all white with snow and dazzling to look at.

Arrived at Khailar [Hailar] at 1.30. Got out for a walk, delightfully exhilarating at first, but the icy wind soon made your ears ache. A man had a thermometer in his hand — it went down to below 20° F, so the real temperature must have been very low.

At Manchuria station [present-day Manzhouli], just at the border of Siberia (we have been in Manchuria up to the present) all the baggage was inspected by the Customs people. Dr Sanders and I went into town and bought some jam; a feat only possible by much expressive pantomime and the recognition of the words 'Conserve' and 'Oranja'.

April 1.

Dressed and went out for a few minutes to see a bit of the town before breakfast. Very cold — saw a Russian peasant with his moustache frozen stiff.

April 2.

Woke at 5 to find the train running beside Lake Baikal, a white snow-covered expanse with occasional men walking on it or driving in sledges. We followed round the lake till 2, when we arrived at Irkutsk, where there was a slight thaw in the streets.

Changed trains. The new one was alongside where we stopped. Got a carriage in exactly the same situation and an identical coupe. After an hour's wait, started off again. Played chess and bridge; talked, ate and slept.

April 3.
Over the Siberian plain. Beautiful white snow and forests of silver birches; the whole scenery exceedingly pretty. Passed Kansk, a biggish town with about six churches. There was some snow falling for about an hour of the journey which made the pine and birch forests even lovelier. Half a dozen horses standing in an open snow plain, with their backs white with the falling snow, made a thorough Siberian picture.

April 5.
Breakfasted just before Kansk. A spring broke in one of the carriages and we spent an hour at Kansk for repairs. A beautiful, sunny, spring morning; the thermometer in the station shows 12° but there is plenty of snow all round.

Arrived at Omsk at 5; a large town some miles from the station. There were two emigrant trains at anchor, full of dirty, bovine people. These Russians are remarkably white under their grime: one hardly ever sees any pink skin or ruddy cheeks; all are dead white, with grey eyes and pale, yellow hair.

April 6.
The trains full of emigrants consist of baggage trucks in which rough shelves and rickety stoves have been fitted. Into these carriages crowd men, women and children all clad in filthy-smelling sheepskins and thick, long boots. The government gives them 150 roubles and 10 acres apiece and only charges a railway fare of 4 roubles to Irkutsk.

At Chelyabinsk, saw a large stuffed bear and wolf and a stall selling articles made from Ural stones. These were mounted in such inferior metal that I didn't feel inclined to buy anything.

We ran into Ural country about lunchtime. The hills are only a couple of thousand feet high and are covered in snow and pines.

April 7.
The first day in Europe was signalised by a splendid sample of European weather — raw cold fog, rain, sleet and slush. The scenery consists of an absolutely flat treeless waste covered with a dirty sheet of melting snow, full of rents disclosing the black mud of the Russian plain.

Had a long discussion with Heponstall, Wallace and Sanders on the subject of the route home. We all want to go by Petersburg [Leningrad], Stockholm and Copenhagen, if the Wagon-Lits people will change our tickets. People say that they are very bad when once you get in their clutches; and they are obstinate as mules in opposing any change.

April 8.
Still crossing the black plain; it is perfectly flat and treeless and depressing to the last degree, partly on account of the weather which is bad.

At Tula occurred a tragic incident. In the cabin next to mine has been an old Jew with his wife and a little almond-eyed daughter of six or so. He has been boxed in all the time and has looked very ill; he objected strongly to any fresh air. However, as the train slowed down at Tula, he ran out of his cabin into the gangway and on the platform he fell down between the two carriages with blood pouring out of his mouth. Dr Sanders ran up and pronounced him dead. His wife raised a weird oriental lament, but otherwise was quite calm and capable. They brought a stretcher and carried off the poor, shrunken old body and the woman and child and all their baggage left the train.

We arrived at Moscow at 7.35, exactly the scheduled time; not bad after nearly 6000 miles (9400km) from Vladivostock. Rather a pandemonium at the station, everybody shouting and nobody doing anything. We eventually drove off to the Metropole Hotel in a cab. The hotel is a magnificent one; splendid marble columns in the halls and the whole place furnished in the 'new' art. My room costs 4 roubles per night. Dined for 1.50 Roubles in the hotel and afterwards went for a stroll in the Kremlin.

April 9.
Sanders, Nuttall, Wallace and myself set off after breakfast for the Kremlin. We climbed the big campanile, at the foot of which lies the big broken bell, and saw the view. It was a perfect day, the atmosphere transparent so that the snow-clad downs and pine forests all round Moscow could be clearly seen. The view is probably unique (of course, every view is — logically). The golden domes, which glittered in every direction and the brilliant colouring of the various buildings are what I remember best, beyond the clearness of the air.

We then went into the 'pineapple' church of St Basil. The interior is cut up into chapels, from the dome of which looks down an immense face — rather awe-inspiring to the simple peasant, I should think. The China Inland missionary with us was struck by the fact that the chapels were too tiny to admit of any preaching; I don't think the orthodox church cares much about teaching or conduct: all that seems to be necessary is to pay the priests and let them do all the work of saving you.

After lunch, Count Ancilotto (Secretary of the Italian Embassy in Tokyo, who happens to be going home) kindly took me to St Saviours where, from a special gallery, we heard the Good Friday Mass. Each person had a candle which, at a given point in the service, they lit from one another till the whole congregation seen from above, seemed to glitter with golden stars.

April 10
Got up at 2 last night (or rather, this morning) and went with Wallace to the Church of St Saviour; Dr Sanders had told us that there was to be a very special procession. We got to the church, found it crowded and a service going on, but after standing listening to the wonderful bottom C of the intoner for 2 hours, we felt we had had enough and left. There are no seats in a Russian church and we really could not stand any more. Consequently, we only just got up in time to join Count Ancilotto in his specially permitted visit to the Imperial Palace. We were shown round by a majordomo with the most perfect manners and a white beard brushed horizontally in two, thick bands. The white hall of the Order of St. George, the gilded avenue of pillars in the throne room, Peter the Great's dining room with the lunette for his harem and the beautiful parquet floors, remain best in my memory.

There was a corridor showing all the small pictures on one side and the gold plates and salt cellars on which was presented the bread and salt from each city of Russia to Alexander II. We happened to pass the Imperial Chapel just at the moment of administering the bread and wine in the mass; there was a family participating, probably some of the people of the Palace.

After leaving the Kremlin, we drove round some of the principal streets. I was struck by the wealth everywhere apparent. The florists are full of magnificent flowers. We went into the Elisieff Freres, a shop for foodstuffs; it is splendidly decorated inside and holds every kind of food arranged to tantalize by every wile that art can suggest.

April 11. Easter Day
Out again at midnight last night for the celebrated Easter Eve service at the Church of the Assumption. Sleeting, and the road disgusting with slush, but a fairly large crowd assembled in the big

square. At midnight all the bells were rung, a few desultory fireworks were let off, and a procession of crowned priests came out of one door of the church and into the other. Probably the outside ceremonial was cut short on account of the indescribably miserable weather. We expected everybody to cry "Xristus voskres" and kiss everybody near; but the crowd immediately began to move off without any outburst of enthusiasm. We followed, thawed our feet in the hotel and turned in, rather disappointed with the whole performance. These recurring feasts of midnight religion are very sleepifying and we did not breakfast till 10. Wrote some letters and postcards and read all the illustrated papers in the hotel reading room. We had to dine in our rooms since the police at Easter insist on the restaurants being closed.

Left at 9 in the hotel motorbus and eventually boarded the Wagon-Lits. The train left at 10, after which oblivion.

April 12.
Woke in the train to find the same scenery that we have seen for so many thousands of miles in Siberia: flat snow plain with pine and birch forests. Got to Petersburg at 9.30am and drove down the Nevsky Prospekt, a magnificent street 4 miles long, to the Hotel de France. After 'café complet' engaged a guide, and the four of us set off with him to the Hermitage. Found it closed for the holidays, but a visiting card to the Governor procured us admission.

We had to wait for an hour though and filled in the time at the Zoological museum, where the mammoth discovered in Siberia is located. It is mounted exactly as it was found, sitting on its haunches and apparently trying to get up by the use of its forepaw. It looks rather pathetic and is probably a small one, as it is not any bigger than an elephant. It has reddish hair remaining on a good part of its body and its tusks are curved in a beautiful arc. Other fine things in this Museum were the white polar bear family standing in a wrecked boat, and a pair of Siberian wolves.

Returned to the Hermitage. Miles of old masters and tons of gilt furniture. The portico is held up by grey granite colossi sculpted by a large-minded Russian. After lunch, an orgy of churches. The Memorial Church built over the spot where Alexander II was assassinated in 1881 was described by the guide as the most beautiful in the world. It most emphatically is not. Outside it is like the pineapple church in Moscow and inside is a discord of blues and greens. The rood screen is surmounted by crosses of enormous topazes which look like glass. The most striking thing is the bit of road where the bomb exploded which has been left in situ and is surrounded by a black marble catafalque.

April 13.
Went to the Winter Palace. While waiting for admission, we met Ancilotto and strolled into St Izak's again. The most striking part is contained in the private rooms of Alexander II, which are in exactly the same state as when he was assassinated. The 30 kopeks in his pocket are shown and his handkerchief; the clocks are stopped at the hour of his death — only the dust which daily falls is removed; it is just as when he left it.

After lunch we went to see the fortress of St Peter and St Paul. The church contains all the silver wreaths presented to the tombs of the emperors who are buried there. They are hung on the pillars and give a very tinselly effect. Also saw Peter the Great's cottage and boat, both of which he built himself. Another house has been built over them to preserve them and the priests have turned his bedroom into a temple which has special efficacy in curing sick persons! Sanders and myself went to the Finnish station, from whence we started for Abo and Stockholm.

¹3⁴
14 May   14 Friday [131 231]   [5th Month] 1909

Dear Sir!

    Your favour of the 2-d inst. to hand, herewith we are communicating to you, that the asked for pair of blue trousers, where not found in the room you occupied after your departure; my be tnat you forgot them elsewhere.

    Regretting that we were not able to help you to get in possesion of the mentioned object, we remain, dear Sir,

        yours very truly

Hotel „METROPOLE" Moscow
    Manager *Richter*

I find on arriving in London that I have not got my blue serge trousers. Thinking I must have left them behind in Moscow I wrote to the Manager of the Hotel + got the above answer in reply.

1970

Hilary Costa Sanseverino, who now lives in Italy, sent this account of a journey with her young son.

Fashions in travel change. In the sixties, all those adventurous souls were hitting the trail to Russia and returning with horror stories about Intourist, lack of bath plugs and two hour waits for their breakfast boiled egg. Now, the intrepid masses go to China and complain about hotel service, the forced visits to factories and communes and the primitive bathrooms.

The way of travelling has also changed. When my father first went out to China in 1906, a few years after the Boxer Rebellion, he travelled out by boat and returning to England after two years, decided it would be more restful, as well as cheaper, to take the Trans-Siberian Railway from Peking to Moscow. As a result, my childhood memories are filled with exotic pictures of this nostalgic train puffing slowly northward, following the Great Wall of China and crossing the plains of Mongolia, before the monotonous days spent chugging through the birch woods of Siberia.

Those were the days when travellers were not tourists and the train was a luxurious hotel with a gleaming samovar at the end of each compartment and everyone had their private suite with anti-macassared sofas and the sheets were changed every day. The menu read like Maxims in Paris, and the three weeks that it took to make the journey passed slowly and pleasantly, talking to friends, playing cards, eating the vast and delicious meals and taking strolls during the frequent stops that the train was obliged to make.

From my childhood onwards, I have seldom heard a train go by and not wished to be on it.

When I was posted to Peking in the late sixties, I decided for sentimental and economic reasons to take the Trans-Siberian back to England with my four-month-old son. As I wished to pass through Mongolia, I chose the Chinese train and travelled 'soft class' for the princely sum of thirty pounds sterling. For a few pounds more, I also bought a book of coupons with which to buy food in the restaurant car. The baby had his case of sieved food and I had my bottle of whisky and ten paperbacks.

Having waved goodbye to my husband, I settled down in my compartment in which my father would have felt perfectly at home. A plush, floral sofa which converted into a bed and a deep armchair which could have come straight out of an exclusive men's club in London.

The crocheted antimacassars were still much in evidence and converted gas lamps were perfectly in keeping with this anachronistic form of travel. Even in the passages the Victorian dream continued. A thick carpet covered the floor and the numerous mirrors reflected the gleaming brass fittings. Tassled swags held back the deep-red, plush curtains which were comforting to draw during a Siberian winter, but oppressive as I sweltered in the Chinese summer heat.

In those days, travel more than fifteen miles outside Peking was only possible with a special permit, so the view from the train was fascinating as we followed the Great Wall which wound up and down the hills and finally snaked off into the distance. The trains on the Trans-Siberian railway have a peculiar gait as the rails have square, rather than staggered joints and for travelling with a young child this is ideal — the equivalent of being in a permanently rocking cradle.

At the Mongolian border the compartment swarmed with small, smiling, moon-faced Mongolians. Passports were checked and although my health papers were solemnly read upside down, I was pronounced fit enough to enter the People's Republic of Mongolia. To the romantically inclined, the view from the window is pure Ghenghis Khan. Mongolian children learn to ride before they can walk and consequently, I have never seen such a nation of bow-legged people. As we chugged towards Ulan Bator, a horseman wearing a glorious, dark-green, brocaded robe (known as a *del*) and brandishing a vicious scimitar, galloped alongside the train for a few hundred yards. My cynical companion observed he had a great future with Metro-Goldwin-Mayer. The station at Ulan Bator was packed with people clutching provisions and the chickens pecked and scratched in the dust. Although the younger men wore Western clothes, their heads were covered with large felt berets of the French variety or those cleverly constructed newspaper hats reminiscent of the carpenter in Alice in Wonderland.

The food in the Chinese restaurant car had been a gastronomic indulgence of the finest quality, but the end came when it was uncoupled at the Mongolian border.

The Mongolian restaurant car arrived in replacement and for two days at breakfast, lunch and dinner, we were offered a monotonous diet of boiled mutton which was fatty, greasy and had a particularly revolting smell, rivalled only by the smell of mare's milk which is considered a great delicacy. The baby and I began to share the baby food. I spurned the milk, or *koumiss*, and sneaked evaporated milk from his tins and consoled myself, as I spooned down a puree of beef and carrots, that things would change with the new restaurant car in Russia.

To mark this occasion, I changed for dinner and beamed expectantly at the vast lady who slapped an enormous and imposing menu down in front of me. Pages of evocative dishes swam before my eyes as I slavered at the mouth, each dish seeming better than the last.

I reached my decision. "I should like the chicken Kiev, please."

"Nyet", she barked, brushing a fly off her ample bosom.

"Well", I hesitated, "In that case, this veal looks rather good, if you could only help me to pronounce it correctly."

"Nyet, nyet". And my hopes faded as a plump finger pointed firmly to borscht which eventually arrived in a stainless steel bowl and ... ten years later, my most evocative memory of the Trans-Siberian Railway is of bowls of borscht on every table in the restaurant car, swilling and slopping as the train rounded the gentle curves through Siberia. The tablecloths were never changed and each day, as I waited for my borscht, I traced my finger through borscht maps on the cloth which started out modestly as Europe and by the time we reached Moscow, had blossomed into huge, mythological maps wih rivers and oceans and ranges of dried cabbage mountains.

After the first day of this diet, I headed towards the *tovarich*, or complaints book, prominently displayed at the end of the dining car but virgin sheets and a venomous look from my only adult contact with food, sent me straight down the thickly carpeted corridor and towards a guilty half-jar of strained prunes.

I cursed myself for not taking a Russian phrase book or roubles. We stopped three or four times a day, but I could not supplement the meagre diet by buying sweet cakes or fruit on the stations during the frequent stops. After my two English companions left the train in Ulan Bator, I decided to investigate the others. All the foreigners had been placed in a special compartment. They were mostly Russians returning home, East Germans or Poles. The uniform train dress was pyjamas which did not look incongruous beside the attendants' Mao jackets and baggy trousers. My efforts at conversation were repulsed by suspicious looks and banging of doors as my new 'friends' retreated into their compartments.

I was the only woman in my section of the train and the second day into Siberia, my contemplative gaze of the pine trees and birch woods was rudely shattered as the door burst open and a stocky, fair-haired man catapulted in. Shutting the door firmly and locking it behind him, he announced with a wide grin "Me

Polish sailor. You have beautiful legs." (This was a hopeful figment of his imagination as, not having pyjamas, the legs were inside trousers). I pointed to the sleeping baby and, with a leer and a wink, he was gone as quickly as he had arrived.

My third Siberian day was spent ejecting numerous Polish sailors out of my compartment. On learning that there were, in fact, thirty of them who had left their ship in Shanghai and were returning to Poland by train, I reported to their Captain and explained, amongst other things, that the baby was getting very little sleep. He did not speak much English but promised that the disruptions would cease and patting me on the shoulder said "But you have beautiful legs." Obviously, their English/Polish phrasebook was a thin volume indeed.

Siberia had a predictable permanence. Despite the July sun, a smoggy fog filtered over identical towns with wooden bungalows, steel derricks and small stations where Lenin's statue, like Big Brother, went unnoticed but still reminded that, for most of my fellow travellers, the ultimate achievement was Moscow. I prefer to remember the forests of pines and silver birch and the magpies, lazily flapping off the tracks.

"One for sorrow, two for joy; three for a wedding, four for a boy", I said to the baby and speculated that the Russian equivalent, if it exists, must go up to fifty to accommodate those hordes of Siberian magpies.

I awoke one morning and saw a vast sea and thought, for one bleary-eyed moment, that the train had rushed backwards with the speed of light. But this was Lake Baikal, so enormous that it took us a whole day to get round it. I know we went through Omsk and Tomsk, which have a Gilbert and Sullivan air about them, and Sverdlovsk, which marks the end of Asia and the beginning of Europe. We must also have stopped at Perm and Kirov, but everybody said "Nyet, nyet" to all my questions, laboured as they were in English, Italian, French and, in extremis, very rusty Latin.

The only place that seemed different was Yaroslavl. At first, I could not understand why my Russian companions emerged from their compartments to gaze solemnly at what seemed to me yet another identical Russian town. I finally understood that the great river, which ran sluggishly and darkly beside the railway tracks, was the legendary Volga.

Life settled down to an orderly routine. As I had to share my bathroom with two Chinese bureaucrats, I would listen until the swishings and scrubbings had stopped and then wash and feed the baby. Once I misjudged the moment and burst upon my travelling companion who was gazing benignly at himself in the glass and forced him to retreat in confusion — pink, giggling and apologetic.

The long railway journey began to induce a trance-like state where reality slipped into distortion. I lost all sense of time but I hoped we were nearing Moscow. The whisky had long since run out, I was on my ninth paperback and the baby had only four jars left. The restaurant car was reduced (or perhaps uplifted) to goat's cheese and black bread. There was that restless stir and snapping of suitcases that precedes the end of a long journey. Everyone came to stand in the corridor, smoking and chatting and then, through the semi-darkness, I saw the onion domes of Moscow, tipped with the early morning sun. After seven days and six nights, we had arrived on time, to the exact minute.

In 1905 a honeymoon couple were travelling on the Trans-Siberian through Manchuria, on their way back to Europe. Since the summer weather was exceptionally hot and the temperature did not drop during the night, the couple kept the large windows open at night and, before retiring to bed, hung their clothes on special hooks on both sides of the window. One morning, Count Ermes Berg, the bridegroom, woke early and discovered that the clothes had disappeared. The Count rang the bell for the steward and asked what could have happened to the clothes since he had, of course, locked the door. 'Oh, your Highness', came the reply, 'You should never have left the window open. It is common knowledge that Chinese thieves secretly travel on the roof of the carriages and carry fishing rods with hooks which they use to fish out all they can reach inside the compartment.' The situation was most embarassing since not only had they lost their clothes, but — alas — their passports and all their money had disappeared as well. (Dagmar de Rehren).

1985

John Fleming, from Lancashire, must be one of the oldest people to have joined a Trans-Siberian tour, but the following extracts from his letter about the trip show that he fully enjoyed it.

I shall be 82 in May. I farmed up to the age of 45 and then worked as a Street Crossing Patrolman (lollipop man) for 15 years. I went to Russia in 1983 for the first time and then booked again for Siberia. There were 17 of us and it was a very happy party; everyone was called by their Christian name. We flew from Manchester to Moscow and then flew all night to Khabarovsk. After staying one night, we set off for the station to board the Trans-Siberian train. While we were waiting, a clock was playing a lovely tune and we all remarked how nice it was.

What a thrill getting all our bags and cases aboard. We soon settled in: me and my three mates had our own carriage and spent three days and three nights we shall never forget. We had a party each night including two Russian lads who worked on the train. There were 17 carriages pulled by two engines and we had to go through seven carriages to get to the dining car, but we made plenty of friends. The food was good, and as much as you could eat. We were all kept busy taking snaps. What a vast country it is.

Our next stop was Irkutsk where I walked around the busy market. One old man looked at me and my badge. In 1942, you see, they were selling this badge (red star with hammer and sickle) for one shilling to help the convoys from England to Murmansk. When he came up to me, he pointed to it and I just said "England". "England", he repeated, and held his hand out to shake hands. Another old man passing, saluted and smiled (old soldier). Several folks asked me where I had got my badge from, so I told them. Some soldiers looked at it stony-faced. But, as I have always said, the Russian folk are no different to us.

After a day or two, our group said they felt as if the ground was still moving under their feet. I would like to go on the full 8-day journey, but I may be too old. Last August, I went up to the Isle of Bute to see some of our group, all glad to see one another and to talk of our trip to Siberia.

'This journey was, for me, one of the outstanding events of my life, and I enjoyed every minute of it to the full.' (D.Abel Smith).

TRAILROVERS

For people who want to discover first hand and for themselves the World as it really is. Since 1975 Trailrovers has offered the best value for money, convenience and security possible, coupled with fellowship, freedom and adventure.

Each Rover is individual in concept and is tailor-made to suit the particular requirements of travellers in each region.

All tours are accompanied by very experienced tour leaders, whose job is to iron out all day to day problems.

The four tours can be done individually or joined together to make a complete journey London to Bali.

*London to Yokohama, the great overland journey via the Trans-Siberian Railway - 21 days. From the magnificent city of Moscow, visit the imperial city of Leningrad before boarding the Trans-Siberian express bound for the Pacific Ocean. Stop en-route at Novosibirsk in the heartland of Russia. Visit Lake Baikal, the Worlds deepest freshwater lake from Irkutsk, the capital of Eastern Siberia, and spend two nights in the Russian city of Khabarovsk. Finally unwind on a two day cruise from Nakhodka to Yokohama, across the Sea of Japan.

* Plus Northern Thailand - 12 days. A fully escorted tour allowing you to experience a wide range of traditional cultures, amid stunning scenery and in a climate dry and clear during the day and refreshingly cool at night. Travel by boat, bus, train, on foot and elephant through this exotic country from Bangkok in the south to the legendary Golden Triangle in the far north.

* And the Bangkok to Bali Rover - 20 days. Our most popular tour as a complete holiday in its own right or as an ideal stepping stone for those on their way to Australia. Relax on the beaches of Penang, 'The Pearl of the Orient', before heading off to the once colonial hill station of the Cameron Highlands. Enjoy a Singapore Sling at the Raffles Hotel. Watch a shadow puppet show or Javanese classical dancers in Yogyakarta. See the sun rise from the top of Mount Bromo. Arrive in Bali feeling a sense of achievement.

To book any Trailrover tour or for further information plus your **FREE** copy of the Trailfinder Magazine:
Call **TRAILFINDERS** on 01-937 9631
42-48 Earls Court Road, London W8 6EJ

Part 2

PLANNING AND PREPARATION

Transit or stop-over?

The Trans-Siberian is becoming especially popular with travellers from neighbouring countries of Eastern Europe (Scandinavia, Germany, Austria, etc.) as a means of low-price overland transit from Europe to Asia or vice-versa. In a sense, it has become a limited substitute for the overland route to India which was once flooded with travellers until events in the Middle East, Iran and Afghanistan reduced them to a trickle. With the opening of Tibet and the border crossing between Tibet and Nepal, as well as the Kunjirap border-crossing between China and northern Pakistan, it has become easier to complete a huge overland circuit around and across the landmasses of Europe and Asia. Since travel in the USSR, compared with travel in Asia, is extremely expensive, the budget-minded either take a student package tour or settle for fleeting impressions of Siberia from the window and put off a full trip to the USSR for some other time.

For some, however, a week on a train without a pause has little appeal. On the route to Japan, there is a compulsory overnight stop-over at Khabarovsk to change trains. Of the other towns open to foreign visitors in Siberia, Irkutsk is a clear first choice for a stop-over, way ahead of Novosibirsk, Bratsk and the less usual or accessible towns of Abakan, Barnaul, Yakutsk, Komsomolsk, Norilsk, Ulan-Ude, Omsk, Tomsk and Krasnoyarsk. Many travellers find Leningrad easier on the soul and, if there is a choice, give Moscow less attention.

Check with Intourist or affiliated travel agencies for package tours with different options in Siberia. Duration of stay in each town is usually a few days, and it is possible to skip an occasional guided tour and browse in town on your own for a while. Stopovers arranged individually for independent travellers have a whopping price tag which is probably only worthwhile for specialists or those who have expenses paid.

☭

An eminent ornithologist from the Soviet bloc was so besotted with the bird potential of the Siberian landscape that he slung his survival pack on his back and jumped off the Trans-Siberian into the wilds near Lake Baikal. After a week of heady bird-spotting, he returned to the line and clambered onto the train to Nakhodka. In Japan, his research funds ran out, but being a tall man he was able to beg from Japanese, who, astounded at the height from which he stooped, poured enough cash into his hat for him not only to complete a tour of all the wildlife parks in Japan, but also to pay for his return ticket.

Independent or packaged travel?

This decision depends on a variety of factors. The two major Soviet travel bureaux are Intourist and Sputnik (specialises in youth travel). Independent or group arrangements are channelled through them. 'The tourist is helpless without Intourist' is the blunt message of one publicity pamphlet.

Most independent travellers either take the cheapest package (which is non-stop) or a package which allows one or more stopovers. Those who travel independently pay higher prices for guides, car hire, transfers etc. They should also be willing to expend an inordinate amount of time on petty requests and possess great patience.

If you know Russian, you may find it easier to arrange deviations from a standard itinerary, but don't count on it.

Group travel (through Intourist) can be easier on your blood pressure and usually includes shepherding by interpreters through visits to factories, schools, industrial sites, youth organisations, etc. For each stop on your tour, it is standard practice to have local Intourist guides as well as your main Intourist guide. Some groups have been surprised to find themselves almost outnumbered by guides.

Tours arranged through other tour operators will still include a local Intourist guide but the itinerary is more likely to suit your interests.

The following selection of tour operators and their tours is intended to provide a rough idea of what is available. Itineraries and prices change constantly, so contact tour operators direct for details.

INTOURIST 1292 Regent Street, London W1R 6QL. Tel: (01) 631 1252.
71 Deansgate, Manchester M3. Tel: (061) 8340230.

For independent tourists or groups travelling via the USSR to Japan and Hong Kong (or vice-versa), Intourist offers itineraries on the Trans-Siberian Railway for travel from Moscow to Nakhodka. The itineraries differ in the number of places visited, the comfort and types of transport used, the length of the trip and the corresponding price. The price will normally include hotel accommodation, three meals a day in the hotel, one guided sightseeing tour in each city visited, transfer services on arrival and departure and domestic transportation. Often excluded in the price are meals on the train (sometimes vouchers are used), international transportation, visas for countries other than the Soviet Union and, of course, personal expenses. Arrangements can also be made for travel between Moscow and Beijing (via Mongolia or via Manchuria). There are many permutations available which could, for example, include international transportation and specific tours of the Soviet Union. Intourist offices can provide a folder with itineraries and prices (from

£300 upwards) for the Trans-Siberian.
The following are a few representative itineraries:

1. Moscow to Khabarovsk (8 hours by air, non-stop); Khabarovsk to Nakhodka (16 hours by rail).

2. Moscow to Irkutsk (82 hours by rail); Irkutsk to Khabarovsk (3 hours by air); Khabarovsk to Nakhodka (16 hours by rail).

3. Moscow to Nakhodka (165 hours by rail with change of train and overnight stop in Nakhodka).

4. Moscow to Irkutsk (5 hours by air); Irkutsk to Khabarovsk (67 hours by rail and stop-over in Khabarovsk); Khabarovsk to Nakhodka (16 hours by rail).

5. Moscow to Bratsk (7 hours by air, non-stop); Bratsk to Irkutsk (1 hour by air); Irkutsk to Khabarovsk (67 hours by rail and stop-over in Khabarovsk); Khabarovsk to Nakhodka (16 hours by rail).

The Scandinavian Student Travel Service (SSTS)
117 Hauchsvej, 1825 Copenhagen V, Denmark. Tel: (01) 21 85 00.

This is a highly recommended organisation which provides, in conjunction with Sputnik, tours to the Soviet Union for budget- conscious student travellers (but it is not necessary to be a student). They have a wide variety of tours, usually in the summer, which can be booked direct (at a slight saving in cost) or through student travel agents in Europe, North America and Hong Kong. Tours include the basics: sightseeing programme, youth-group meeting, accommodation, meals and transport. Since the tours start and finish within the Soviet Union, you must either arrange inward and outward transport yourself, or, if you feel less adventurous, let SSTS book you on their connecting flights. The following is a sample of their Trans-Siberian programme:

1. Helsinki — Leningrad — Moscow — Novosibirsk — Irkutsk — Khabarovsk — Nakhodka — Yokohama. Duration 20 days.

2. Helsinki — Leningrad — Moscow — Irkutsk — Bratsk — Irkutsk — Khabarovsk — Nakhodka — Yokohama. 20 days.

3. Leningrad — (Moscow) — Novosibirsk — Irkutsk — Khabarovsk — Moscow. 18 days.

Prices range between US$700 and US$950 and can be chosen to include or exclude connecting flights.

Yorkshire Tours

149 Thornton Lodge Road, Huddersfield HD1 3JQ. Tel: (0484) 24269.

This company offers tours including travel on the Trans-Siberian and uses bus transport between England and Budapest. Groups include all ages and are often large and cheery. Prices range from £325 for an Irkutsk tour, to £885 for a China tour returning on the Trans- Siberian via Moscow.

Explore Worldwide

7 High St., Aldershot, Hants GU11 1BH. Tel: (0252) 319448.

These adventure tour operators offer a Trans-Siberian itinerary from £995. They also provide an interesting tour along the following route: Moscow — Irkutsk (by rail) — Ulan Bator (by rail) — Beijing (by rail) — Pyongyang (N.Korea).

Society for Anglo-Chinese Understanding (SACU)

152 Camden High Street, London NW1. Tel: (01) 482 4292.

SACU has a wide range of functions which include organising travel and tours to China. Part of their tour programme offers the opportunity to follow Trans-Siberian routings which are then merged into various China tours:

1. **Winter Special** Leningrad — Moscow — Irkutsk — Harbin — Beijing — Xian — Beijing — Moscow.
   This tour by air and rail lasts 23 days and includes Christmas in Moscow and New Year on the Trans-Siberian.

2. **Russia — China Express** Moscow — Irkutsk — Beijing —Shanghai — Hangzhou — Guilin — Guangzhou — Hong Kong.
   This 21-day tour includes a Trans-Siberian element between Irkutsk and Beijing.

3. **Mongolia — China Express** Moscow — Ulan Bator — Datong — Beijing — Xian — Shanghai — Wuyishan — Fuzhou — Xiamen — Hong Kong. This 28-day tour follows the Trans-Mongolian route.

4. **From the Steppes to the Yellow River** Moscow — Hailar —Beijing — Xian — Luoyang — Gongxian — Zhengzhou — Beijing. This 24-day tour follows the Trans-Manchurian route.

5. **China Express and the Yangzi Gorges** Moscow — Beijing — Chengdu — Emeishan — Chengdu — Chongqing — Yangzi — Wuhan — Guangzhou — Hong Kong. This 30-day tour combines a Trans-Siberian rail trip with a Yangzi boat ride.

Prices for these tours start at £1,358.

Voyages Jules Verne
Travel Promotions Ltd, 10 Glentworth Street, London NW1 5PG
Tel: (01) 486 8080.
Hong Kong office: Office 203/204 2/F Arcade, Lee Garden Hotel, Hysan Avenue, Causeway Bay, Hong Kong. Tel: 5-7953181.
Voyages Jules Verne offers a wide variety of sophisticated tours, including some on the Trans-Siberian Railway, such as:

1. **Red Arrow Express** By rail from London to Hong Kong via Moscow — Irkutsk — Ulan Bator — Beijing and Canton. Duration 21 days. Tour also operates in opposite direction.

2. **St Petersburg Express** By rail from Leningrad along the Trans-Siberian Railway to Irkutsk with return by air. Duration 13 days.

3. **Tian An Men Express** By rail and air from London to China via Leningrad, Moscow, Irkutsk, Ulan Bator, Datong, Beijing and Hong Kong. 20 days.

4. **Central Kingdom Express** By rail from London to Hong Kong via Paris, Berlin, Warsaw, Moscow, Irkutsk, Ulan Bator, Datong, Beijing, Xian, Luoyang, Nanking, Shanghai and Canton. 42 days. Distance covered: 15,017km (9,331 miles).

5. Golden Road to Samarkand A journey from London to the USSR and

Prices for these luxurious tours start at £1420.

When to go

In the winter, temperatures in Siberia and Mongolia often drop to -20°C and sometimes to -40°C. Snowfall is most common at the beginning of the season, so the weather is often crisp, clear-skied and calm from January to March. Apart from Christmas, when bookings are heavy, reservations are easier to obtain at short notice in the winter, a season which appeals to many Trans-Siberian travellers for its bleak, snowy landscapes and relative absence of foreign tourists. The windows on the train are locked in the winter and often grubby, so photography is restricted.

The Siberian summer is short-lived with temperatures rising as high as 35°C. The peak period for travel in this season is June to August and demand for a limited supply of seats is heavy, so book at least eight weeks in advance.

Spring in Siberia lasts from late April to late May. Some travellers feel that it matches the floral delights of summer but with a heavy dose of melting slush and mud. The Siberian autumn, which lasts approximately from September to early October, is the time when the immense forests put on a colour spectacular with the birch playing a leading role.

Visas

If you are travelling eastwards to Japan, you will only be granted a visa for the USSR if your passport is valid for entry to Japan. If you are transiting Mongolia to China, you will have to play ring-a-ring-of-roses with visas. Since each of the countries en route demands to see a visa for the next country as the reassurance that you won't stay, this means you must start in reverse order. So, for those travelling east, the order would be China, Mongolia, USSR, Poland then East Germany. For the sake of clarity, the following section provides only a general outline of requirements; addresses and other details for individual countries are given in *European Gateways* and *Oriental Gateways* later in the book. It is clearly in your own interest to check with the relevant consulates or agencies on the latest requirements.

Before you start pursuing visas, stock up with plenty of passport photos. They should be approximately 4.5cm x 4cm, on a white background, show facial features clearly and not be too dark or otherwise spoilt.

USSR

If you are a national of an Eastern bloc country, Vietnam, North Korea or Mongolia then you are saved the hassle of a visa and can skip this section. For those travelling from Hong Kong, Beijing etc., further details are provided in the relevant sections later in the book (*Oriental Gateways*) but most of the following also applies.

If you book an Intourist package tour or a group tour arranged through an affiliated travel agency, your visa application can only be made after your travel arrangements have been accepted and confirmed by Intourist. This rule also applies to independent travellers who wish to organise their own itinerary by using the obligatory services of a travel agent or going direct through Intourist. Once approval and confirmation have been supplied, a visa application can be made through Intourist or an affiliated travel agency (for which a small handling fee will be charged) or in person. At present visas are issued free of charge to citizens of the UK, Ireland, USA, Canada, Australia and New Zealand.

To apply for a visa you must supply the following

1. Three identical passport-type photographs trimmed to size and affixed to passport/application form as per visa instructions.

2. Visa application form, properly completed.

3. Either your passport or clear photocopies, trimmed to size, of the first five pages of your passport.

NOTE: British citizens must have a full 10-year passport. If you hold a non-British or non-Commonwealth passport, check if there are any restrictions on travel to the USSR. All passports must be valid for at least 3 months after the scheduled return from the USSR. If you are in transit through the USSR, your passport must be valid for entry to the destination country.

4. If you are going to the embassy or consulate in person, you should also present a voucher from a travel agency with the confirmation number from Intourist.

You will be issued with a business, tourist or transit visa. No stamps or entries are made in your passport. The visa is a separate document which is retained at your exit point from the USSR. A tourist visa is normally valid for the duration of your itinerary and will be issued if you are stopping off or touring in the Soviet Union. This type of visa is extendable. A transit visa is usually valid for a maximum of 10 days and is non-extendable. If you take the Trans-Siberian to or from Moscow, this leaves just enough time to get there, stay overnight and then travel straight out of the USSR without a stopover.

Japan

To enter Japan you must either have a visa or your country must have reciprocal visa exemption with Japan.

If you are from one of the countries listed below, you will not require a visa for the period of days given, but do remember, this only applies if you are a tourist and not going to work or seek work in Japan. Immigration officials may want to see an onward ticket and proof of sufficient funds when you land.

The following lists are restricted to countries considered relevant for readers and are a rough guide only. Apply to your nearest Japanese Consulate for fullest and latest details.

Visa Free Status (not to exceed 180 days): Germany, France, Ireland, United Kingdom, Austria, Switzerland.

Visa Free Status (not to exceed 90 days): Belgium, Canada, Denmark, Finland, Italy, Netherlands, Norway, Spain, Sweden.

Visa Free Status (not to exceed 30 days): New Zealand.

If you are from the United States or Australia, you will require a visa which is issued free of charge and is usually valid for 60 days. Multiple visas are also issued.

Mongolia
Most travellers who take the Trans-Siberian, cross Mongolia on a transit visa which is overpriced and usually available in 24 hours. A transit visa is only granted if your passport is valid for entry to your next country of destination. One photo is required.

China
Visas for China are now easier to obtain. Transit visas, valid for 10 days but non-extendable, are readily available in Europe, and obtaining a tourist visa is no longer a complicated procedure (see page 75).

However, if you can obtain only a transit visa, the best solution is to cross China rapidly and enter Hong Kong where Chinese visas for periods ranging from 1 month upwards are easy to obtain.

Another possibility for China-bound travellers became available in February 1986, when a law was enacted which allowed foreigners to apply, 'under special circumstances', for entry at designated points in China. The only snag at present is that it seems to work for some (especially for business travellers with invitations), but not for others. On paper, you can arrive at airports such as Beijing, Tianjin, Shanghai, Hangzhou, Fuzhou, Xiamen, Guilin, Kunming or Xian and at railway stations such as Manzhouli, Erlian or Shenzhen and request a visa (entry/exit only, not multiple entry) valid for one month, six months or even one year.

However, a friend of mine followed the policy sheet and travelled via the Trans-Siberian to Erlian where the perplexed Chinese border officials had never heard of the idea, but finally told him it was a good try and politely let him in.

Hopefully, this will be sorted out soon officially. Meanwhile, it's probably best to stick to the standard procedures whilst keeping in touch with the CTS for the latest developments.

Poland
Transit visas should be obtained prior to travel since obtaining the visa on the train can be dodgy and much more expensive.

East Germany
A transit visa can be obtained within 24 hours or on the train.

The world's longest train journey is from Lisbon in Portugal to Nachodka in the USSR. It takes nine days and two hours.

VISA AGENCIES

If the whole rigmarole of visa hunting threatens to drive you barmy or your time is more usefully employed elsewhere, the agencies below will, for a fee, obtain them for you:

Thomas Cook Passport Dept. 45 Berkeley Street, London W1A 1EB.
Tel: (01) 499 4000.

Travecour
Tempo House, 15/27 Falcon Road, London SW11 2PH. Tel: (01) 223 7662 (ext 35) or (01) 223 4772.

Visa Shop 44 Chandos Place, London WC2N 4HS.
Tel: (01) 379 0419/0376.

Money matters

There is, at present, no limit to the amount of foreign currency, travellers' cheques, etc. that can be brought into and out of the USSR. *But* you are forbidden to bring in or take out roubles, and when you leave the USSR, any unspent Soviet money must be converted back to foreign currency immediately before departure at the border or airport. Since the rouble is not quoted on international money markets, the exchange rate seems somewhat arbitrary. When you enter the USSR, you will have to complete a currency declaration form on which you must declare all the currency and valuables you are bringing into the country.

Most of the costs on a package tour are prepaid, so you probably won't spend much money. Only change small sums into roubles since you will be paying for optional excursions and purchases in foreign currency bars and *Beriozka* (foreign currency shops) in foreign currency anyway.

When you do change money, make sure you get a properly stamped receipt, otherwise on departure there could be problems accounting for your remaining currency.

Travellers cheques and cash should be taken in small denominations. US dollars in small denominations are very handy. Out on the street there are plenty of people offering high rates but be warned, this is illegal.

Apart from the standard sources of travellers cheques, such as Thomas Cook, American Express, etc., the Bank for Foreign Trade of the USSR also advertises travellers cheques in roubles with free conversion and no commission charge when they are used at Soviet banking institutions, Beriozka shops and 'foreign currency only' restaurants and bars. However, reconversion of unused cheques could prove tricky back home.

Plastic money

The following credit cards can now be used in the USSR: Diner's Club; Eurocard (Master Charge, Access); Carte Blanche; American Express and BankAmericard (VISA). Credit cards are accepted by Intourist for its services; by specialised national cuisine restaurants in Moscow, Leningrad and other cities; by department stores such as GUM and TsUM in Moscow and at hard currency shops.

'Some of our relatives were worried that we were going by ourselves to the Soviet Union and suggested we obtain the advice of the Foreign Office. I wrote and received information on how to behave and seek help if necessary. I was asked to complete and return a form giving details of our names, addresses, passport numbers, itinerary, and dates of travel. Having done this, I felt happier.' (Lucie Lomax).

Borders and customs formalities

Lengthy and rigorous inspections are the norm in the USSR and the customs officers take their business seriously. Searches are usually restricted to baggage, clothing lying around in the carriage, seats, luggage racks and stowage space.

Books or magazines which are pornographic, decadent, violent or anti-Soviet will be confiscated. No halt is made at your personal diaries, address books, notebooks and letters. Certain Russian authors are 'approved' others are 'damaging' and will be confiscated. Eric Newby's *The Big Red Train Ride* is on a blacklist, but passes unnoticed sometimes. I travelled once with a Dutchman who put up a tremendous fight on the Mongolian border but finally lost several huge bundles of Dutch newspapers (reading matter for a week on the train) to a meticulous commanding officer who was taking no chances.

Letters or manuscripts aimed at Soviet citizens or written by them for attention outside are clearly liable to confiscation. An American told me how he crossed the border by train in the early hours of the morning and, after the customs official had spent half an hour going through every item in his toilet bag as a type of English lesson, he was asked if he was sure he didn't have any letters from Soviet citizens.

PHOTOGRAPHY

The following is an extract from a booklet by Intourist.

Coming to the USSR you will certainly find many interesting things you would like to film or photograph. You will doubtlessly take back home a multitude of landscape, genre or documentary photos or cine pictures.

We advise amateur photographers and cameramen to study the rules cited below, in order to avoid possible misunderstandings.

While travelling in USSR on Intourist routes, foreign tourists may photograph, film and make drawings of architectural monuments and buildings; cultural, medical and educational institutions; theatres, museums, recreation parks, stadiums, streets and squares, houses and landscapes.

When taking pictures of individuals, please remember that some people do not like being photographed without their consent.

It is PROHIBITED to photograph, film or make drawings of all kinds of military hardware and military objects, seaports, large hydroengineering works, railway junctions, tunnels, railway and motor bridges, industrial enterprises, scientific research institutes, design offices, laboratories, power stations, radio beacons, telephone and telegraph exchanges.

It is PROHIBITED to take pictures from planes, to take long-range overland pictures and make drawings within the 25km border zone.

At industrial enterprises, state and collective farms, government offices, educational establishments and public organisations, photographing, filming and drawing can only be done with permission of the managements of the said enterprises, establishments and organisations.

Film shooting in the USSR is allowed exclusively for personal (non-commercial) purposes.

Intourist winds up with the hope that you will have a pleasant journey and take home many interesting pictures.

In fact, photography on the Trans-Siberian has become easier over the years and station interiors are a permitted subject now. During the summer, windows on the train can be opened for an unimpeded shot, but watch out for smuts and general dirt flying into the compartment. During the winter, windows are locked and it is a tough proposition to take photos through grimy glass even if you use a polarising filter (to cut out reflection) and keep the lens close to the window. Other hazards include aerial cables that swoop into the viewfinder with maddening irregularity and the poles to which they are attached must top the list of uninvited subjects in Siberian photography.

En route, station and platform photography is much more closely monitored than you might think. Keep your camera ready for use, comfortably zippered under your jacket, and produce or replace it calmly and smoothly. Dangling it round the neck is an advertisement for attention from plainclothed and uniformed officials who can kick up a fuss about what may seem the most trivial subject and there is little point in arguing.

Photography of subjects which, perhaps unknown to the photographer, detract from the modern image can provoke unexpected reactions. In my experience, subjects which have fallen into this category include the samovar in the carriage and steam locomotives.

A German traveller also reported, several years ago, that he had his film confiscated at a stop because, several hours before, someone must have spotted him taking a picture, from the corridor of the moving train, of some (long-range?) forbidden landscape.

Confiscation of film is imposed if you blatantly ignore an official request not to take photographs or you have snapped something clearly prohibited. If you feel there are no grounds for confiscation, gentle but firm remonstration sometimes works. Should you openly and aggressively flout the rules, you will be in real trouble.

In Mongolia, the officials, who are not noted for their affability, can turn photography into a most unpleasant experience. Theoretically, the same rules should apply here as in the USSR, but in practice, application is random and ruthless.

A birdwatcher from eastern Europe who, as he phrased it, was tramping 'inhibited areas' in Mongolia in search of black vultures, told me of the deep unease he felt when, from a large hillock behind him, there suddenly burst out not a vulture, but a missile.

Catherine Treasure wrote: "At the first station in Mongolia, many people got off with cameras and snapped away happily until, suddenly, the stationmaster approached one American and wordlessly removed the zoom lens from his camera. He then led the American round behind the end of the train, out of sight, where he produced a pair of nail scissors and deliberately scratched the inner lens (irreparably) and then handed it back to its apoplectic owner. A few of us tried to protest by refusing to reboard the train, but to no avail — the train started to move off without us, so we had to leap on. The Trans-Siberian waits for no-one."

In China, the present attitude towards photography is refreshingly relaxed, probably because the Chinese are themselves in the middle of a severe epidemic of joyful photomania.

Film and photographic equipment
The basic rule here is to take more than you need and spares of everything since you will be unlikely to find what you want in the USSR or Mongolia. Subzero temperatures, such as those encountered in the Siberian winter, can cause the film to turn brittle and crack in your camera. Camera batteries are quickly exhausted in these conditions, so fit new ones before you go and take spares. In China, hotels in major cities have limited stocks at high prices. Stock up in Europe, Japan or Hong Kong.

Health
Medical treatment in the USSR is free, but medicines are not. You should bring all your routine potions for 'tummy trouble', colds, coughs etc. Leningrad has a nasty parasite, *Giardia Lamblia*, which causes diarrhoea, skulking in the tapwater. Buy botted drinks or tea, where the water has been boiled.

A wise precaution, especially if you intend to travel into Asia, is to take out travel insurance which includes medical cover.

> Ensure that you have all the relevant vaccination certificates. Failure to do so will result in the required jab(s) being given to you, there and then, as happened to a Spanish woman on my journey. (Joan Smith.)

What to bring

Bedeker's Guide to Russia (1914 edition) included the following under practical notes:

> The traveller should be provided with a pillow or an air cushion, linen sheets, towels, a small india-rubber bath and some insect powder ... High goloshes or 'rubber boots' are desirable, as the unpaved streets of the towns are almost impassable in spring and autumn; in winter felt overshoes or 'arctics' are also necessary. A mosquito veil is desirable in eastern Siberia and Manchuria during the summer. It is desirable to carry a revolver in Manchuria and on trips away from the railway. The hotels are almost invariably dear and indifferent. Bed-linen, soap, etc. should always be taken. A disturbing feature is the inevitable concert or 'singsong' in the dining-room, which usually lasts into the night.

Perhaps the revolver was also effective against singsongs.

West European Trans-Siberian travellers will find themselves travelling considerably lighter than their Eastern bloc counterparts. Rita Wikner, travelling second class from Berlin to Moscow, met a lady from Poland, returning from East Germany. "Into our compartment she brought eleven packages — others were stowed elsewhere — a mattress roll, later prodded by various officials boarding the train and, to our consternation, a stainless-steel kitchen sink and draining board. We were very glad to leave her in Warsaw."

Others travel light but imaginatively. "My most astonishing memory was of my one lady companion. She packed her battered old case before leaving the train at Irkutsk and brought out a huge, old-fashioned corset, cut open a seam and produced a sheaf of roubles!" (Dorothy Abel Smith)

Trans-Siberian travellers who replied to the advertisement in The Times were asked to give tips in general and a list of things they considered useful for the trip. Here are some of their comments followed by a check-list compiled from all their 'what to bring' suggestions.

> You can get Russian tea and sugar from the provodnik (train attendant), but if you enjoy a cup of coffee, take some with you from home (Russian coffee can be dreadful), together with dried milk, as you can obtain hot water at any time from the coke-fired samovar at the end of every coach.
> Take toilet requisites, as loo paper is usually non-existent and soap a rarity. (Philip Robinson)

> If the washbasin in your carriage doesn't have hot water, take along a container (thermos, water-bottle etc.) so you can carry away hot water from the samovar. (Lucie Lomax and Nancy Webber)

Space in the 4-berth compartments is not abundant. If you want to avoid dragging out suitcases or large bags, use string and simple cotton bags (like pillow cases) to improvise 'hanging hold-alls' which can be slung up on the wall behind your seat. (Lucie Lomax)

Packets of small dressings, such as Elastoplast or Airstrip, are much appreciated as presents, particularly by mothers travelling with children. (Lucie Lomax)

Take lots of postcards of your home town and country. Many people, especially those living in the Soviet Far East, have very little idea about Great Britain, and one man I spoke to thought it was permanently covered in fog. (Joan Smith)

Apart from delicious fresh fruit on sale on the platform at small stations, I sometimes bought carrots, which keep better and can be peeled with another basic necessity, a sharp penknife or Swiss army knife. (Joan Smith)

I'm glad I took my Walkman. Chinese 'tunes' got a bit much sometimes, as did 'By the Rivers of Babylon'. (Rossana Tich)

Restaurant food is best during the first three days before stocks begin to run out. If you have a stock of goodies, use the restaurant car at the beginning of the journey so you can dig into your stache when dining car opening times and the food supply become erratic. (Rossana Tich)

The only thing I wished I could do during the six days but couldn't, was wash my hair. A thermos flask for hot water from the samovar and a universal plug would have done the trick. (Rossana Tich)

Paper knickers (or to put it more delicately, disposable underwear) are essential. Even though the Trans-Siberian has water, with shared bathrooms it is hardly fair to expose some wretched fellow traveller to a labyrinth of sodden knickers. (Hilary Costa Sanseverino)

CHECK-LIST OF MISCELLANEOUS ITEMS

Universal bath plug (squash ball works too); face wipes; fresh- air spray; films and spare batteries for photo gear; Walkman radio (with batteries and cassettes); old classics (to give away to guides etc.); badges (to swap or give away); pens, notebook; maps; Russian phrase book/dictionary; stamps and foreign currency of minimal value; picture postcards and photos from home; glossy picture magazines (no porn); chess set, cards, crosswords, Scrabble; Rubik's cube; sticky tape (or glue); large envelopes; plastic bags (plenty, large and small); torch (with spare batteries); toilet roll; soap; paper tissues; clothes pegs; towel (small); Elastoplast;

Lipsalve; hand lotion; throat lozenges (Strepsils, etc.); medicines (Panadol, Lomotil, etc.); tampons; scissors and nail file; suntan cream and mosquito repellant (vicious bugs in Siberia!).

Culinary delights
The food provided on the train is adequate but lacks variety so it is highly advisable, especially in the winter, to take along supplementary provisions. What you don't need you can barter or give away. 'Pot Luck' meals with passengers from other compartments can lead to a surprising mixture of foods.

Here's a list of utensils and foods which contributors either dearly missed or highly valued:

Plates, bowls etc. (polystyrene or paper); mug and glass; Swiss army knife (or tin-opener, penknife, compact cutlery set etc.); Thermos flask.

Sardines; baked beans; Marmite; cheese; coffee; tea bags (but note, tea is provided on the train); cocoa; dried milk/coffee creamer; 'Quick Soup'; potato crisps; fruit juice (concentrated or powdered); potted shrimps; sausage; pumpernickel bread; pickles; muesli; instant noodles; melba toast; Ryvita; tinned salmon; rice pudding; pate; tinned fruit; peanut butter; corned beef; sweet corn; nuts and raisins; dried fruit; chocolate bars; bottles of water/tonic/whisky/beer/brandy.

CLOTHES
For the Siberian winter you should take a warm hat (preferably fur or wool, with ear flaps), stout boots (waterproof and felt or fur-lined), down jacket or heavy overcoat and extra-thick or warm underwear (thermal or silk). Remember, however, that the compartment heating is very efficient, and this warm clothing will only be needed off the train.

Other clothing recommendations include: track suit (can double as pyjamas); jeans; shoes for relaxing (sneakers, slippers, joggers etc.); disposable underwear (or panti-liners); gloves and scarf.

'I travelled at the end of May. Be warned, even though it was like an oven in Mongolia, we woke up to snow blizzards next day. Keep a thick jumper at the top of your luggage.' (Rossana Tich).

Part 3

EUROPEAN GATEWAYS

European gateways to Moscow

This section is for travellers interested in European rail connections with the Trans-Siberian and is divided into three parts to provide advice and practical information on selected countries — Western Europe, Eastern Europe, and Scandinavia.

To organise your trip yourself will need careful planning and the persistance of a bulldog. Booking and reservation of tickets is much easier in the winter than in the peak summer season.

WESTERN EUROPE

Two of the best places to purchase tickets to Moscow and obtain visas are London and West Berlin. London has all the embassies, national tourist organisations and plenty of expert travel specialists for advice. Berlin plays a key role, since many of the international trains from London, Brussels, Paris, Bern, Hamburg, Aachen, etc. are timed to meet up there before proceeding to Moscow, and visas for Eastern European countries can be picked up quickly in East Berlin.

Travellers who are not happy at fasting for 12 hours should remember to stock up on food and drink for the trip. There is no restaurant car service through Poland, and the Russian service is limited.

The route from Berlin to Moscow runs via Frankfurt a.d. Oder (the East German border post, about 90km from Berlin) to Kunowice (the Polish border post). From there, the train rolls for about 12 hours across the flat Polish countryside, halting at Poznan (270km from Berlin) and Warsaw (576km from Berlin), before reaching Terespol (a further 210km from Warsaw, on the Soviet-Polish border).

After crossing into the Soviet Union, the train halts for a couple of hours at Brest where several sets of officials perform various functions: one detachment inspects fruit and meat (don't take large quantities, as they are liable to confiscation/quarantine); another group hands out and collects currency declarations; more officials peruse passports and visas, perform baggage inspections, assess your stock of literature and search the compartment.

At Brest, to save passengers the inconvenience of changing trains, the European narrow-gauge bogies are changed to Soviet broad-gauge. The train pulls into a large shed where individual carriages are gently lifted by motorised jacks; the narrow-gauge bogies are then rolled off and replaced by broad-gauge ones. Photography of this astounding procedure is, it seems, forbidden, although a Russian-speaking traveller has reported success in pursuading the train attendant to allow photo-taking.

After foodless Poland, the restaurant car joins the train here.

For the remaining 1,100km from Brest to Moscow (Belorusski station), the train continues along the route used in 1812 by Napoleon's armies and

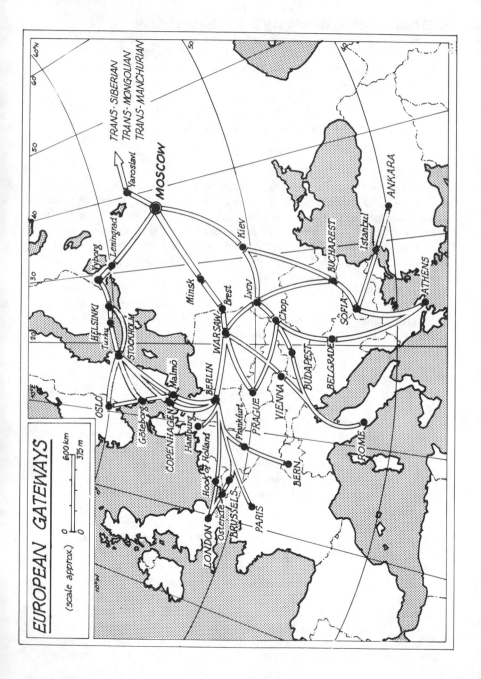

again in 1941 by Hitler's invading forces. Many famous battles are associated with places along this route, such as Minsk, once a Napoleonic battlefield, now the capital of the Belorussian Soviet Socialist Republic; Smolensk, the scene of great carnage in 1812 and again during World War II; Borodino, where in 1812, Napoleon's army of 130,000 met a Russian army of 110,000 under Kutusov and almost 100,000 soldiers perished.

ENGLAND

There are two international express trains which run daily direct to Moscow from London (Liverpool Street Station or Victoria Station):

Ost-West Express
London (Victoria) — Oostende — Brussels — Berlin — Warsaw — Moscow.
  Distance covered: 3,061km; time required: approx. 48 hours.

This same express has a daily connection from Paris which links up in Poland: Paris (Nord) — Berlin — Warsaw — Moscow.
  Distance covered: 2,969km; Time required: approx. 44 hours.

Hoek-Warsaw Express
London (Liverpool Street) — Hoek van Holland — Rotterdam — Berlin — Warsaw — Moscow.
  Distance covered: 2,928km; Time required: approx. 50 hours.

Visas

Information on visa requirements can be found on page 63. The following addresses will help set the wheels in motion:

Intourist
292 Regent Street, London W1R 6QL. Tel: (01) 631 1252.
  Also at: 71 Deansgate, Manchester M3. Tel: (061) 834 0230.

Soviet Consulate
5 Kensington Palace Gardens, London W8 4QS. Tel: (01) 229 3215.
Office hours: Mon—Fri, 10am to 12.30pm.

Embassy of the People's Republic of China
Visa Section, 13 Weymouth Mews, London W1. Tel: (01) 580 2268.
  A single entry tourist visa from the Chinese Embassy costs £8, but is

usually only available here during the low season (November to March).

U.K. China Travel Service Ltd. (UK CTS)
24 Cambridge Circus, London WC2H 8HD. Tel: (01) 836 9911.
The services available from this very helpful and newly opened office include tours to China (also organised via the Trans-Siberian Railway) and visas for groups or individuals. They charge from £25 to £45, depending on how quickly you need it.

Japanese Embassy
43—46 Grosvenor Street, London W1X OBA. Tel: (01) 493 6030.

Japan National Tourist Organisation (JNTO)
167 Regent Street, London W.1. Tel: (01) 734 9638.

Mongolian Embassy
7 Kensington Court, London W8. Tel: (01) 937 5238.
Office hours: Mon—Fri, 10am—1pm and 2pm—5pm. The visa fee is now a massive £9 and you will also need one photo, one completed application form and a photocopy of the relevant pages of your passport.

Polish Embassy
47 Portland Place, London W1. Tel: (01) 580 4324.
Closed on Wednesdays. Transit visa available within 2 days; 2 photos; £5 (approx.).

Information also available from the Polish National Tourist Office. Tel: (01) 637 4971; (01) 636 470.

Embassy of the German Democratic Republic
34 Belgrave Square, London SW1. Tel: (01) 235 4465 (Visa section); Office hours: Mon—Fri 9—10.30am. Visa available same day or on the train; £1.40 (approx.).

Other useful addresses
China International Travel Service (CITS)
4 Glentworth Street, London NW1. Tel: (01) 935 9427.
Abundant general information can be obtained here, including details about visas, but not the visas themselves. Helpful.

Moscow Narodny Bank
24—32 King William Street, London EC4P 4JS. Tel: (01) 623 2066.

The Great Britain - USSR Association.
14 Grosvenor Place, London SW1. Tel: (01) 235 2116.

Collet's Bookshop
129—131 Charing Cross Road, London WC2H OEQ. Tel: (01) 734 0782.

WEST GERMANY

Since Berlin is a funnel for rail connections with Moscow, it is also a popular waystation for Trans-Siberian travellers. Those coming from Russia and the east can tumble back into the maelstrom of Western life at ungodly hours, and find a strong drink and a place to recuperate.

If you are coming in from Moscow by rail with a ticket only as far as Berlin, it is important to remember that you arrive in **East** Berlin, at Ostbahnhof. The following transit information on East Berlin, kept as brief as possible, belongs theoretically under Eastern Europe, but is included here to complement the section on West Berlin.

East Berlin

From Ostbahnhof you can take the U-Bahn (subway) to Friedrichstrasse which has both the border checkpoints for foreigners towards each end. Checkpoint Charlie is for pedestrians and motorists; Friedrichstrasse Bahnhof is for pedestrians only, and closes after midnight. If you cross early you may avoid long lines of grannies heading for a visit to the West and take only 20 minutes. If you are unlucky, the grannies will box you in and, as once happened to me, you will spend 45 minutes having six different border bods inspect every inch of your facial features at close range in order to compare them with your passport photo.

Do your best not to get stuck in East Berlin which has exorbitant prices for accommodation. A bed at one of the state-run INTERHOTELS will cost a minimum of US$50. The Interhotel close to Friedrichstrasse Bahnhof has an all-night bar above the lobby which sells booze, coffee and frankfurters in comfortable surroundings which might appeal until the checkpoint opens. The bouncer, if he is still there, is quite the most enormous one I've seen. For about US$30 you could try the Christliches Hospiz, Augustenstrasse, but phone before you go (Tel: 282 53 21). East German Marks cannot be imported or exported, so make sure you have a supply of low-denomination notes in foreign currency (preferably US dollars or West German marks).

Useful addresses

Informationszentrum am Fernsehturm
(Information centre beneath the TV tower)
Alexanderplatz. Tel: 212 46 75.
Maps and sightseeing guidance.

Reiseburo der DDR
Alexanderplatz 5. Tel: 215 44 10.
Queue upstairs to change money, organise hotel rooms or camping vouchers, grapple with visa arrangements; queue downstairs for train tickets, bus tours, tickets for cultural events etc.

U.S. Embassy
Neustadtische Kirchstrasse 4—5, 108 Berlin-Mitte. Tel: 220 27 41.

U.K. Embassy
Unter den Linden 32—34. Tel: 220 27 41.

West Berlin
Having made it across from points East, where consumption is a challenging pursuit, this place can provide a momentary dazzle of easy abundance.

Bahnhof Zoo is where you surface in West Berlin after taking the U-Bahn from the border at Bahnhof Friedrichstrasse (or if coming from western Europe). If it is very late at night, the Bahnhofsmission in Bahnhof Zoo can help direct you to simple, bunk bed accommodation (approx. DM15). Otherwise, you are within a few minutes walk of two excellent sources of information:

Verkehrsamt Berlin
Europa Center, Budapesterstrasse. Tel: 262 60 31.
Office hours: 7.30am—10.30pm.
Pick up maps, brochures and accommodation details here. For DM2 they will organise a place to stay, not necessarily budget-priced.

ARTU Reiseburo
Hardenbergstrasse 9, Berlin 12. Tel: 310 771.
This organisation can offer help with student travel, accommodation, student cards for Eastern Europe, etc.

Informationszentrum Berlin
Hardenbergstrasse 20. Tel: 310 040.

Ask at any of the above offices for two publications, *Tips for Young Berlin Visitors* and *Berlin for Young People* which have most of the answers for budget travellers.

Getting out

Air connections with the rest of Europe are plentiful and subsidised. Pan Am, Air France, British Airways, etc. offer standby and student fares. Rail passes are not valid for the routes from West Germany to Berlin, but, for those under 26, BIGE tickets are available.

Buses run from the Zentral Omnibus Bahnhof (ZOB), Masurenallee 4—6, 1 Berlin 19. Tel: 301 80 28 (information). Most major German cities are served and student reductions are available.

It is possible to hitch from one of the checkposts back into West Germany, but hitchhiking by foreigners in East Germany is forbidden, so make sure you get a ride straight through.

An organisation which arranges rides for a fee (petrol costs are split with the driver), is **Mitfahrzentrale** with branches at Kurfursten–damm 227 (tel: 882 76 06) and Arndtstrasse 42 (tel: 693 60 95).

The recently published *Berlin Transit* guide from Thomas Cook will considerably ease your passage through East and West Berlin.

Useful addresses for Berlin and the rest of Germany

Intourist
Olivaer Platz 8, 1000 West Berlin 15. Tel: 881 56 57.
Also at: Stephanstrasse 1, 6000 Frankfurt a.M. Tel: 28 57 76

Embassy of the Chinese People's Republic
Konrad Adenauer Strasse 104, 5307 Wachtberg-Niederbachern.
Tel: (0228) 34 50 51.

Mongolian Embassy
Fritz Schmenkel Strasse 81, Berlin-Karlshorst. Tel: (00372) 50 90 119.
(OK, this is in fact East Germany, but Mongolia has no representation in West Germany, so this is the closest embassy for most West Germans, particularly those living in West Berlin.)

Embassy of the Soviet Union
Waldstrasse 42, 5300 Bonn 2. Tel: (0221) 31 20 89.

Polish Embassy
Leyboldstrasse 74, 5000 Köln. Tel: (0221) 38 70 13.

SWITZERLAND

Bern — Moscow Express
Bern — Basel — Berlin — Warsaw — Moscow
This service runs four times a week. Distance covered: 2,882km; time required approx. 45 hours.

Intourist
Usteristrasse 9, Löwenplatz, 8001 Zürich. Tel: (01) 2113355.

Embassy of the Soviet Union
Brunnadernrain 37, 3006 Bern. Tel: (031) 440567.

Chinese Embassy
Kalcheggweg 10, Bern.

SSR
Leonhardstrasse 10, Zurich. Tel: 47 30 00.
SSR has offices in major cities in Switzerland and specialises in budget travel, including Trans-Siberian tours.

Eastern Europe
The main headaches for travellers interested in connecting with the Trans-Siberian from Eastern Europe are visas, travel restrictions, bureaucracy and a requirement to change a minimum amount of currency daily. The least complicated country in all these respects is Hungary. Budapest, the capital, offers a stylish atmosphere and very reasonable prices. As a result, it has acquired the reputation, for those who cannot make it to the real thing, of being 'The West of the East'. In the summer, the city attracts a huge volume of visitors including East German youth groups, Czech migrant workers, Polish hookers, Arab students, backpackers falling off the edge of Europe, Danube daytrippers and occasionally, in their midst, a Trans-Siberian transient.

HUNGARY
For information about Hungary and a generous supply of maps and brochures, you should enquire in your country at the office of the Hungarian National Travel Bureau (IBUSZ) or the Hungarian Embassy. Ask specifically for *Travel Information Hungary* and a catalogue of accommodation in Hungary, which are excellent.

Visas

If you fly or drive into the country, visas are issued on the spot. Rail and boat travellers must obtain their visa prior to entry. Transit visas and tourist visas are valid for 48 hours and 30 days respectively within 3 months from date of issue. Multiple entry and double transit or double entry visas are also available. All that is required for a tourist or transit visa, is a passport (valid for 6 months), two passport photos, a completed application form and a fee (approx. equivalent of US$15). Visas are usually issued within 24 hours, sometimes on the same day, for a surcharge.

Money and customs

The Hungarian Forint is divided into 100 Fillers. In November 1986 the rate of exchange was £1= 46Ft.

Foreigners are allowed to import or export banknotes not exceeding 100 Ft. For exchange of foreign currency into Forints or vice-versa, you must only use official places (National Bank of Hungary, travel agencies, tourist offices, hotels, camping sites, etc.).

The unofficial market is illegal and really isn't worth the risk when Hungary offers such value for money through official channels.

Customs will confiscate pornographic, racist, offensive or damaging publications, pictures, videos, etc.

Travelling to/from Hungary

Air Hungarian Airlines (MALEV) and most of the major international airlines operate flights to and from Budapest. Reductions are available for APEX — return tickets (usually cheaper than a single) and young people under 26 ('standby' and youth tickets).

Bus Budapest has bus connnections with Munich, Vienna and Eastern European countries. For details in Budapest, contact Central Coach Terminal, V. Engels Ter. Tel: 172-562.

From Amsterdam there is, reportedly, a cheap bus connection (approx. US$38) to Budapest run by Magic Bus, Rokin 38 (Tel: 264334).

Boat A hydrofoil service operates on the Danube, two to three times daily, between Budapest and Vienna from 1 April to 26 October. Passport and visa control take place one hour before departure. Single fares cost approx. US$23 (£12), double for return and there are no other concessions for the 5½ hour trip.

In Budapest, tickets are available from MAHART International Boat Station, Belgrad rakpart. Tel: 181 953 or 181 704.

Or from IBUSZ, VII., Tanacs korut 3/c. Tel: 423 140.

In Vienna, tickets are available from IBUSZ Reiseburo,

Kärntnerstrasse 26. Tel: 52 29 67.
Or from DDSG Schiffsstation Praterkai, Mexiko Platz 8.
Tel: 26 56 36/450.

Rail All main cities of Europe are connected by rail with Budapest. The InterRail card (age limit 26) is valid for a 50% reduction on tickets and the Eurotrain card gives reductions between 25% and 50%. Holders of the RES (Rail Europe Senior) card get a 33% reduction on domestic routes within Hungary. The Eurail Pass is not valid in Hungary.

Accommodation
The range available includes hotels (1-star to 5-star), private rooms, student hostels, youth camps and camping sites. Hotels are expensive and private rooms, from as little as 150 Ft., are a real bargain. IBUSZ, EXPRESS and TOURINFORM (addresses below) are just a few of the organisations that can help. Roll up early if you want to avoid spending hours in a queue.

Transport in Budapest
The system which is efficient, cheap and extensive, includes trams, buses, taxis and a Metro. Tickets cost between 1 and 3 Ft and can be bought at automatic machines, tobacconists' kiosks, tram and bus terminals and railway stations. Operating hours are generally from 4am to 11.30pm but there are also night services for buses and trams.

Eating
Prices are very reasonable from snackbars, self-service restaurants and bistros all the way to elegant and top-class establishments. There are numerous specialities, many using paprika, and some soul-destroying desserts. Hungarian wines are worth trying, especially in a *borok* (wine cellar) where you can have it ladled out by the glass or the litre. Budapest also has wonderful old coffee-houses (*cukraszda*).

The Hungarian connection

Hungarian State Railways (MAV) also offer, on the basis of reciprocal international agreements, a concessionary fare for travellers to Hungary. This concession allows a 50% reduction for traffic between socialist countries AND is available to travellers not arriving from socialist countries provided their tickets for travel from Hungary are purchased in convertible currency (e.g. US dollars, pounds Sterling etc).

The good news is that this applies to rail travel between China and Hungary, which means that a ticket from Budapest to Beijing via the Trans-Siberian can cost approximately US$70. The bad news — of course there has to be some — is that seat reservations are under a state of siege for most of the year and the booking procedure involves plenty of time and often diabolical complication. This is *not* a route for those with little time and lacking in patience — try at all costs to avoid booking during the summer season or book well in advance.

The sequence for booking varies, but the following is a rough guide:

1. Order your ticket for the Trans-Siberian from one of the organisations listed below, preferably two months in advance, possibly less if travelling during the winter. IBUSZ offices abroad may be amenable. At the same time, you will have to pay for the ticket and probably for telex and handling charges as well.

2. Your travel organisation will telex Moscow for a reservation and await official confirmation which will include a seat number. For the blessed, a mere 10 days elapse before a reply comes back (yes, telex takes a long time). To avoid a negative reply, you may be able to offer alternative days, in case the one you want is booked solid.

3. Meanwhile, providing your request has been made well in advance, you can assume your booking will succeed and apply for Chinese and Mongolian visas. If you are uncertain, you could wait until you have the confirmation and then race for your visas. Chinese visas (especially for transit, which is what you'll have to go for if you can't obtain a tourist visa in time) are no longer such a major problem, and a Mongolian transit visa is quick too.

4. Once you have your confirmation, you can proceed to the Soviet Embassy or Consulate to apply for your visa which can take 5 days, but could take a day or two less if your case is urgent.

Prices are raised annually, so take the following as a very rough guide. For a ticket from Budapest to Beijing, expect to pay approx. US$70 (3,000 Ft.). With an IUS card (see below for details) the price drops to approx.

US$50 (2,000 Ft.). However, simple as the price may sound, you will have incurred a few other expenses too. For a clearer picture of the real cost, you should, depending on how you booked, add the costs of your transport to Budapest, ticket handling and telex charges, visa fees and related charges, food and accommodation, IUS card fee (approx. US$10).

Regarding booking on the Trans-Siberian to Japan, it may be possible to book as far as Nakhodka at a socialist discount, but the ferry from Nachodka to Yokohama could be interpreted into a different price category — I have no information on this routing from Budapest yet, so any you can send me would be most welcome.

The following is taken from an official reply to a request I sent for information:

> In Hungary the IBUSZ Travel Office issues tickets for the Trans-Siberian Express and undertakes reservations. Unfortunately, however, this is a rather difficult process.
>
> On the basis of the order sheet sent out by IBUSZ and the transferred advance in foreign currency, the office makes reservations by telex and we have to wait 2 weeks and — even by express — nearly 10 days for confirmation and to know whether or not there is a place available for the requested date. The Soviet transit visa is issued only on production of the prepurchased tickets. The waiting time is 10 days and, for trains running through Mongolia, a Mongolian transit visa is necessary.
>
> According to the manager of the Budapest office of Intourist, at present it is not advisable to start powerful publicity for the Trans-Siberian Express, because the services are booked up almost any time.

An Austrian who travelled this way to Beijing many times used to make a reservation for a ticket on the Trans-Siberian from Moscow to Beijing, at least two months before departure, with the head office of IBUSZ in Budapest. Since it took at least 10 days for a reply to come from Moscow, he had several choices: a) stick around in Budapest until the answer arrived; b) go back to Budapest a second time; c) do nothing more about it and roll up in Budapest the day before departure of his Budapest connection (an optimistic approach which worked then, but probably won't now); d) find someone in Budapest to check the reply and tell him; e) call IBUSZ direct. This left him just under two months to organise Chinese, Mongolian and Russian visas.

Two Germans successfully arranged their Trans-Siberian journey the following way: They each bought a Beijing to Budapest ticket, not in Beijing but in Budapest. They were able to get the tickets quickly for the equivalent price of $US60 each — valid for two months and no reservation needed. They then flew to Hong Kong, entered China and only needed to make a reservation with CITS in Beijing (see *Oriental Gateways*) before obtaining the relevant transit visas.

The two train connections from Budapest (Kaleti station) to Moscow are the Tisza Express/Maestral (Rome — Budapest — Kiev — Moscow) which leaves at 20.15 daily and the Budapest Express (Budapest — Kiev — Moscow) which leaves at 23.10 daily in the summer and three times a week during the rest of the year. These trains are often packed, so make your reservation early. Since the Trans-Mongolian (Train No. 4) leaves Moscow once a week at 21.10 on Tuesdays, the last day to catch your connection from Budapest is Sunday. The Tisza Express and the Budapest Express (check the winter schedule carefully) arrive in Moscow on Tuesday morning at 7.38 and 11.55 respectively. If you want to be safe and see more of Moscow, you could leave Budapest a day earlier, but departure on Sunday means you save the cost of a hotel room (approx. US$40) or an overnight in Kievskaya station.

Budapest has three stations (Eastern, Western and Southern) all easily accessible by Metro. The Eastern Station (Palyaudvar Keleti) handles domestic and international trains, including those to and from the Soviet Union and Vienna. The Western Station (Palyaudvar Nyugati) serves routes to and from Romania, Czechoslovakia and East Germany.

If you are heading into Hungary from the Soviet Union, The Budapest Express departs Moscow at 22.08 and the Tisza Express at 23.52 — useful departure times if you want to make the most of Moscow on a transit visa and save on hotel costs by overnighting on the train!

Providing your routing keeps within socialist countries, tickets from Budapest are great value. Avoid expensive tickets which are charged in foreign currency from Hungary into capitalist countries by buying a ticket in forints to the border. As an example, from Budapest to East Berlin (via Czechoslovakia and East Germany) costs about 300 Ft., excluding visa fees.

Useful addresses
IBUSZ, Head Office
1051 Budapest VII., Tanacs krt. 3/c. Tel: 423-140; Telex 22 5650.

IBUSZ, Central Office
Budapest V., Felszabadulas ter 5. Tel: 186 866; Telex 22 4976.

IBUSZ has many branches in Budapest; you can book a room in a private home, hotel accommodation, arrange domestic and international travel (including Trans-Siberian ticketing), change money, etc.

EXPRESS (Youth and Student Travel Bureau)
Head Office, 1052 Budapest V., Semmelweiss utca 4.
Tel: 176 634; Telex 22 7108.
Express have several offices in Budapest. They provide the same type of service as IBUSZ, but oriented towards budget, youth and student travellers. ISIC student cards are not generally valid for travel discounts in Eastern Europe, but their Eastern European equivalent, the IUS card, is available at EXPRESS for a fee and entitles the holder to a reduction (25% or more) on train tickets to socialist countries. This can shave yet more dollars off the price of a Trans-Siberian ticket. Express also handle reservations for cheap hostels and rooms.

Tourinform
Budapest V., Petofi Sandor u. 17/19. Tel: 179 800
This is another major tourist information office which handles reservation of hotels, private rooms, travel arrangements etc. And there are even more, such as Cooptourist and Volantourist.

Intourist
1053 Budapest V., Felszabadulas ter 1. Tel: 171 795.

Embassies

Soviet Embassy
1062 Budapest VI., Bajza u. 35. Tel: 320 911; 324 748; 327 729.
Consulate: 1062 Budapest VI., Nepkoztarsasag u. 104. Tel: 318 98.

Mongolian Embassy
1121 Budapest XII., Istenhegyi u. 59—61. Tel: 556 219.

Chinese Embassy
1068 Budapest VI., Benczur u. 17. Tel: 224 872.

East German Embassy (GDR)
1143 Budapest XIV., Nepstadion u. 101—103. Tel: 635 275; 299 015.

Polish Embassy
1068 Budapest VI., Gorkij fasor 16. Tel: 228 437; 425 566; 428 135.

Czechoslovakian Embassy
1143 Budapest XIV., Nepstadion u. 22. Tel: 636 600; 636 608; 834 552.

American Embassy
1054 Budapest V., Szabadsag ter 12. Tel: 126 450; 126 451.

British Embassy
1051 Budapest V., Harmincad u. 6. Tel: 182 888.

Scandinavia

For non-Scandinavians, the one problem with entering or leaving the Soviet Union from Scandinavia is the high cost of living. For Swedes, Finns, Danes and Norwegians it is no real problem to skip across to Leningrad and on to Moscow for the Trans-Siberian. As a result, there are several agencies specialising in organising travel to the USSR at reasonable rates and with highly-recommended efficiency. For travellers from the East or Europe who are going as far north as Moscow, this is an option worth considering, even if the budget dictates quick transit.

FINLAND

For general information, a liberal supply of maps and brochures is usually available at your nearest Finnish Embassy or consulate and the Finnish Tourist Board has offices in most parts of the world. A visa is not necessary for most residents of Western countries, including the United States and Britain.

Travel to/from Finland

For ease of reference, I have concentrated on the capital, Helsinki, and Turku, a port near Helsinki.

Bus There are bus connections between many European cities and Helsinki and Turku. Between Finland and Sweden the bus goes on the ship.

Ship Silja Line and Viking Line operate ferries with several sailings daily, between Stockholm, Turku and Helsinki. Price reductions of up to 50% are available to students.

On the Silja Line, ticket prices start at approx. US$18 to Turku (10½ hours); approx. US$28 to Helsinki (15 hours). Interail cards qualify for 50% reduction; holders of Eurail cards go free.

On the Viking Line, ticket prices start at approx. US$17 to Turku and US$27 to Helsinki. 50% reduction for holders of Eurail or Interail cards.

There is also the Finnjet Line, which operates between West Germany

(Travemunde) and Helsinki (up to 37 hours).

Rail Rail routings run from Copenhagen, Stockholm and Hamburg and are connected by ferries with Turku and Helsinki. From London to Helsinki (approx. 50 hours) the standard second class single fare is approx. £115. For under 26's, much cheaper tickets are available.

Air Helsinki is about 3 hours from London by air. Discounted student fares are available from the Finnish Student Travel Service (FSTS) and other members of the Student Air Travel Association (SATA).

Train connections from Finland to the Soviet Union
There is a daily train (excluding Saturdays in the winter) which leaves Helsinki at midday and arrives at 20.10 in Leningrad (443km).

From Helsinki, a train leaves daily at 17.00 and arrives in Moscow (1,117km) at 9.22 the next morning.

There are several companies, such as The Finnish Student Travel Service and The Finnish Travel Association, which arrange trips into the Soviet Union (see addresses below).

Helsinki
This is an extremely expensive city. Try the following addresses for assistance:

Helsinki City Tourist Office
Pohjoisesplanadi 19, 00100 Helsinki 10. Tel: 169 3757 or 174088.

Travela-FSTS, Finnish Student Travel Service.
Mannerheimintie 5C, 00100 Helsinki 10. Tel: 90 624 101.
They act as agents for SSTS tours to the USSR, issue IUS cards and provide budget and student travel advice.

Finnish Travel Association
Mikonkatu 25, 00100 Helsinki 10. Tel: 170 868
Travel information and tours to the USSR.

Hotellikeskus
Asema-aukio 3. Tel: 171 133
For a fee, this office can find you a room. Maps, city information and youth hostel lists available here too.

Embassies
American Embassy
Itoinen Puistotie 14B, 00140 Helsinki 14. Tel: 171 931.

British Embassy
Uudenmaankatu 16—20, Helsinki 12. Tel: 647 922.

Chinese Embassy
Gamla Kalkbacken 9—11, Helsinki 57.

Soviet Embassy
Bergmansgatan 6, 00140 Helsinki 14.

SWEDEN
Stockholm, the capital, is as pricey as Helsinki, but there are some useful travel connections with the USSR.

Connections
The Sassnitz Express Stockholm — Malmo — Sassnitz — Berlin — Warsaw — Moscow. (Distance covered: 2,900km; time required: approx. 55 hours). This train leaves once a week, on Tuesday.

The Tolstoy Express Stockholm — Turku — Helsinki — Moscow. (Distance covered: 1,626km; time required: approx. 36 hours).

Ferry Scansov Line run a ferry connection between Stockholm and Leningrad.

Useful addresses
Scansov Line
Stureplan 2, Box 7474, 10392 Stockholm. Tel: 08 18155.

SFS-Resor
Drottninggatan 89, 113 60 Stockholm. Tel: 340180.
Budget travel information and tickets and SSTS tours to the USSR available here.

Stockholm Tourist Office
Sverige Huset (Sweden House), Kungstradgarden.
General information and accommodation bookings (for a fee).

Embassies

American Embassy
Strandvagen 101, Stockholm. Tel: 6305 20.

British Embassy
Skarpogatan 6, Stockholm. Tel: 6701 40.

Chinese Embassy
Bragevagen 4, 11426 Stockholm. Tel: 08 217539.
Consular section: Baldersgatan 7B, 11427 Stockholm. Tel: 08 200542.

Soviet Embassy
Kungsgatan 48, Stockholm. Tel: 08 208652.

DENMARK

Copenhagen is expensive, but has direct connections with the USSR and is the originating point for SSTS tours.

Rail connections run to Moscow and Leningrad via Finland or via Berlin to Moscow. Via Finland, connections take approx. 36 hours to Leningrad and approx. 46 hours to Moscow. Via Berlin, connections to Moscow take approx. 39 hours.

Useful addresses

Danish Tourist Board (Danmarks Turistrad).
H.C. Andersens Boulevard 22A, 1553 Copenhagen V. Tel: 11 13 25.
Scandinavian Student Travel Service (SSTS)
Hauchsvej 17, 1825 Copenhagan V. Tel: (01) 21 85 00; Telex: 16320.

This is the head office of SSTS who specialise in budget travel to the USSR, including Trans-Siberian tours. They have offices abroad, but it is also possible to deal with them direct. Their specially arranged connecting flights leave from Copenhagen.

Use It (Huset)
Radhusstraede 13, Copenhagen.
Virtually encyclopaedic source of assistance and information. Ask for their guide *Playtime* which has addresses, facts and a city map.

Dis Rejser
Skindergade 28, 1159 Copenhagen. Tel: (01) 11 00 44.
Another source for budget tickets.

Embassies
American Embassy
Dag Hammarskjolds Alle 24, 2100 Copenhagen. Tel: (01) 42 31 44.

British Embassy
Kastelsvej 36-40, 2100 Copenhagen. Tel: (01) 26 46 00.

Chinese Embassy
Oregards Alle 25, 2900 Hellerup. Tel: (01) 62 58 06.

Soviet Embassy
Kristianiagade 3, 2100 Copenhagen. Tel: (01) 38 23 70.

国 际 旅 客 订 票 书 RESERVATION SHEET ЗАЯВЛЕНИЕ НА БИЛЕТ		订票日期　　　月　　　日 Date Дата заказа мес чис
订票单位 Organization Организация		
订票人姓名 Booked by Фамилия заказчика	电 话 Telephone Телефон	住 址 address Адрес

'I had the most worrying time of my whole journey at the Russian/
Hungarian border. As I was the only 'Westerner' on the train, only I got
off at 4am to change my roubles back to dollars. The carriages had all
been split up and raised on so the wheels could be changed. I had to walk
quite a long way in the dark to the huge station which was more like an
airport. Lack of communication was the main problem. It took a long
while to wake up the bank! Then I wasn't allowed back on the train. I
didn't know why, and my passport etc was on board. Half an hour later,
the train had joined together again, but with extra carriages, so I didn't
know where mine was. Passengers started getting on. Eventually I was
spotted and was rushed towards customs. Obviously, since I had got off
the train I was supposed to go through customs, only no one could tell me!
Then I had to find my carriage and have more customs officials visiting
my compartment.' (Rossana Tich).

Part 4

ON THE MOVE

The Soviet Union

For many, the Union of Socialist Soviet Republics (USSR) is a monolithic entity, a shape vaguely remembered from history books or newspaper headlines. The reality is the largest country in the world — nearly three times the size of the United States or ninety times the size of the United Kingdom. Over 10,000 kilometres in breadth, the equivalent of the distance between London and Beijing or between Edinburgh and Cape Town, this is also a land with eleven time zones — breakfast time in Nakhodka (Soviet Far East) is midnight in Moscow. Although the Soviet Union covers over 22 million square kilometres, well over half is composed of permafrost and desert areas which are scarcely inhabited.

Within the 15 republics that constitute the Union of Soviet Socialist Republics, a population exceeding 270 million and containing over 100 ethnic groups speaks 80 different languages and writes in 5 different alphabets. The largest, most densely populated, highly developed and obviously dominant of these republics is the Russian Soviet Federated Soviet Republic (RSFSR), the European part of which is, strictly speaking, the area referred to when we talk of Russia or Russians. Whether heading east or west, almost all who travel on the Trans-Siberian will pass through Moscow, the capital of the RSFSR and of the entire USSR.

MOSCOW

Matushka Moskva ('Mother Moscow') is the nerve centre of the Soviet Union, an urban conglomerate of gargantuan proportions for a population of over 8 million.

Moscow's origins are traced back at least as far as 1147 when it was a minor outpost. In 1238 it fell to the Mongols but by the 15th century their influence had been lost to the Muscovite princes who had established Moscow as the state capital. Although the capital was moved to St Petersburg in 1703, Moscow retained importance and emperors were still crowned there.

In 1812, during the Napoleonic wars, Moscow was pillaged and almost completely burnt to the ground. After the October Revolution of 1917, it again became the capital.

Arrival in Moscow

If it seems crowded at the station, be comforted that you are only one of more than 400 million who use Moscow's nine railway stations annually. The following stations are the ones most commonly used by Trans-Siberian travellers and are all connected on a ring line of the Metro system.

Byelorusski station, terminus for train arriving in Moscow from Europe.

Byelorusski Station (Byelorusskogo *Vokzal)
The terminus for trains to/from London, Paris, Berlin, Warsaw, Minsk, Brest, Smolensk and Vilnius. Metro Station: Byelorusskaya.

Yaroslavl Station (Yaroslavski Vokzal)
The terminus for Trans-Mongolian, Trans-Manchurian and Trans-Siberian trains. Metro Station: Komsomolskaya.

Leningrad Station (Leningradski Vokzal)
Next to Yaroslavl station and the terminus for Helsinki, Vyborg, Leningrad, Kalinin and Tallinn. Metro Station: Komsomolskaja.

Kievskaya Station (Kievsky Vokzal)
The terminus for trains to and from Budapest, Prague, Sofia, Istanbul, Belgrade and Bucharest. Metro Station: Kievskaya.

Arrival in Moscow can be confusing, especially if it is late and freezing cold. If you are travelling westwards independently, you will probably have to make a reservation for onward travel or even buy your ticket. Officials often supply conflicting advice on where to do this. The foreigners' ticket office next to the Hotel Metropol (but this was closed for renovation in 1986) is the usual source, but for same day tickets you may also be sent to pick up reservations/tickets at Byelorusski station (Intourist office on first floor; open 9am-8pm).

There are luggage lockers tucked beneath the stations (look for the suitcase signs) and if you intend staying overnight for a connection next day, baggage is certainly safer in the locker. Some tired travellers have not done this and lost valuables in the waiting-room.

Although the lockers are not fool-proof, they are surrounded by the daunting paraphernalia of surveillance — armed police, flashing red lights, closed circuit TV and alarm bells — that shred your nerves. When the locker door is opened, alarm bells sound and red lights flash.

I was once in a group of three dumb foreigners who tried to figure out the system on separate lockers. The effect was awesome: like 10,000 alarm clocks being unleashed or the discovery of a breakout at Alcatraz. Within seconds, a policeman had arrived on the scene and unhitched a megaphone from his belt. He then aimed it at a peasant lady extracting vegetables from a locker next to mine, and let fly with orders. Unfortunately, we were both only 3 feet from the megaphone, so were blasted speechless. The peasant lady disappeared sharply with her veg, the trio of foreigners grinned feebly and the policeman found a language

---

*Vokzal is the Russian for 'station' and, reportedly, derived from Vauxhall station in England.

student to show us how to do the trick and silence the infernal jangling.

As I remember, the system works like this.

1. With the locker door open, insert one 15-kopeck coin.
2. On the inside of the door, there are four dials; the first one on the left is a letter of the alphabet, the others are numbers. Make a note of the right combination which should be composed of a letter and three digits (e.g. A121).
3. Close the door and *make a note of the locker number.*
4. When you return, insert another 15-kopeck coin and twiddle dials to the right combination. If you get stuck, keep a pair of ear-plugs handy and keep trying.

At some stations there are manned left-luggage places.

City transport

Metro The Moscow Metro is the busiest underground system in the world with over 7 million passengers travelling daily between 115 stations on more than 180km of track. Far more than a mere means of transport, with its huge chandeliers and wall decoration in a classico-political style, it is a work of art too. From 6.30am to 1am, trains leave the stations within minutes of each other — the quickest and surest way to get around. Maps of the Metro in Roman script are usually available at stations or from Intourist offices, but on the trains, announcements for the next stop are made in Russian and all station names are in the cyrillic alphabet. Interchanges can be a problem, so try and have the name of your destination written down in Russian before you set off. As a pivot point, the Metro station Prospekt Marxa, linked to Ploshad Revolution and Ploshad Sverdlova, is worth remembering, a few hundred metres away from the Hotel Metropol and Red Square. There is a flat fare of 5 kopecks. Obtain change for 10-, 20-, or 30-kopek coins from the machines at station entrances and insert your 5-kopeck coin in the turnstile-automat. The stations are sunk deep: art-deco bomb shelters.

Taxis Intourist offers pre-paid transportation or transfer (prices start at 16 roubles) as part of their package tours. It is also possible to organise this on arrival at their station office or, at other times, try the reception desk of your hotel. This could be worthwhile if there are four of you or you have mountains of baggage to move.

On the other hand, since there are over 10,000 of them out there, you could also try a taxi rank or flag one down. Taxis are easily recognised by the chequered strip on the doors and the green light on the windscreen which indicates whether the taxi is for hire. On the street, expect to pay a

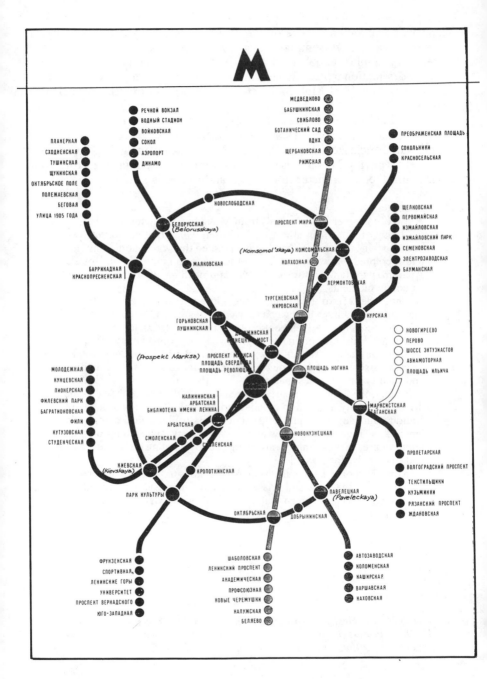

service charge (approx. 20 kopecks) and a distance charge (approx. 20 kopecks per kilometre). The drivers are a receptive lot and keen on a western cigarette. Assuming you are not a Russian speaker or have forgotten your phrasebook, show the driver a piece of paper with the name of your destination written in Russian or use simple language for a simple destination (i.e. 'otel Metropol', 'otel Intourist, Byelorusski Vokzal or Yaroslavski Vokzal').

John Harrison, who lived in Moscow, reports: "Taxi touts are common, especially at main stations and large hotels. Travellers are often approached and asked, in broken English, where they are going, then find themselves paying 3 or 4 times the normal fare. It is essential, therefore, to make sure there is a meter in the taxi, and that it is switched on."

A taxi tale

A trio of foreigners, late arrivals from Mongolia, got lost somewhere in the Lenin Hills at 1 am after they had been wandering around for two hours looking for a hotel. One woman pointed this way, another muffled figure pointed that way, and finally there were no more figures to ask. Apart from the temperature, which was approaching -20°F the scene had its comic moments.

Since the Metro had long since closed down, they positioned themselves on a huge highway and tried to flag down helpful motorists. One stopped, but clearly flabbergasted to find foreigners, leapt back into his car and screeched off in first gear. Two taxis stopped but were either on their way home (well, that was the excuse) or too nervous to take foreign passengers. A decision was made to change tactics — get in first, and then explain the destination.

Finally, the lady in the party flagged down a decrepit bus which the driver cheerfully allowed to be hijacked several kilometres to a Metro station. Outside the silent Metro station a patrolling guard completely ignored a request for assistance — perhaps, patrolling at that temperature, he was simply conserving heat by opening his mouth once, and once only, for a rapid negative.

'Most Welcome Taxi of the Year Award' goes to the stout driver who spun round in the snow and was surprised in a monosyllabic way at the enthusiastic reception given to him by frozen souls, delighted to escape frigor mortis.

The Siberian electricity transmission system is the only one to use 1000k.v. to reduce power losses over the huge distances between their generating stations and the industrial users. (Brian Cross).

The Moscow Metro.

Hotels and overnighting

Most travellers will already have vouchers for a hotel booking. At the hotel, you present your voucher at the desk and receive a room card for security checks at the door. Until their recently proposed abolition is put into effect, there will be another hurdle on your floor — the *dezhurnaya* (floor attendant). This is usually a lady of imposing girth and stature who zealously watches over items in the room and keeps the keys. It is important to keep the room card with you at all times, otherwise you may be prevented from re-entering the hotel by the doorman.

Sometimes, you may arrive in transit without a booking and decide on a night in a hotel — Hotel Orlyonok (same address as Sputkik) is budget-priced even though you may be urged to go to the Intourist hotel. If you don't, and stay over at a station waiting-hall (best at Byelorusski or Kievskaya) because you came in late or are leaving early, stache baggage in lockers (see above), valuables next to the skin, and muffle up good and warm in the winter.

Eating

Russian food is functional. Hotel restaurants vary, but the Rossia (21st floor restaurant), Intourist (the self-service on the first floor does buffet breakfasts and lunches), and National seem consistent. City restaurants are often booked out by the late afternoon and service can take hours. On request, Intourist will advise and make reservations in the morning.

The ice-cream in Russia (Soviet consumption is approaching 400 tons daily!) is excellent. "This is perhaps the only country in the world where you will see people queueing up for ice-cream when the temperature is -15°C!" (John Harrison).

Alcohol laws, introduced in 1985, forbid the sale of spirits (e.g. vodka) before the afternoon, although this does not apply to hard- currency bars in the hotels. Pravda recently criticised an employee who smuggled alcohol out of his firm in a rubber tie and questioned the extraordinary amount of methyl alcohol used for cleaning telephones in ministries. "A sure way of getting on good terms with Russians is with a bottle of Vodka. Getting drunk together is a way of cementing friendships."

Shopping

The country's largest department store, built in 1841, is the famous **GUM** (Gosudarstvenny Universalny Magazin). Long queues, unexciting products, but dramatic architecture.

For souvenirs, try the *beriozka* (little birch) shops which take foreign currency only. The most expansive of these is in the Rossia Hotel. Apart from GUM, there are other large stores such as TsUM at 2 Ul. Petrovska. For browsing, wander along Gorky street, Kalinin Prospekt, Kuznetsky Most and Arbat street which are all near the centre.

A good shop for **records** is Melodiya, Prospekt Kalinina 40 (Metro Kalinski Prospekt). **Maps and books** can be bought at Dom Knigi, Kalinin Prospekt 26.

Financial deals are offered by wheeler-dealers (*fartsovschchiki*), who will approach you with fluent English directly or indirectly by seeking favours after providing a hospitable atmosphere. The exchange of a present or two is one thing, but dealing on the black market is illegal and considered a grave offence against the State. Since the best of the souvenir items are

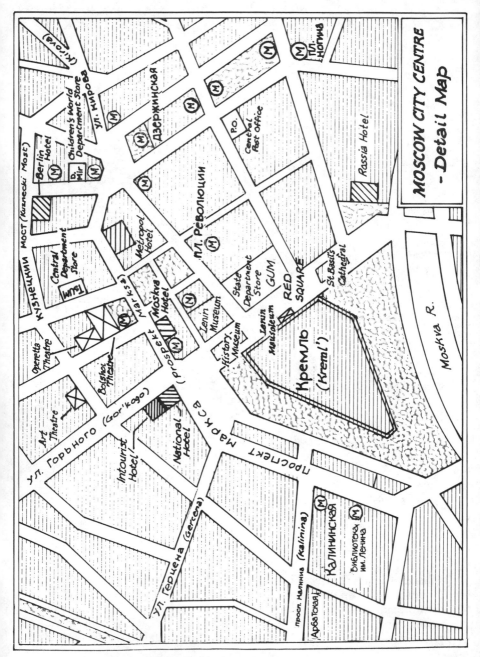

MOSCOW CITY CENTRE – Detail Map

found in hard-currency shops, it seems crazy, for the sake of a few roubles, to compromise yourself into possibly the hottest water of your life, by dabbling in jeans (Levi, Lee, Wrangler), watches, calculators, radios, walkmans, music cassettes, T-shirts with and without logos, sneakers (Nike), down jackets, money or hip pouches, nylon stockings, Chinese tea, perfume, cigarette lighters, pens, foreign magazines (fashion, news), western cigarettes, nylon stockings, quadruple rates for greenbacks, etc.

Entertainments
Tickets can be bought at street kiosks, but you will find it simpler to head straight for the Central Reservation Bureau (see *useful addresses*) in the morning and pay in hard currency. Every evening there are performances of opera, ballet, theatre, concerts, circus (ice-skating bears!), mime, puppet theatre and dancing. Famous names include the Bolshoi Opera and Ballet, The Moscow Art Theatre, the Taganka Drama and Comedy Theatre, the Tchaikovsky Concert Hall and Obraztsov Puppet Theatre. Ten minutes before the show starts, or earlier if you want to bargain longer, ticket operators work outside some venues, for example, the Bolshoi.

Sightseeing
The stock of sights is seemingly endless, but personal interest and available time or funds will soon sort out priorities. There are monuments to history, revolutions, heroes, political figures, revolutionary movements, scientists, art explorers, space explorers and one with the expressive title: 'The Worker and the Collective Farm Woman'. And when you've had a rest, there are well over 75 museums to choose from. Distances in Moscow should be treated with respect — what looks like a short walk on the map can be a lot longer out on the street, so it's best to use a taxi for places not served by the Metro. Depending on the time available, sights can be divided into *Red Square*, *Beyond Red Square* and *Out of Town*.

Opening hours vary but the best general advice is to do indoor sightseeing between 10am and 5pm. Unfortunately, almost every attraction also closes on two days of the week according to an arcane system which often includes an additional day in the last week of the month. If you want to weigh the odds in your favour, draw up a list of hopefuls and ask at an Intourist office/hotel desk for precise information.

Red Square This is the centre of Moscow and for many a harassed Trans-Sib transient on a 10-day visa, is the scene of the fastest tour in town. To the west lie Lenin's Mausoleum and the Kremlin, to the north is the

Historical Museum, to the south is St Basil's Cathedral and to the east is GUM. Some of the sights require a dogged pursuit of interest. It's best not to do the lot in one swoop, but perhaps take a break in Alexander Park in the summer, or, before your face freezes off in the winter, retreat and regroup with an Armenian brandy at the Hotel Metropol (closed for renovations in 1986).

Lenin's Mausoleum Keep your hands out of your pockets, a solemn face and be prepared to queue for a brief view of the preserved remains of Lenin. Behind the mausoleum are the tombs of such historic figures as Dzerzhinsky, Stalin, Gorki, Gagarin and John Reed (the American journalist portrayed in the film *Comrades*). On Saturdays, scores of bridal pairs come here straight from mass weddings and then pop round the corner for a photo at the Tomb of the Unknown Soldier. Just off Red Square and close to the Metropol Hotel is the Central Lenin Museum (over 45 million visitors since its opening in 1936) which gives the complete picture, in minute detail, of his life and work.

The History Museum The 300,000 pieces on display have been selected from a collection of some 3 million items and grouped according to the Marxist-Leninist concepts of history. Perhaps rooms devoted to proletarian movements, liberal intelligentsia, the development of capitalism and agriculture etc. will appeal, otherwise, keep going.

St Basil's Cathedral This is the cluster of multi-coloured, architectural 'onions' immediately associated with Russia. The central structure is surrounded by eight domes each of which honours a saint on whose day Ivan the Terrible was victorious against the Tartars. However, the architects, Barma and Postnik, received less recognition. Ivan, reputedly, had their eyes put out to ensure their work would never equal this one in beauty.

The Kremlin From a small rampart of oak and earth built on this site in 1156, the Kremlin, which means 'fortress' or 'citadel' in Russian, was soon provided with white stone walls and developed to its present size. The present red-brick walls (over 2km long, up to 10m thick and up to 20m high) with 21 towers date back to the late 15th century. Just as Moscow is considered the heart of Russia, so is the Kremlin considered the heart of Moscow. Once the residence of Grand Princes and Church Patriarchs, it is now the seat of the Soviet government. The Spassky Gate on Red Square is for official use only and whistle-blowing guards will boss you away to the Borovitsky Gate about 20 minutes walk away on the southwest corner. You will not be permitted to take large bags or backpacks in with you. These can be deposited in a left luggage store underneath the entrance.

This is a visit not to be missed and an Intourist tour (approx. US$12) is good value in this complicated, collection of buildings. A second, unguided visit is worthwhile to do justice to some of the following:

The Armoury Museum* including the Diamond Fund; the Assumption Cathedral; the Great Kremlin Palace; Rizpolozhensky Church; the Annunciation Cathedral; the Archangel Cathedral; the Facets Palace (Granovitaya Palata); the Church of the Twelve Apostles and the Patriarch's Palace; the Ivan the Great Bell Tower; the Tsar Cannon; the Tsar Bell and the Palace of Congresses.

Beyond Red Square

The following is a selection of places to visit: Novodevichi Convent, Smolensky Cathedral and Cemetery (Metro station: Sportivnaya). Pushkin Museum of Fine Arts (Ul. Volhonka; within walking distance and to the south-west of the Kremlin). Tretyakov Art Gallery (Metro station: Novokuznetskaya). Kolomenskoye Summer Residence (Metro station: Kolomenskaya). Kuskovo Palace (Metro station: Rjazanski Prospekt, then walk to Park Kuskovo). Exhibition of Achievements of the National Economy (VDNKh). (Metro station: VDNH.) Ostankino Palace (just west of VDNKh; Metro station VDNH). Archangelskoye Palace (25km northeast of Moscow).

Of these, the VDNKh, despite its rather uninviting name, is highly recommended. In a lovely park setting you will find an excellent exhibition of space technology, along with natural history and Russian crafts. This is a good place to go to see Russians enjoying themselves — strolling around, picnicking, and relaxing.

Out of town

For those with more time, there are places worth visiting beyond the official 25km limit. You will have to organise permission or book, at a price ranging from 20 roubles upwards, on a tour (see below for address of Intourist excursion office). Give at least a day's notice for the following: Zagorsk; Pereslavl-Zalessky; Rostov; Yaroslavl; Vladimir; Suzdal.

---

*The Great Siberian Railway Easter Egg.

Amongst the wealth of sumptuous exhibits, don't miss one on the Upper Floor (Hall III, Case 23). The huge silver egg inscribed with a map of the Trans-Siberian Railway and containing a platinum, wind-up replica of the Trans-Siberian Express, complete with five gold coaches, was a gift to Tsar Nicholas II on the occasion of the opening of the Trans-Siberian Railway. Michael Perkin, a craftsman at the workshop of the court jeweller, Carl Faberge, designed this masterpiece of a working model in 1900 and included astounding details, such as a ruby for the headlight and a church car in Orthodox splendour.

Useful addresses
**Travel Dept. of the Moscow Branch of VAO
(Central Reservation Bureau)**
1 Ulitsa Gorkogo.

Services at this office, paid for in hard currency, include: over 60 different types of excursion in Moscow, the surrounding area, or to other cities (ask for their leaflet); obtaining tickets for performances at the theatre, ballet, circus etc; provision of guides or interpreters; extension of hotel stay, visas and itineraries (if you're keen and have money, it's worth enquiring even if your current visa is for transit).

Intourist Hotel
Ulitsa Gor'kovo 3-5, Moscow. Tel: 203 6962.

Sputnik (Youth Travel Agency)
15 Ul. A.N. Kosygina, 117946 Moscow. Tel: 139 86 65.

This is also the address of the Hotel Orlyonok which takes youth groups and has easier rates.

Intourist
Head Office. 16 Marx Prospekt, Moscow. Tel: 229 42 06.

Embassies
British Embassy
Naberezhnaia Morisa Toreza 14, Moscow. Tel: 231 95 55.

American Embassy
Ulitsa Tchaikovsky 19-23, Moscow. Tel: 252 24 51.

Canadian Embassy
Starokonyushenny Per. 23, Moscow. Tel: 241 90 34, 241 91 55; 241 90 34 (night).

Australian Embassy
Kropotkinsky Per., Moscow. Tel: 241 20 35; 241 20 36.

Mongolian Embassy
Spansepeskovski 7/1, Moscow (Metro station: Smolenskaya).
Visas have been obtained here, on the spot, but try not to leave plans that late.

Danish Embassy
9 Pereulok, Ostrovskovo, Moscow. Tel: 201 78 60.

Finnish Embassy
Kropotkinski Pereulok 15/17, Moscow.

Swedish Embassy
Ulitsa Mosfilmovskaya 60, Moscow. Tel: 147 90 09.

Swiss Embassy
Ulitsa Stopani 2-5, Moscow. Tel: 295 53 22.

German Embassy (FRG)
Ulitsa Bolshaya Grusinskaya 17, Moscow. Tel: 255 00 13.

The Novodevichy convent in Moscow. Krushchev and Molotov are buried in the adjoining cemetery.
   Note the little platform and cabin in the lake, provided for the ducks, which are being fed by the group in the foreground.

The Trans-Siberian
Station stops

Between Moscow and Nakhodka there are, according to various estimates, over 800 stations, but the train only stops, on average, two or three times a day. Time spent at the station varies between 2 and 20 minutes — check the timetable (in the *Appendix* or in the train corridor) or ask the provodnik. *Don't* expect bells or whistles: a flag may be waved but the clearest indication that the train is about to move off is when the provodnik starts pulling up the steps. "... make sure you are back aboard in good time. If you need to cross any tracks to go to shops, etc, look out for other trains coming along and cutting off your return to your own train." (Philip Robinson).

In spite of vigilant attendants, passengers do get left behind and the thought of being stranded, horror of horrors, without passport, money and baggage, chills my blood to sub-Siberian temperatures. Apparently, though, the experience is not quite so desperate: "An American and a Canadian were left behind whilst queuing for the excellent ice-cream available in Novosibirsk station. There are no warning bells before departure and it seems people quite regularly get left behind in Siberia. Never fear, should this happen the unfortunates are either put on a plane (free) to Moscow, or on the next local train. These two were put on a train two hours behind us and collected their luggage, money and passports at the next station where we had left them for collection." (Catherine Treasure).

During stops locomotives are changed, bogies are checked according to the ringing sound made when whacked with a steel bar and fresh water supplies are pumped through hosepipes.

Passengers take the opportunity of jogging along the platform, having snowball fights, poking around the waiting room, trading or taking quick pics under the noses of surly monitors.

Station kiosks ... depending on their size and the time of year ... have a limited selection of Russian newspapers and magazines, cigarettes, pearjuice, *pirozhki* (a type of sausage roll) and *blini* (a form of pancake), buns, cakes, chocolate, ice-cream, fried fish and roast chicken. Little old ladies with headscarves also run private enterprises from tables and buckets. Winter fare is often displayed on sledges and very limited, but in the summer some of the goodies available include apples, tomatoes, redcurrants, raspberries, wild strawberries, carrots, turnips, *kartofski* (potatoes in dough), *valinski* (boiled potatoes with herbs), pickled mushrooms, corn-on-the-cob, sunflower seeds, pine kernels, bread, kebabs, bottles of milk, yoghurt and *pryaniki* (gingerbread).

Chinese 'fuwuren' keep the train spic and span

Philip Robinson commented on a special, unscheduled stop:

> In spring and summer the Siberian steppes are ablaze with wild flowers, a fact not unnoticed by train crews and passengers. In fact, flower-picking stops are quite a tradition on the Trans-Siberian Railway. Whenever there are flowers to be had, and presumably when the timetable allows it, the train stops, the provodniks lower the steps and everyone goes off flower-picking. After five or ten minutes, the driver toots the horn, everyone clambers on board and the train continues.
>
> Occasionally, only the driver or his assistant will do a quick spot of flower-picking, which leads to a romantic rumour among the passengers that his wife or girlfriend is waiting at the next station. Normally, everyone joins in and the escapade is followed by a search along the 'dry' train for bottles to be used as vases for the flowers to brighten up compartments on the train.

ROUTE DESCRIPTION

The following route description is not an exhaustive, station-by-station account, but a concise selection of items of general interest. The route maps in cyrillic (or English and Chinese) accompany the text, cross-referenced to the numbers behind the town-names in the description. Major stops are shown in English on the maps and in capitals in the text.

The timetables at the back of this guide and the cyrillic ones in the train corridors will also help you keep track, as will the kilometre markers beside the line, unless covered by snow.

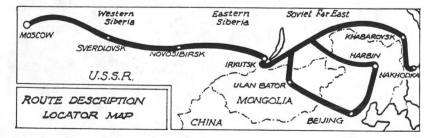

Western Siberia   Eastern Siberia   Soviet Far East

MOSCOW   SVERDLOVSK   NOVOSIBIRSK   IRKUTSK   KHABAROVSK   HARBIN   NAKHODKA   ULAN BATOR   MONGOLIA   BEIJING   CHINA   U.S.S.R.

ROUTE DESCRIPTION LOCATOR MAP

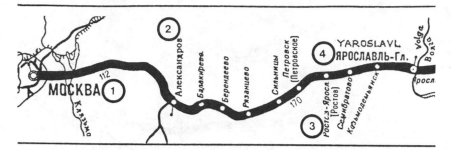

From **MOSCOW (1)**, the train passes through Zagorsk (km70), famed for the Trinity Monastery of St Sergius with its golden domes, seen from the left (northern) side of the train. Founded in 1340 by St Sergius of Radonezh, later known as the "Builder of Russia", the monastery is still revered by large numbers of pilgrims as the centre of Russian Orthodoxy, the hub of religious activity in Russia. The theological academy is over 300 years old and still trains clergymen.

Alexandrov (km112) **(2)**, reached after 2 hours, was chosen by Ivan the Terrible in 1564 as a retreat where he organised his own autocratic and gruesomely cruel system of government.

The train passes **Rostov** (km224) **(3)**, also known as Rostov Veliki ("Rostov the Great"), which lies on the bank of Lake Nero and is one of Russia's oldest settlements.

Yaroslavl (km282) **(4)** was founded almost 1,000 years ago by Prince Yaroslav the Wise who, it is said, used his battle-axe to kill a bear sent by the local pagans to kill him. By the middle of the seventeenth century this was the second largest city in Russia, after Moscow. Its importance declined after Peter the Great built St Petersburg and its present population is 600,000.

At Yaroslavl, the train crosses a massive bridge spanning the Volga, the longest river in Europe, as it flows 3,700km to the Caspian Sea.

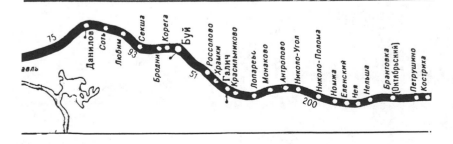

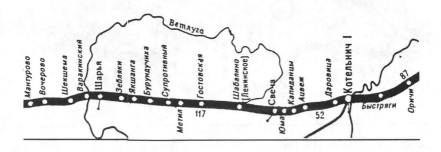

Kirov (km957) **(5)**, now an industrial city with a population of 350,000, received its present name to honour Sergei Kirov who was assassinated in December 1934. This prompted Stalin — perhaps it was merely a convenient pretext — to unleash mass purges and within four years, millions — some estimates say twelve million — had been executed, exiled or imprisoned.

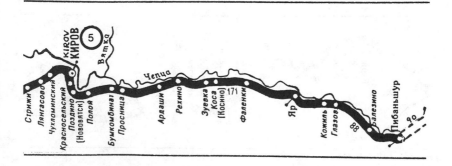

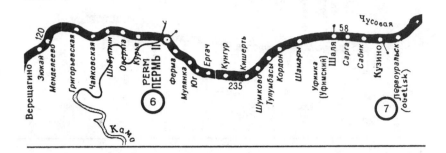

Perm (km1437) **(6)**, known as Molotov between 1940 and 1957 (when Vyacheslav Molotov and other Stalinists were demoted by Khruschev), is reached approximately 9 hours later. It is one of the chief ports on the River Kama.

Before the railway was constructed, Perm was the start of the Trakt or Great Siberian Post Road which was a narrow track, usually in unbearably muddy or dusty condition, running to Irkutsk and the Nerchinsk silver mines. One of the earliest links in the Trans-Siberian Railway was the section from Perm to Sverdlovsk, completed in 1878.

The train now enters the Urals, less like mountains, more like a succession of undulating hills.

Shortly after **Pervoralsk (7)**, approximately 4½ hours after Perm, at kilometre marker 1,777, the train thunders past a white obelisk (about 4m high) on the southern side of the train. No stop is made, but there is sometimes an announcement before reaching this unexciting monument which has the Russian for 'Asia' carved on one side and 'Europe' on the other.

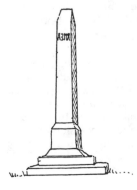

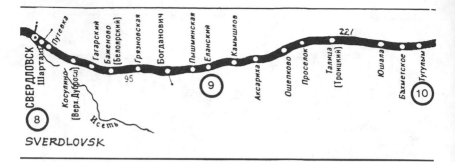

SVERDLOVSK

Western Siberia

About an hour after the obolisk, the train pulls into **SVERDLOVSK** (km1818) **(8)** which was founded in 1721 during the reign of Catherine the Great and, until 1924, known as Yekaterinburg. Sverdlovsk, the capital or 'Pittsburgh' of the Urals, has a population of over a million and a centre of heavy industry.

It is also a major railway junction and official surveillance of platform photography is strict. Back in 1960, another keen photographer, the American pilot Gary Powers, was brought down over this town in his U-2.

Sverdlovsk was also the scene of a grim, historic event when, early in the morning of July 17, 1917 — the exact details are not known — Bolshevik agents hustled Tsar Nicholas II, his wife, young son and daughters into a dingy cellar where they were shot.

At frequent intervals along the Trans-Siberian line there are steam locomotive graveyards where splendid steam engines and rolling stock quietly rust. One of the largest is on the north side of **Ilansk** station (km1945) **(9)**.

In 1885, two Americans, George Kennan and George Frost were commissioned by the American *Century Magazine* to write about penal conditions and exile life in Siberia. Close to **Tugulym** (km2080) **(10)** they came across the site of the Siberian boundary post known as the 'Column of Tears' and gave this description:

> As we were passing through a rather open forest between the villages of Markova and Tugulimskaya, our driver suddenly pulled up his horses, and turning to us said, 'Vot granitsa (here is the boundary)'. We sprang out of the tarantas (horse-drawn conveyance) and saw, standing by the roadside, a square pillar ten or twelve feet in height, of stuccoed or plastered brick, bearing on one side the coat-of-arms of the European province of Perm, and on the other that of the Asiatic province of Tobolsk. It was the boundary of Siberia. No other spot between St Petersburg and the Pacific — has for the traveller a more melancholy

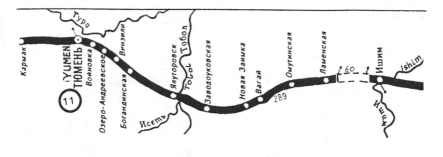

interest than the little opening in the forest. Here, hundreds of thousands of exiled human beings — men, women and children; princes, nobles and peasants — have bidden good-bye forever to friends, country and home.

The next major halt is **Tyumen** (km2144) **(11)**, the oldest settlement in Siberia, founded in 1586. Before completion of the railway to the River Ob in 1885, Tyumen was a forwarding post for criminals and exiles who were shipped to Tomsk in crowded prison barges for a voyage lasting a week or more.

After crossing the Tobol and Ishim rivers, the train reaches **OMSK** (km2716) **(12)** which originated as an *ostrog* (fort) in 1717 on the banks of the River Irtysh. Once a major centre for exile, it was here that Fedor Dostoyevski arrived in 1849 to spend four years of exile during which he was repeatedly flogged and wrote his *Recollections of A Dead House* (variously translated into English as *Buried in Siberia*). After his discharge, he served with the army in Semipalatinsk.

As the train crosses the Barabinskaya steppe, the numbers of passing freight trains keep increasing until they are passing virtually every two minutes and, in fact, this is the most densely travelled section of railway in the world.

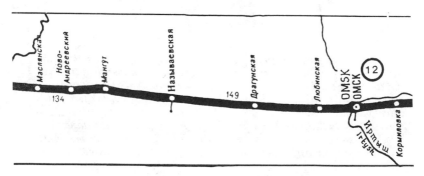

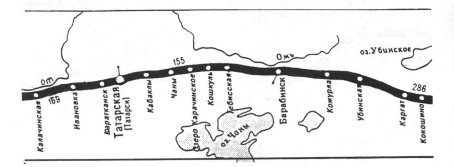

In the eighteenth century, John Bell was intrigued by the tale of a hunter near Barabinsk (reached 4 hours after Omsk):

One of these hunters told me the following story, which was confirmed by several of his neighbours. That, in the year 1713, in the month of March, being out hunting he discovered the track of a stag, which he pursued; at overtaking the animal, he was somewhat startled on observing it had only one horn, stuck in the middle of its forehead. Being near this village he drove it home, and showed it, to the great admiration of the spectators. He afterwards killed it, and ate the flesh; and sold the horn to a comb-maker, in the town of TARA, for ten alteens, about fifteen pence Sterling. I inquired carefully about the shape and size of this unicorn, as I shall call it, and was told it exactly resembled a stag.

The horn was of a brownish colour, about one archeen, or twenty eight inches long; and twisted, from the root, till within a finger's length of the top, where it was divided, like a fork, into two points very sharp.

'The subject of Russian place names is as complicated as Russian grammar, as each place name can exist as either a noun or an adjective, and the latter can have three genders. However, on the Siberian line, the name usually refers to a "stantsiya" or station and is in the feminine, adjectival form which ends in -skaya. The station-sign at Karimsk, for example, reads Karimskaya. Karimskoje or -oye is the neuter, adjectival form and so refers to the town, rather than the station. Station-signs, however, are almost always in the feminine -skaya form.' (Philip Robinson).

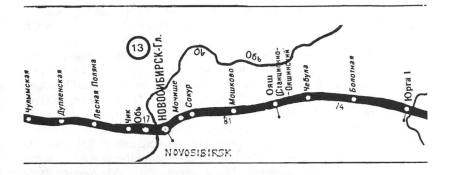

NOVOSIBIRSK (km3343) **(13)**, previously known as Novonikola-yevsk, was founded in honour of Tsar Nicolas II in 1893 when the population was a mere 3000. It is now, with a population approaching 1.5 million, the largest city in Siberia and the eighth largest in the Soviet Union. Novosibirsk is untiringly cited as 'Chicago of Siberia' since it functions as a major river port on the River Ob, a vast centre for heavy industry and an important rail hub.

The Trans-Siberian line is joined here by the Turkestan-Siberian Railway (1442km long), completed in 1931, down which grain and timber are supplied in return for cotton from Central Asia.

Novosibirsk is on the Intourist map and can also be reached by air from Moscow in about 4 hours. To demonstrate the wearying size of this city, it has a main street, Krasny Avenue, which is 10km long. Novosibirsk station is constructed in the shape of a vast locomotive and copes with over 70,000 passengers and 60 passenger trains daily. Inside the station building, watchmending and patching/sewing services are provided. Beer is obtainable by the wise, stooges abound and the British newspaper 'Morning Star' is sometimes sold.

Foreign tourists are usually placed in The Hotel Novosibirsk. The sanitary installations can dismay and the orchestra at evening meals has an eclectic choice. Standard sights include the largest Opera House in the Soviet Union, the local museum with a mammoth and exhibits about the exile system, a technical library, a circus, etc.

Akademgorodok ('Academy Town'), about 30km south of Novosibirsk, is the location of the Siberian branch of USSR Academy of Sciences, which is often visited on a tour from Novosibirsk (taxis can also be hired for an independent trip). On the way you pass the Ob power-station with a huge reservoir approximately 180km long and 14km wide. Over 40,000 scientists have moved to Akademgorodok with their families since its founding in 1961.

In effect, this is a massive Siberian 'think tank' on which the State has lavished funds. The department store in the centre has an amazing variety of goods. The scientists here are expected to ponder and solve economic, technical and ecological problems in Siberia. Probably the most controversial projects at present involve changing the course of some Siberian rivers so that they will empty, not into the Arctic Ocean, but into the desiccated regions and expanding deserts of Central Asia. One such proposed project would link up the Tobol, Irtysh, Ob and Yenisei river areas to create a colossal reservoir, the Tobolsk Sea, from which water would then be channelled south in a canal to the thirsty deserts. Another proposal considers using pumps powered by atomic energy to rocket the water down massive pipes (over 6m in diameter) and thereby avoid water loss due to evaporation or leaks. More recently, the Communist Party published draft guidelines for the economy up to the year 2000 and included a project to divert water from the Onega and Pechora Rivers as well as 'the project to divert part of the flow of the northern rivers to the Volga basin and from the Volga to the Don and the Kuban'.

There is growing opposition to these ideas, particularly amongst Russian intellectuals, and even scientists from Akademgorodok have protested against the incalculable damage which could result to the environment and climate, and not only of Siberia. A group of leading Russian writers recently published an article in the Soviet newspaper *Sovietskaya Rossiya*, which expressed serious doubts: "Its expense is without precedent ... and those who initiate the project do not know the consequences of reducing the water flow to the Arctic Ocean, whose ecology affects weather in the Northern Hemisphere."

'This ride is like a lesson in human and physical geography; as the miles go by, you see the landscape, architecture and people change slowly, and it's odd to think of this snake-like Chinese capsule chugging its way across Siberian lands never visited by foreigners, containing people from all over the world and leaving behind a trail of international waste: American peanut butter jars, French instant coffee jars, Chinese instant noodle packets, Canadian apple-cores, English chocolate wrappers and Australian Vegemite jars." (Catherine Treasure).

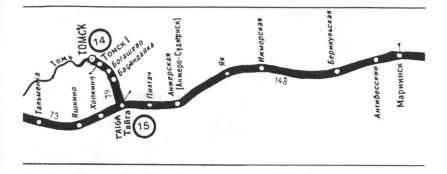

Eastern Siberia

Shortly after leaving Novosibirsk, the train passes the huge marshalling yards of the Turk-Sib line. **Tomsk (14)**, contrary to popular opinion about the Trans-Siberian, does not lie on the route (supposedly because the town merchants refused to come up with the expected bribe to the railway builders) but 95km north of **Taiga** (km3571) **(15)** which *is* on the route. The next major stop after **Achinsk** (km3920) **(16)** is **KRASNOYARSK** (km4104) **(17)** on the Yenisei river.

After crossing the Yenisei, the route enters the *taiga*, a predominantly coniferous forest occupying a massive 40% (895 million hectares) of the USSR. During his travels across Siberia, Anton Chekhov described this region: "Soon beyond the Yenisei there starts the celebrated taiga. They have spoken and written so much about it, that one expects more from it than one finds. On both sides of the road there stretches the usual forest of cedar, pine, larch, birch and spruce ... Its strength and magic lie not in the size of its giant trees nor in the depth of its deathly silence, but rather in the fact that perhaps it is the migrant birds alone of all living creatures that know its limits."

The taiga was also the setting, near the basin of the Podkamennaya Tunguska (Stony Tunguska River), for an extraordinary phenomenon,

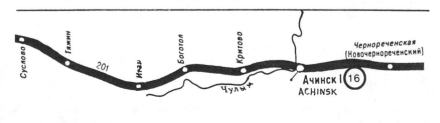

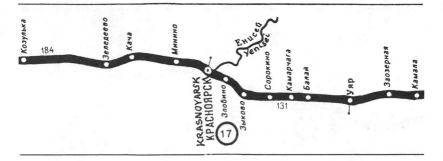

The Tunguska Explosion, sometimes also called The Great Siberian Blast Mystery.

At 7.17 on the morning of June 30, 1908, close to Vanavara, a small trading post some 650km north of Krasnoyarsk, there ocurred a cataclysmic explosion, 'like millions of suns', followed by pressure waves and firestorms. Within a radius of hundreds of kilometres, the forest was flattened, trees were torn up or singed. The seismic shock was registered all over the world and ascribed to atmospheric disturbance or a falling meteorite. However, in 1927 a Soviet expedition found the blast area which had been well preserved by the climate. Since the scale and type of the damage did not resemble that normally caused by meteorites or gas comets, experts were puzzled.

Theories are still being advanced to this day. Some experts consider that the explosion was caused by an ice comet, others propose an 'anti-matter' explosion. Alexander Kazantsev, a Soviet scientist, was struck by the similarity between the damage caused by the atomic bomb at Hiroshima and that of the Tunguska Explosion. He then formulated a theory, later backed by UFO specialists, that the explosion was an atomic one which resulted when interplanetary visitors landed or lost control of their spaceship over Siberia.

'I was struck by the enormity of Russia, vast distances between stations, and the silence was uncanny. No people nor animals around ... miles of fir and silver birch forests covered the countryside, and the sun-rises were spectacular. It was the same distance as travelling from London to Cape Town, and it was hard to believe that we were travelling through just part of one country.'(D.Abel Smith).

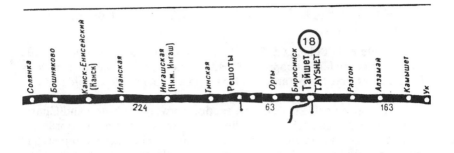

After brief stops at Uyar and Kansk, the train reaches **Tayshet** (km4521) **(18)**, is of special importance now as the starting point of the BAM (see below) and most of the passengers who leave or board the train here are engineers engaged on this project.

BAM (Baikal Amur Mainline)

Starting at Tayshet and terminating at Sovetskaya Gavan on the Pacific, this is in fact a northern branch of the Trans-Siberian. Plans for BAM were already being made in the 1920s and some construction took place until the early 1940s when track already laid was torn up and transported to the west to repair sections of rail damaged by bombing. After extensive surveys of the area north of the Trans-Siberian in the 1960s, construction was resumed and Brezhnev proclaimed the completion of BAM as part of the 1976-1990 Fifteen Year Plan.

By the time the last sections of basic (there is far more planned) tracklaying had been completed at Kuanda on September 29, 1984, this line had already required over ten years for 3,145km of track at a cost, in approximate monetary terms, of £30 billion.

The task has proved a colossal challenge. Millions of trees were felled, over 3,000 streams and rivers required 2,400 bridges and seven large tunnels were constructed through mountainous terrain. A large part of the route runs through permafrost areas, whilst avalanches, mudflows and earthquakes pose additional hazards.

The severity of the climate around Yakutsk was noted by John Bell in 1720:

> The winter here is very long, and the frost so violent, that it is never out of
> the earth, in the month of June, beyond two feet and an half below the
> surface. When the inhabitants bury their dead above three feet deep, they
> are laid in frozen earth; for the heat of the sun never penetrates above two
> feet, or two feet and an half: so that, I am informed, all the dead bodies

remain in the earth, unconsumed; and will do so till the day of judgement.

The climate hasn't changed since then. In Udokan, for example, an area with some of the largest copper deposits in the world, winter lasts as long as 232 days and temperatures hit 56 degrees below zero. Clearly this pushes both men and machines to their limits.

The Kodar tunnel (2km), on the section between Taksimo and Chara, proved a giant headache for drillers who were unable to coordinate concreting fast enough after preliminary tunnelling had been completed in February 1984. As a result, warm air inside the tunnel melted the permafrost in places, causing sudden roof collapses. An attempt was made to solve the problem by squirting concrete from ground level down into the tunnel and then drilling out the tunnel again. However, concrete shortages hindered this plan and, following criticism of 'inappropriate technology', the tunnel was bypassed temporarily.

To encourage pioneers to work under these conditions, wages are offered as much as three times higher than the norm, holidays are provided in the warmer European part of the Soviet Union, retirement is allowed earlier and highly-coveted residence permits for Moscow are easier to obtain.

According to Soviet officials, development of 100 towns and 11 production complexes and industrial hubs along this line is part of a concerted economic drive to populate the eastern part of the USSR. BAM will provide impetus for huge-scale development, particularly of coal and iron deposits, timber enterprises, oilfields and international freight from the Pacific to Europe, as well as domestic freight transport.

There is another less publicised, but crucially important purpose behind the construction of the BAM. It represents a strategic link in the growing political arena of the Pacific region and is far less exposed to possible Chinese encroachment than the Trans-Siberian Railway which has long sections running within a hair's breadth of the Chinese-Soviet border.

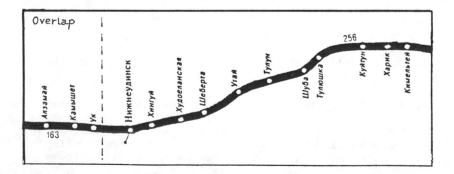

Foreigners wishing to visit Bratsk are not usually allowed to travel along the BAM via Tayshet, but have to fly from Moscow, Khabarovsk or Irkutsk.

John Bell kept meticulous notes on the indigenous tribes he encountered in Siberia. Close to present-day Tayshet, he came across members of the Tungu tribe (now called Evenks) and observed a lifestyle which has long since disappeared:

The TONGUSY, so called from the name of the river, who live along its banks, are the posterity of the ancient inhabitants of SIBERIA, and differ in language, manners, and dress, and even in their persons and stature, from all other tribes of these people I have had occasion to see. They have no houses where they remain for any time, but range through the woods and along rivers at pleasure; and, wherever they come, they erect a few spars, inclining to one another at the top; these they cover with pieces of birch bark, sewed together, leaving a hole at the top to let out the smoke. The fire is placed in the middle. They are very civil and tractable, and like to smoke tobacco and drink brandy. About their huts they generally have a good stock of reindeer, in which all their wealth consists.

The men are tall and able-bodied, brave and very honest. The women are of a middle size, and virtuous. I have seen many of the men with oval figures, like wreaths, on their fore-heads and chins; and sometimes a figure resembling the branch of a tree, reaching from the corner of the eye to the mouth. These are made, in their infancy, by pricking the parts with a needle and rubbing them with charcoal, the marks whereof remain as long as the person lives. They are altogether unacquainted with any kind of literature, and worship the sun and moon. They have many shamans (tribal priests) among them and I was told of others, whose abilities in fortune-telling far exceeded those of the shamans at this place, but they lived far northward. They cannot bear to sleep in a warm room, but retire to their huts and lie about the fire on skins of wild beasts. It is surprising how these creatures can suffer the very piercing cold in these parts.

The women are dressed in a fur-gown, reaching below the knee, and tied about the waist with a girdle. This girdle is about three inches broad, made of deer's skin, having the hair curiously stitched down and ornamented; to which is fastened, at each side, an iron-ring, that serves to carry a tobacco-pipe, and other trinkets of small value. Their long black hair is plaited and tied about their heads, above which they wear a small fur-cap, which is becoming enough. Some of them have ear-rings and their feet are dressed in buskins, made of deer-skins, which reach to the knee and are tied about the ankles with a thong of leather.

The dress of the men consists of a short jacket with narrow sleeves, made of deer's skin, having the fur outward; trousers and hose of the same kind of skin, both of one piece, and tight to the limbs. They have besides a piece of fur, that covers the breast and stomach, which is hung about the neck with a thong of leather. This, for the most part is neatly stitched and ornamented by their wives. Round their heads they have a ruff made of tails of squirrels, to preserve the tips of the ears from cold. There is nothing on the crown, but the hair smoothed, which hangs in a long plaited lock behind their backs.

Their arms are a bow and several sorts of arrows, according to the different kinds of game they intend to hunt. The arrows are carried in a quiver on their backs, and the bow always in their left hand. Besides these, they have a short lance and a little hatchet. Thus accoutred, they are not afraid to attack the fiercest creature in the woods, even the strongest bear. In winter, which is the season for hunting wild beasts, they travel on what are called snow shoes, without which it would be impossible to make their way throgh the deep snow. These, however, can only be used on plains.

They have a different kind of shoe for ascending hills, with the skins of seals glued to boards, having the hair inclined backwards, which prevents the sliding of the shoes; so that they can ascend a hill very easily; and, in descending, they slide downwards at a great rate.

The nation of the TONGUSY was very numerous; but is, of late, much diminished by the small pox. It is remarkable, that they knew nothing of this distemper, till the RUSSIANS arrived among them. They are so much afraid of this disease, that, if any one of a family is seized with it, the rest immediately make the patient a little hut, and set by him some water and victuals; then, packing up everything, they march off to the windward, each carrying an earthen pot with burning coals in it, and making a dreadful lamentation as they go along. They never revisit the sick until they think the danger past. If the person dies, they place him on a branch of a tree, to which he is tied with strong withes, to prevent his falling.

When a TONGUSE goes hunting into the woods, he carries with him no provisions; but depends entirely on what he has to catch. He is never at a loss for fire, having always a tinder-box about him; if this should happen to be wanting, he kindles a fire by rubbing two pieces of wood against each other. I have been told by some of these hunters, that, when hard pinched with hunger on such long chases, they take two thin boards, one of which they apply to the pit of the stomach, and the other to the back opposite to it; the extremities of these boards are tied with cords, which are drawn tighter by degrees, and prevent their feeling the cravings of hunger.

I shall only remark further, that from all the accounts I have heard and read of the natives of CANADA, there is no nation, in the world, which they so much resemble as the TONGUSIANS. The distance between them is not so great as is commonly imagined.

Zima (km4941) **(19)**, the name of a station between Tayshet and Irkutsk, appropriately means 'winter' in Russian.

IRKUTSK (km5184) **(20)**. The regional centre of Eastern Siberia, Irkutsk originated as a winter camp for Cossacks in 1652. Under orders from the Tsar, the Cossacks exacted a tribute of furs and skins from the native Buryats who were understandably hostile to the idea. In 1661, the camp was fortified and received its present name. The wealth that earned Irkutsk the title 'Paris of Siberia', was earned through furs, tea, gold and ivory which were traded along a caravan route running through the Gobi Desert between Peking and Kyakhta on the Sino-Soviet border. The Chinese caravans brought in tea, silks and porcelain and departed with furs of black fox and sable as well as ivory tusks taken from frozen mammoths in Arctic regions.

John Bell also came across tusks from mammoths although, at the time, he believed them to come from elephants:

> Mammon's horn resembles, in shape and size, the teeth of a large elephant. The vulgar really imagine mammon to be a creature living in marshes and under ground; and entertain many strange notions concerning it. The TARTARS tell many tales of its having been seen alive. But to me it appears that this horn is the tooth of a large elephant. When, indeed, or how, these teeth came so far to the northward, where no elephants can, at present, subsist during the winter season, is what I am unable to determine. They are commonly found in the banks of rivers which have been washed by floods.
>
> I have been told by TARTARS in the BARABA, that they have seen this creature, called mammon, at the dawn of day, near lakes and rivers; but, that on discovering them, the mammon immediately tumbles into the water and never appears in the day-time.
>
> They say it is about the size of a large elephant, with a monstrous large head and horns, with which he makes his way in marshy places, and under ground, where he conceals himself till night. I only mention these things as the reports of a superstitious and ignorant people.

Traditional 'wooden lace' decorates this 'izba' near Irkutsk.

Some Chinese considered these tusks to be from a celestial rat (*Tian shu*) which lived in dark holes in the interior of the earth and caused earthquakes.
John Bell also describes a conversation with a Lama (learned priest) in Mongolia who ascribed earthquakes to a different cause:

> This day, a lama from the Kutuchtu (High Priest), going to PEKIN, joined our company, who, by his habit and equipage, seemed to be a person of eminence. In marching along the tedious desert, the conversation turned on a terrible earthquake which happened during the month of July last, in CHINA, between the long wall and PEKIN; and had laid in ruins several villages, and walled towns, and buried many people in their ruins. The lama enquired what was the opinion of the learned men in EUROPE concerning the cause of this phenomenon. We told him, it was commonly reckoned to be subterraneous fire; and then asked, in our turn, to what cause such extraordinary appearances were imputed by his countrymen? He replied, that some of their learned lamas had written that GOD, after he had formed the earth, placed it on a golden frog; and, whenever this prodigious frog had occasion to scratch its head, or stretch out its foot, that part of the earth, immediately above, was shaken. There was no reasoning on a notion so fantastical; we therefore left the lama to please himself with his hypothesis, and turned the discourse to some other subject.

Cultural and political importance came to Irkutsk in the nineteenth century, through a growing stream of political exiles. The foremost group of exiles were the Decembrists who were banished to Siberia after the failure of a coup d'etat in 1825. Polish exiles arrived after an uprising in 1863 and were followed at the turn of the century by notorious figures, such as Molotov, Kirov and Dzerzhinsky. During the winter of 1903, a period of exile was spent here by Josip Vissarionovich Djugashvili, alias Stalin.

In 1879, Irkutsk suffered almost total destruction as the result of a fire. Today, Irkutsk is fast replacing the *izbas* (log houses) with modern unappealing blocks of housing. The izbas have ornately carved eaves, known in Russian as 'wooden lace', and brightly painted window frames and shutters.

Irkutsk can also be reached with a 7 hour flight from Moscow and is the most popular stopover for travellers in Siberia. Apart from hotels in Irkutsk, there is also the Baikal Hotel on the shores of Lake Baikal.

Standard tours often include visits to the Irkutsk Fur Centre and School of Trapping; Church of the Holy Cross; Church of the Holy Saviour, Znamensky Convent and Church of the Apparition of Our Lady; The Decembrists' Museum; the Local History Museum; the Homes of the Decembrists, Sergei Trubetskoi and Sergei Volkonsky; the Art Museum and Siberia's only planetarium.

Other excursions are possible, with or without guidance, to Listvyanka on Lake Baikal. Listvyanka's chief attraction is the Limnological Institute which has fascinating exhibits of Lake Baikal's natural history, including a model of the lake bed showing its great depth. A hydrofoil leaves from the centre of Irkutsk (close to the Central Hotel) and it's cheaper to buy a ticket yourself than take the over-priced Intourist tour. Taxis will also do the same route for about thirty roubles and offer more flexibility than tour buses. Some boats also do a short cruise on the Angara river for a few kopecks.

On the Angara River, just above Irkutsk, is a huge dam supplying hydroelectic power to the area. This dam is rock-filled (rather than concrete) and was the forerunner to the Russian-built Aswan dam in Egypt.

Typical Siberian 'Izba' in the village of Bolshaya Rechka (Big Stream) by the Angara river.

Lake Baikal, 'The Glorious Sea'

Lake Baikal, 640km in length and 80km at its widest part, covers an area equivalent in size to a quarter of England. A depth of 1620m measured at one point on its bed, makes it the world's deepest lake, holding the largest volume of fresh water on our planet. It contains 20% of the world's surface fresh water resource and is also claimed to be the oldest lake in the world. Although over 300 sources flow into the lake, which is of exceptional clarity, the Angara River is its only outlet. The Buryats, a local tribe descended from Mongol stock, called this lake Bai-kul or 'Rich Lake', and amongst their legends is one about the Shaman Rock which juts out of the Angara River:

> A tyrant, known as Starik Baikal ('Old Man Baikal') lived in the lake with 336 sons (the number of rivers emptying into the lake) and his beautiful daughter, Angara.
> His sons faithfully poured in their water, but Angara was kept imprisoned because she refused to marry the Irkut River. Water birds from the north brought her news of Yenisei, a handsome giant, and in time she fell in love with her unseen hero. One restless, stormy night, Angara broke out of her prison to be united with Yenisei. The tyrant woke too late to stop her exit, but launched a cliff after her. The rock missed, and now stands in mid-stream.

Of the 500 plants and 1,200 animals found in and around the lake, two thirds are found nowhere else. A flourishing population of Arctic seals or *nerpas* is an oddity since they are strictly salt-water animals. One explanation is that they migrated down the Yenisei and Angara rivers. Of the many types of fish to be found in the lake, the *omul*, sturgeon and golomyanka are of particular interest. The omul is a type of salmon which is fished in huge quantities and appears in one form or another at almost every meal. The Baikal sturgeon can grow up to two metres long, weigh as much as 200kg and produce over 8kg of black caviar. The golomyanka is a cold-water fish which is killed by temperatures over 45°F and produces live young, not eggs. Some of the adult fish die during the process and, whilst the dead males sink to the bottom, the dead females float ashore in large numbers. These golomyanka contain a special oil, rich in Vitamin A, which is prized both as a cure for rheumatism and as a fuel for lamps.

The whole area around the lake has been designated a national park, partly in response to public outcry when wood-processing plants threatened wholesale pollution and destruction of the delicate ecological balance. A report from the Soviet Academy of Sciences recently concluded that pollution posed an increasing threat to the lake which was on the brink of irreversible changes.

As the train pulls out of Irkutsk, a sign passed on a level crossing indicates the half-way point (km5204) between Moscow and Vladivostock. Shortly after this the railway passes through a tunnel — the first since Moscow.

John Bell describes a strange meeting in 1720, close to Lake Baikal:

Walking along the bank of the river, I was a little surprised at the figure and dress of a man standing among a number of boys who were angling for small fishes, The person bought all the fishes alive, and immediately let them go again in the river, which he did very gently one by one.

The boys were very civil to him, though they looked upon him as distracted on account of his behaviour. During this ceremony he took little notice of me, though I spoke to him several times. I soon perceived, by his dress, and the streak of saffron on his forehead, that he was one of the Brahmins from INDIA.

After setting all the fish a-swimming, he seemed much pleased; and, having learned a little of the RUSSIAN language, and a smattering of the PORTUGUESE, began to converse with me.

I asked him the reason why he bought the fish to let them go again. He told me that perhaps the souls of some of his deceased friends, or relations, had taken possession of these fishes; and, upon that supposition, it was his duty to relieve them: that, according to their law, no animal whatever ought to be killed or eaten; and they always lived on vegetables.

After this interview, we became so familiar that he came every day to visit me. He was a cheerful man, about seventy years of age. He had a bush of hair growing on his forehead, very much matted, and, at least, six feet in length; when it hung loose, it trailed along the ground behind him; but he commonly wore it wrapped about his head, in the form of a turban. The hair was not all his own; but collected as relics of his friends, and others of his profession, reputed saints; all of which he had intermixed, and matted, with his natural hair. Persons of this character are called Fakirs, and esteemed sacred everywhere.

He told me he was a native of INDOSTAN, and had often been at MADRAS, which he called CHINPATAN, and said it belonged to the ENGLISH. This circumstance, added to several others, made me believe he was no impostor, but an innocent kind of creature, as are most of that sect. He came to this country, in company with some others of his countrymen, on a pilgrimage, in order to pay their devotions to the Kutuchtu (High Priest) and Dalai Lama.

They had been twelve months on their journey, and had travelled all the way on foot, over many high mountains and waste deserts, where they were obliged to carry their provisions, and even water, on their backs. I showed him a map of ASIA, whereon he pointed out the course of his journey; but found many errors in the geography; and no wonder; since few EUROPEANS would have had the resolution to undertake such a journey as this man had done.

The route continues round the southern tip of Lake Baikal, with a stop at Slyudianka, passes **Mysovaya** (km5482) **(21)**, formerly Babushkin, on the eastern shore and then crosses the Selenga river before reaching **Ulan-Ude** (km5647) **(22)**, the capital of the Buryat ASSR.

A meeting of the Buryat tribe close to present-day Ulan-Ude was described by John Bell:

> The BURATY are stout active men, but hate all kind of labour. They choose still to live in their tents and tend their flocks, on which their subsistence entirely depends.
>
> The chief exercise of the men is hunting and riding. Their arms are bows and arrows, lances and sabres; all of which are used on horse-back; for, like the KALMUCKS, they have no infantry. They are dexterous archers, and skilful horsemen.
>
> The men wear a coat, or rather gown, of sheep-skins, girt about the middle, in all seasons; a small round cap, faced with fur, having a tassel of red silk at the top; which, together with a pair of drawers and boots, makes up the whole of their apparel. The women's dress is nearly the same; only their gowns are plaited about the waist, and hang down like a petticoat. The married women have their hair hanging in two locks, one on each side of the head, drawn though two iron rings to prevent its floating on the breast; and looking very like a tie-wig.
>
> Round their forehead they wear a hoop of polished iron, made fast behind; and on their head a small round cap, faced with fur, and embroidered, in their fashion, to distinguish it from those of the men. The maids are dressed in the same manner; only their hair is all plaited, hanging in separate locks round their head, and is black as a raven.
>
> Both the men and women are courteous in their behaviour. I should like them much better if they were a little more cleanly. Both their persons and their tents are extremely nasty, from their using only skins to preserve them from the cold; on these they sit, or lie, round a little fire, in their tents.

A winter scene near Irkutsk. Milk is often sold in frozen blocks, each with a stick with which to carry it.

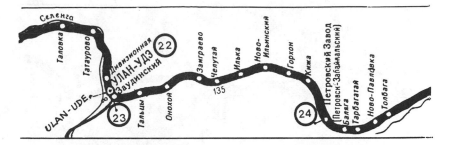

Bell later found himself invited to tea with the Buryats:

> Our horses having swum the river, we went into one of the BURATSKY tents, till they were dried. The hospitable landlady immediately set her kettle on the fire, to make us some tea; the extraordinary cookery of which I cannot omit describing. After placing a large iron kettle over the fire, she took care to wipe it very clean with a horse's tail, that hung in a corner of the tent for that purpose; then water was put into it, and, soon after, some coarse bohea tea, which is got from CHINA, and a little salt. When near boiling, she took a large brass-ladle and tossed the tea, till the liquor turned very brown. It was now taken off the fire, and, after subsiding a little, was poured clear into another vessel... The mistress now prepared a paste of meal and fresh butter, which was put into the tea kettle and fried. Upon this paste tea was again poured; to which was added some good thick cream, taken out of a clean sheep's skin. The ladle was again employed, for the space of six minutes, when the tea, being removed from the fire, was allowed to stand a while in order to cool. The landlady now took some wooden cups, which held about half a pint each, and served her tea to all the company.
>
> The principal advantage of this tea is, that it both satisfies hunger and quenches thirst. I thought it not disagreeable; but should have liked it much better had it been prepared in a manner a little more cleanly.

At **Saudinski** (km5654) **(23)** there is a junction where the Trans-Mongolian Railway, in operation since 1965, branches off and crosses the border at Naushki before entering the People's Republic of Mongolia and continuing via the capital, Ulan Bator, to Beijing in China.

Further details of the Trans-Mongolian route are included under the Trans-Mongolian section.

On the Trans-Siberian line the route continues to **Petrovsk Zabaikalsk** (km5790)**(24)**, formerly Petrovski Zavod. In the 1830s, the Decembrists were moved here from Chita to a windowless prison, 'like a stable with a row of stalls', reputedly designed by the Tsar himself. On the station platform there is an elaborate monument to the Decembrists: bronze busts of eight of their leaders, enclosed in alcoves along a marble wall, with a full length bronze Lenin perched on top.

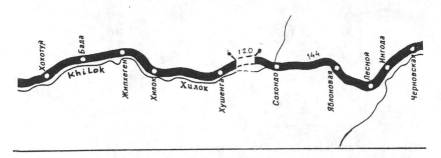

The line follows the Khilok river, running through the Yablonovy mountains to **Chita** (km6203) **(25)**, once the site of a Decembrist prison. Shortly after **Karimskoye** (km6300) **(26)** there is a junction at **Tarskaya** (km6311) **(27)** where the Trans-Manchurian line branches off to Zabaikhalsk and Manzhouli on the border of the People's Republic of China, follows the old route of the Chinese Eastern Railway as far as Harbin and then curves down to Beijing. Details of the Trans-Manchurian route are included under the Trans-Manchurian section.

From Tarskaya, travellers continuing on the Trans-Siberian line follow the Ingoda river which meets the Onon river to then become the Shilka river. The lands between the Onon and Kerulen rivers were the traditional hunting grounds of a Mongol Khan, Yesugei Bagatur, whose son Temuchin was born here in 1162. Temuchin later changed his name to Jenghiz Khan ('Ruler of the World') before carving out a Mongol Empire through Asia to Europe.

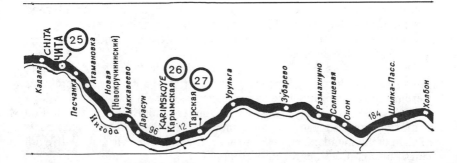

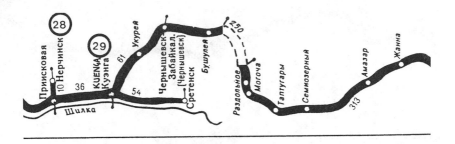

At **Priiskovaya** (km6495) **(28)** a branch line leads off to Nerchinsk. The Treaty of Nerchinsk, signed here in 1689, is still a source of historical and hence border disputes. Nerchinsk also became the centre of the infamous Nerchinsk Silver Mining District where gold and silver were mined for the Tsars. Thousands of convicts and exiles who had survived a two month march from Irkutsk lived and worked in atrocious conditions at the mercy of sadistic guards.

The line heads north at **Kuenga** (km6531) **(29)**, the starting point in 1908 of the Amur Railway, built to replace the previous connection between Sretensk and Khabarovsk by steamer.

As the train enters the Soviet Far East — the largest region in area but with the smallest population density and lovely scenery — it passses through the station of **Yerofei Pavlovich** (km7119) **(30)**, named after the Cossack explorer Yerpfei Pavlovich Khabarov, who also, of course, gave his name to the main city of the region.

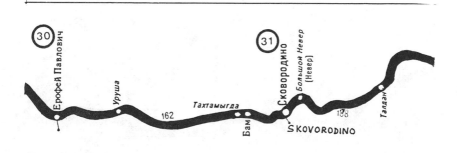

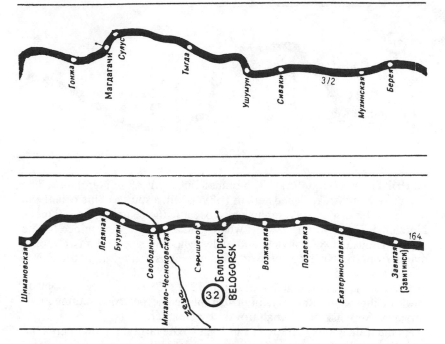

The route continues through **Skovorodino** (km7317) **(31)** and **Belogorsk** (km7873) **(32)** along the sensitive border area (with attendant military hardware) formed by the Amur river (known in Chinese as Heilongjiang or Black Dragon River) which is concealed by undulating hills. This 560km stretch is scenically very pleasing, as the railway crosses the river Zeya to the fertile 'Granary of the Far East', then over the Bureya river to an area particularly rich in flora and fauna. This is the Khingan Preserve, set aside as a wildlife sanctuary in 1963.

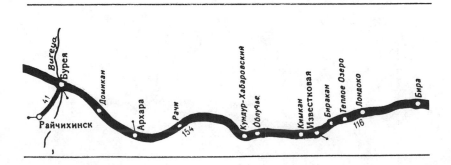

Birobidzhan (km 8358) **(33)** is the capital of an autonomous Jewish region, founded in 1934, but today barely 10% of its population is, in fact, Jewish.

About three hours later, the train reaches **KHABAROVSK** (km8531) **(34)** where travellers continuing by boat to Japan usually stay overnight, boarding a boat express the next evening. Travellers going westwards can change trains the same day.

Khabarovsk is one of the major cities of the Soviet Far East, founded in 1858 by Count Muravyev-Amursky beside the Amur river. The name commemorates a Cossack pioneer who reached this point in 1649. The tourist trail includes the Museum of Local History, the Art Gallery, the Arboretum of the Far East Forestry Research Institute and assorted monuments and busts.

> If you go to Khabarovsk, and the circus is in town, go and see it. I have never laughed so much at clowns in my life — and I couldn't understand a word they said. (Barbara Taylor).

From Khabarovsk to Moscow takes 8 hours by air and there is also an air connection with Niigata, in Japan, which explains why virtually every other foreigner seems to be a member of a Japanese shopping tour.

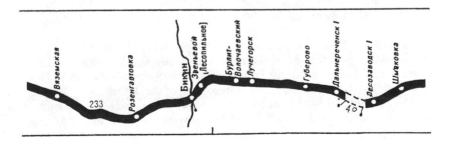

From Khabarovsk to Nakhodka is less than 1,000km, but the line runs through the politically and strategically sensitive area along the Ussuri river — in 1969 there were serious border disputes with China here. To keep prying eyes away from military sights (over 50 divisions reportedly stationed here), foreign tourists have to spend a night in Khabarovsk and take a special train which leaves at night. The boat train is built in palatial style — certainly in first class, where there are fittings made from mahogany and brass, armchairs, immaculate white curtains, plush carpets and grandiose bathrooms.

Vladivostok (km9297) **(35)** was founded as a military outpost in 1860. Since then, its ice-free harbour has become of crucial strategic importance to the Soviet navy and is the home base of the Soviet Pacific Fleet. Not surprisingly, it is most firmly off-limits to foreigners.

At Nadezhdinskaya (km9249), the boat train branches off to **NAKHODKA** (km9428) **(36)**. Just south of Nakhodka is the port of **Tikhookeanskaya** (km9438) **(37)**, the departure point for the boat to Japan. Buses ferry passengers from the station to the quay. Before the boat can be boarded, long queues have to be joined in a jumbled and confusing sequence which includes: currency exchange; inspection of currency declarations; inspection of visas; collection of passports, for which receipts are handed out in the form of numbered scraps of cardboard, which are then swapped for the passport again on the boat; baggage inspection.

The M/V Khabarovsk operates on the sailing to Hong Kong via Yokohama, and the M/V Dzerzhinsky ends at Yokohama. Felix Dzerzhinsky, after whom the boat is named, was the founder, in 1918 of the CHEKA (secret police), the forerunner of the KGB.

The 52 hour sailing to Yokohama provides unexpected luxuries, such as spacious cabins with hot showers, blow-out meals and ballroom dancing.

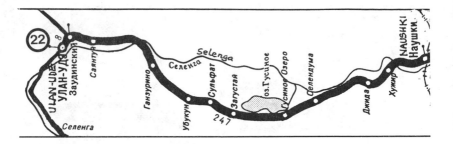

TRANS-MONGOLIAN ROUTE DESCRIPTION

From Ulan Ude, after changing to a diesel locomotive, the train continues to a junction at Saudinski, where it leaves the Trans-Siberian line. This branch of the Trans-Baikal line which was constructed as far as the border town of Naushki in 1940, was extended in 1949 to Ulan Bator. In 1953, Russia, Mongolia and China continued with construction of a link through the Gobi Desert to Beijing. The Trans-Mongolian Railway was opened to traffic on January 1 1956, and has been open for continuous transit since 1965. Further details about the history of this route and the Chinese Eastern Railway can be found earlier in this book. At **Naushki**, where there is a 1½ hour stop, Soviet border officials will check your passport, visa, currency declaration, baggage and compartment. At the far end of the platform, providing frost-bite doesn't deter you, is a bank which will unbar its vault-like exterior on request. This is the place to sell roubles and, more importantly (for those travelling west), to buy them if you want to eat in the Russian dining-car.

The Mongolian border officials here are especially keen on film belonging to travellers leaving Mongolia (see below for details). The train swaps the Russian dining-car for a Mongolian one and covers just over 400km from Naushki to Ulan Bator in about 10 hours.

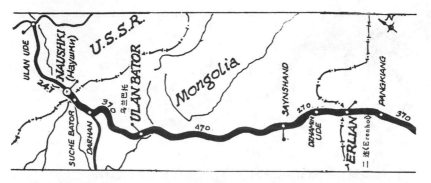

The People's Republic of Mongolia

Ulan Bator ('Red Hero'). Formerly known as Urga, the capital of the People's Republic of Mongolia is a small town with 300,000 inhabitants, approximately one fifth of the total population. In the vastness of the steppes, gently rolling towards distant mountains, the drab hand of monumental architecture has created factories and blocks of flats, with the welcome visual relief in the suburbs of groups of tents, referred to individually as a *ger* or *yurt*. These circular tents, made from layers of cotton and felt, are constructed for easy dismantling and transport on camels, although TV aerials also indicate co-habitation with modern technology.

Accommodation is as expensive as in the Soviet Union — don't be surprised by US$60 per night — and extends to two hotels: Hotel Ulan Bator 'A' and — you've guessed — Hotel Ulan Bator 'B'. These are two tower blocks with a common dining room/lounge area. Plumbing is of the imaginative variety and food adequate but uninspired. *Pelmeni*, boiled dumplings filled with meat, are a local speciality.

The standard itinerary includes a visit to the Palace of King Bogdo with the thrones and bedchambers of the former King and Queen. At The Ganden Lamasery, with its chanting monks, butter lamps, horns, bells and conches, the influence of Tibetan Buddhism, introduced by Kublai Khan, is still on show. This was once the religious centre of Urga, the seat of the 'Living Buddhas'.

Ulan Bator has the usual crop of museums: The Revolutionary Museum with a yurt exhibit and a home movie from the 1920s; The Fine Arts Museum with special exhibits of applique and The National History Museum with ethnographic, plant and stuffed fauna exhibits. The latter is worth visiting for the dioramas. Mausoleum lovers should visit those of Choibalsan and Sukhe Bator, two heroes of the 1921 Revolution. Evening entertainment is a choice between the State Opera and Ballet and the State Circus.

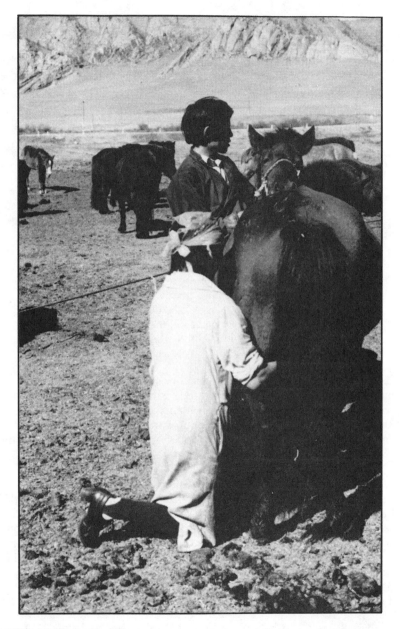

Milking in Mongolia. The foal is held near the mare's head to encourage her to release the milk.

Standard tours are offered out of town to Mandshir and an overnight stay is possible in the mountains at Terelj. Hire of a jeep and driver for other options is very expensive.

An extract from the diary of a 1986 Trans-Siberian traveller who stopped off at Ulan Bator (on an organised tour) gives an idea of the pleasures of the surrounding area:

October 4
Temperature at 8am was 2° Centigrade but rapidly rose to 10° with cool air and bright sunshine. Jam pancakes for breakfast. Coach trip through eastern suburb of city and impressed with very extensive district heating system. Entered an open, wide valley with larch woods perching on the tops of the valley walls. Dry dusty scrubby grassland and a sizeable river were the only features of the valley floor. Forked due east after 10km and continued for some 40km up a spectacular tributary valley going southwards into the main river. Wonderful granite rock ridges and spurs ... Stopped and took photos of this entrancing landscape. Second stop for watching a herd of yak being rounded up by the yakherd mounted on a neat and agile horse. Sat on a friendly and long-skirted yak and found him (her?) more comfortable than the bare back of a horse. Third stop for watching a herd of mares being milked. Sampled mare's milk. Bearable, but only just! (Brian Cross).

There are, apparently, plans to boost tourist numbers from the present figure of 6,000 a year and introduce stopovers for rail travellers (connections and cost are the main problems) plus full tours further afield. If the Beijing/Ulan Bator air connection is re-introduced, a stopover in Mongolia may become an easier, and hopefully cheaper option for travellers on the Trans-Mongolian.

One of the richest areas in rare species, almost certainly a happy result of its inacessibility, is the Mongolian Altai. An acquaintance and zoologist (of Russian extraction) who trekked without official sanction, told stories of abundant snow leopards, eagles which hunted wolves in pairs (one holds the jaws shut, the other breaks the backbone) and of Mongolians who hunted bear by strapping a spike to their chest and allowing themselves to be 'embraced by the bear'!

John Bell passed through Urga (Ulan Bator) and became interested in the rhubarb trade:

What they call URGA is the court, or the place where the prince and high priest reside; who are always encamped at no great distance from one another. They have several thousand tents about them, which are removed from time to time. URGA is much frequented by merchants, from CHINA, and RUSSIA, and other places; where all trade is carried on by barter, without money of any kind. The CHINESE bring hither ingots of gold, damasks, and other silk and cotton stuffs, tea and some porcelain; which are generally of an inferior quality, and proper for such a market. The RUSSIAN commodities are chiefly furs of all sorts. Rhubarb is the principal article which is exchanged for these goods, great quantities whereof are produced in this country, without any culture. The MONGALLS gather and dry it in the autumn; and bring it to this market, where it is bought up, at an easy rate, both by the RUSSIAN and CHINESE merchants.

... After digging and gathering the rhubarb, the MONGALLS cut the large roots into small pieces, in order to make them dry more readily. In the middle of every piece they scoop a hole, through which a cord is drawn, in order to suspend them in any convenient place. They hang them, for most part, about their tents, and sometimes on the horns of their sheep. This is a most pernicious custom, as it destroys some of the best part of the root; for all about the hole is rotten and useless; whereas, were people rightly informed how to dig and dry this plant, there would not be one pound of refuse in an hundred, which would save a great deal of trouble and expense, that much diminish the profits on this commodity. At present, the dealers in this article think these improvements not worthy of their attention, as their gains are more considerable on this than on any other branch of trade.

I have been more particular in describing the growth and management of the rhubarb; because I never met with an author, or person, who could give a satisfactory account where, or how, it grows. I am persuaded, that, in such a dry climate as this, it might easily be so cultivated as to produce any quantity that could be wanted.

Most passengers stay on the train and are content with the half hour stop at Ulan Bator station. Photography is discouraged/prohibited, sometimes violently. Mass expulsions of Chinese took place recently and travellers have witnessed them receiving special animosity. In addition to a reputed five divisions of Soviet military in Mongolia, many of whom use the train when on leave, the space between Ulan Bator and the Sino-Mongolian border has an inspiring assortment of martial hardware above and below ground. So your 'Sunset over the Steppes' pic has a content as unpredictable as the reaction of Mongolian officials.

The scenery does indeed have an uncluttered beauty, as the train rolls past groups of yurts and birds of prey circling above numerous animal skulls and bones, bleached by the sun and gently rocked by the wind, in the fence beside the track. To add to the effect, the occasional horseman, brightly dressed in the traditional *del* (a short, wrap-around coat, tied at the waist with a cummerbund), rides full tilt at the passing train and laughs as the horse rears.

About 12 hours after leaving Ulan Bator, the train reaches Dzamyn Ude, the Mongolian side of the border.

Watch how you greet Mongolian officials. I was awoken in the middle of the night at the Mongolian frontier by a very small man in a very large uniform who saluted me. As I am left-handed, I returned the salute with my left hand which was treated as a great insult. Production of my transit visa and profuse (and, I suspect, misunderstood) apologies finally appeased him, but the military atmosphere was slightly unsettling. (James Stratford).

Officials respond well to decorative magazines with a predominance of pretty pictures of landscapes and people of USA, Europe, etc. (but no porn!) spread out randomly on the seat. But they are nervy and fickle so may possibly demand your film for confiscation. Go for gentle persuasion/remonstration; use the pretty magazines or pics of family and family pets to illustrate your photographic goal in life; perhaps your film contains 'no Mongolia' but Lenin and Moscow. Cheap, unexposed or unwanted ('waste') rolls, preferably already in the camera, can sometimes function as a sacrifice to placate/avoid wrath and/or searches. Camera and film should not be visible; wind film back almost flush with the roll. Unfortunately, this is sometimes in vain and film is ripped out of the camera. Other border stories include demands for 'fees' and excessive attention to lone, female foreigners. There are also stories of pleasant officials and no harrassment.

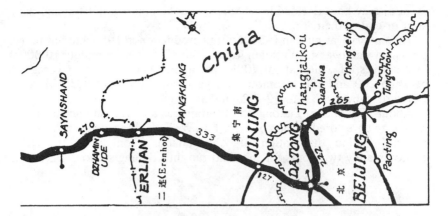

Erlian The Chinese border at Erlian has all the health, visa, baggage and currency declaration formalities, but they are executed in an atmosphere of comparative sweetness and light. Here, customs formalities are relaxed and, while the dining-car and the bogies are changed, you can wander round the station building. As a change from the atmosphere on the other side of the border, Chinese railway workers seem delighted with foreigners clicking pictures in the long shed where bogie-changing (Chinese gauge is 1,435mm; Russian gauge is 1,524mm) takes place with the aid of an overhead crane running on rails and individual jacks for each carriage. If the Russian broad-gauge track laid from Mongolia to Beijing in the early 50's was still there, no change would be necessary, but within a few years of the breakdown in Sino-Soviet relations, the Chinese converted to narrow gauge.

Changing foreign currency into Chinese currency poses no problems at the bank in the station building, but if you are changing back into foreign currency you will have to take whatever there is, literally, in the sack behind the cashier's window. Apart from the post office, another facility worth visiting is the cinema on the first floor which sometimes shows an old and stunning movie about a martial arts festival in Kaifeng.

From Erlian onwards, the virtually empty Mongolian landscape is replaced with large settlements, intensive agriculture and light industry. On this section you are likely to be hauled by a steam train, past **Jining**, the junction with the Beijing-Urumqi line, and at least as far as Datong, which is just under 7 hours from the border.

Datong is of special interest to railway buffs because it is probably the only place left in the world still producing large numbers of steam locomotives. The place is thick with them. Since tours round the Datong Steam Locomotive Factory are organised about three times a week, steam fanatics may have decided in advance to make Datong, not Beijing, the start or end of their trip.

The factory was built in 1956, started production in 1959 and has now produced well over 4,000 steam locos. China has approximately 10,000 locomotives, of which about 70% are steam. Annual output averages between 200 and 300 locomotives a year, mostly 2-10-2 'QJ' 'March Forward' types with a few 2-8-2 models.

About 200km after Datong, the train makes a convenient scenic stop beside an unrestored section of the Great Wall of China, seen snaking up the hill behind the station of Zhangjaikou. From there it takes approximately two hours for the final run into Beijing station.

"I climbed out of the carriage into a refreshingly spectacular world, and the annoyance passed. The Trans-Siberian Express sprawled foolishly down the embankment. The mail-van and the dining-car, which had been in the front, lay on their sides at the bottom. Behind them the five sleeping-cars, headed by my own, were disposed in attitudes which became less and less grotesque until you got to the last, which had remained, primly, on the rails. Fifty yards down the line the engine, which had parted company with the train, was dug in, snorting, on top of the embankment. It had a truculent and naughty look; it was defiantly conscious of indescretion."(Peter Fleming, 'One Man's Company').

THE TRANS-MANCHURIAN ROUTE

At Tarskaya (formerly Kaidalovo), a junction 12km from Karimskaya and 354km from the Sino-Soviet border, the train leaves the Trans-Siberian Railway and continues across the border along the route of the former Chinese Eastern Railway (completed in 1904) as far as Harbin, before turning south towards Beijing.

On the Soviet side of the border, all visa, customs and currency formalities are performed at **Zabaikalsk**, a tiny station dominated by a large, white and yellow tower. A tank stands on a pedestal in front of martial posters proclaiming peace (*mir*). Photography is officially prohibited and zealously enforced at the bogie-changing shed. In the station building, there is a bank on the first floor. On the ground floor, the waiting room has literature in Vietnamese, French and German; the post office sells garish 'Power to the People' postcards with 35 kopeck stamps for overseas postage. If you want to make a phone call to Moscow it is a bargain at 1.20 roubles for three minutes. A Russian friend bought a ticket in China as far as this border where he then bought a ticket to Moscow for about 50 roubles. From Chita, which is 400km away, there are also flights to Moscow at about the same price.

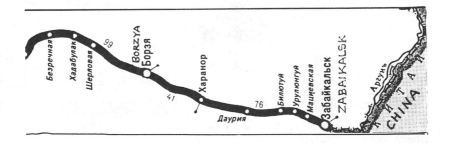

Manzhouli, the Chinese border post, has an easy-going atmosphere as station loudspeakers blare out 'Funkytown' and railway officials even hold tripods for Japanese photographers who are going bananas about bogie-changing and the steam leviathans used in Manchuria.

Customs formalities lack all grimness; the health inspector appears to enquire "How are you?", with a glowing smile that makes you feel better, although I'm not quite sure how you could convey the precise problem if you didn't.

The other good news is that it's only another 2,323km to Beijing, or 6,678km to Moscow. Meanwhile, in the waiting room there's free tea, a video with twirling dancers, a post office, a food and drink counter, a souvenir counter (thermos flasks and pens) and the Bank of China. For many travellers, the main event at Manzhouli is the sad loss or welcome addition of the Chinese dining-car.

Leaving Manzhouli, the train passes a huge lake (Hulun Nur) and passes through **Hailar** and below **Qiqihar**. These are centres for the Daur and Evenki ethnic minorities, who, until recent settlement, were migrant hunters living in birch-bark and hide tents. Flat steppe and sparse tree cover predominate in a landscape dotted with occasional mud-walled villages, horse-carts and smoking industrial complexes. Before reaching Harbin, the route continues through the oilfields of Daqing, an industrial model and source of political propaganda in the 1970s.

'I remember the beautiful sky in Siberia. It is different from other skies, and I have seen many. Also the rivers we saw from the train window — vast, winding silver ribbons.' (Barbara Taylor).

Harbin, the capital of Heilongjiang province, was under Russian influence from the beginning of this century until the end of the Second World War and Russian architecture still sets the style of the city today.

From Harbin, the train crosses Jilin province to its capital, Changchun, which is famous for its automobile factories and film studios. The north east of China has several such centres of heavy industry including Shenyang, the capital of Liaoning province, which is reached four hours later. Travellers to Pyongyang, the capital of North Korea, change here for a rail connection via Dandong on the Sino-Korean border. From Shenyang the route continues through Shanhaiguan (the eastern end of the Great Wall) and Tianjin, before reaching Beijing eleven hours later.

"At the more westerly stations ... you pace the platforms vigorously, in a conscientious British way. But gradually this practice is abandoned. As you are drawn further into Asia, old fetishes lose their power. It becomes harder and harder to pursuade yourself that you feel a craving for exercise, and indeed you almost forget that you ought to feel this craving. At first you are alarmed, for this is the East, the notorious East, where white men go to pieces; you feel that you are losing your grip, that you are going native. But you do nothing about it, and soon your conscience ceases to prick and it seems quite natural to stand limply in the sunlight, owlish, frowsty, and immobile, like everybody else." Peter Fleming ('One's Company').

part 5

ORIENTAL GATEWAYS

Oriental Gateways to Moscow

Many Trans-Siberian travellers prefer to travel west from one of the eastern terminuses of the railway. This section covers China, Hong Kong and Japan, and gives information for the arriving passenger as well as those departing.

The People's Republic of China
BEIJING

Information The Foreign Language Bookstore in Wangfujing (the street next to the Beijing Hotel), the Friendship Store and most of the major hotels in Beijing have bookstalls with maps and guidebooks.

Money The following is a simplified sketch of a perplexing currency system. Two types of currency are used in China: Renminbi (RMB) and Foreign Exchange Certificates (FEC).

Renminbi, also referred to as People's Money, is the currency all the millions of Chinese locals use for everyday life.

Foreign Exchange Certificates, or tourist money, are intended for use by tourists, overseas Chinese, diplomats, etc. for rail and air tickets, taxis, hotels and imported or luxury items. Reportedly, these are now being phased out.

In practice, many travellers pay a mixture of RMB and FEC. The problem, at present, is that the rules are being applied inconsistently. FEC (Chinese: *WaiHuiZhuan* or abbreviated to *WaiHui*) is very much in demand with locals as a means of acquiring items unobtainable with RMB. As a result, you may be approached to change your FEC for more than the equivalent in RMB (rates vary between 30% and 80% extra). This is illegal and heavy fines are imposed if you are caught.

The monetary unit is the yuan (Y) devided into 100 fen. In late 1986 the exchange rate was Y3.20 to US$1, or Y5 to £1.

Transport in Beijing

Taxis Taxis are quick and relatively cheap when shared. Three places where taxis are easily obtained are the station (HuoChe Zhan), the Friendship Store (YouYi FanDian), and the Beijing Hotel (Beijing FanDian — or any hotel that caters for foreigners). Depending on the quality of taxi (clunky Warszawa or stylish Toyota), prices vary between Y0.50 and Y0.80 (FEC or RMB, depending on the type of vehicle — and driver!). A slip of paper with your destination written in Chinese is useful.

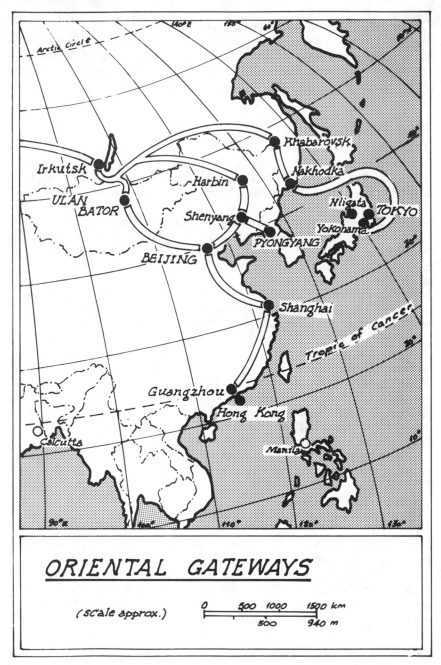

ORIENTAL GATEWAYS

(scale approx.)

Bus Beijing's buses are extremely slow and invariably packed tight. Maps showing bus routes are available (see above for information sources) and tickets cost a few fen.

Subway Recommended as a quick and cheap method to get around, but you are limited, at present, to a line running west from the station.

Bike Biking gets you around the centre of town rapidly and saves delays when waiting for other transport. There are several bike hire shops with the majority of bikes in poor condition. One is opposite the Friendship Store, another is about 10m north of the Chongwenmen intersection. Arrive early, check brakes, saddle, tyre pressure, etc. and, if you find a good roadster, consider hiring for several days at a discount. Rates vary from Y0.60 per hour to Y2.20 per day and Y10 for 5 days. Usually your passport or a deposit of about Y50 is required.

Eating Beijing has hundreds of restaurants with a wide range of specialities and prices. Peking Duck, originally a Mongolian speciality prepared according to a recipe many pages in length, has become the most famous dish in Beijing and, properly prepared, it merits all the accolades. Evening meals are queued for and eaten late in the afternoon, but some hotel restaurants stay open a little later. Here are some suggestions:

Beijing Roast-Duck Restaurant (Quanjude), Hepingmen. Tel: 33 8031. Also at Shuaifuyuan, near Wangfujing Dajie. Peking duck for Y12.

Bianyifang Roast-Duck Restaurant, Chongwenmenwai Dajie. Tel: 75 0505.

Donglaishun Restaurant, Jinyu Hutong. Tel: 55 7840. Good mutton dishes and Mongolian hotpot.

Sichuan Restaurant, Rongxian Hutong, Xuanwumennei. Tel: 33 6348. Fiery food, Sichuan style.

Huadu Restaurant, 76, Dongdan Dajie. Run by ex-chef of the Russian Embassy in Harbin. The menu includes filet mignon, borsch, chicken Kiev, Wiener schnitzel and souffle.

Transport out of Beijing
Officially, foreigners have to pay at least 75% surcharge for rail travel and over 100% surcharge for air travel. Obtain tickets at least four days in advance or be prepared for endless queueing and frustration.

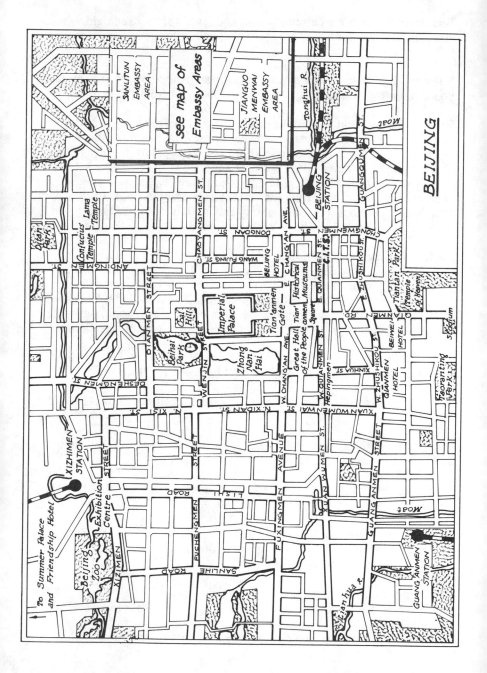

Air The Civil Aviation Administration of China (CAAC) has its main booking office at 117 Dongsi Xi Dajie. Domestic flights: Tel: 55 0497 or 55 3245. International flights: Tel: 55 6720; 55 4175; 55 7319; 55 0626.

Rail Rail tickets can be booked in advance from the CITS office at Chongwenmen or go to the main station where there are special offices for foreigners. Train no 15 is a direct express to Shenzhen (border with Hong Kong and China).

Places to Stay
During the summer there can be a severe shortage of rooms, especially in budget accommodation. At present there appears to be a variable policy, enforced at random, requiring travellers to report first to CITS (address below) who then allocate them a hotel. Since the office closes in the afternoon, hotels have to deal with late arrivals direct. Of the budget hotels listed below, only the Guanghua and Beiwei were unwilling to deal direct.

Qiao Yuan Hotel, Dong Bin He Lu, You An Men Wai, Beijing. Tel: 33 8861. Bed in dorm 8Y; double 32Y; triple 30Y
   Bike hire: 100Y deposit or passport; 3Y per day. Ticket reservations; luggage check; phone (long-distance); shop; Travellers' noticeboard; restaurant.
   This hotel is quite a distance from the centre, close to Yongdingmen station which is the terminus for bus nos 106, 203, 14, 20 or 102.

Tiantan Sports Hotel, 10 Tiyuguan Rd. Tel: 75 2831.
   Favourite with budget travellers and the restaurant has been recommended too. From Chongwenmen (just west of the station) take bus nos 39, 41 or 43.

GuangHua Hotel, 38 Donghuan Beilu. Tel: 59 2931.
   Newly renovated and consequently now higher priced. Take bus no 9 from the station.

Beiwei Hotel. 13 Xijing Lu, Xuanwu district. Tel: 33 8631 Reception not always easy at budget prices. Bus no 20 from the station.

The Beijing Hotel
Not a budget abode, but the bars, lounges, restaurants and coffee shops are popular meeting points for travellers staying further out of town. For Y0.50 a piece, you can check baggage here, although a sign forbids radioactive items.

Public Security, visas, Aliens' Travel Permits, open places

Public Security Bureau, 85 Beichizi Dajie, Beijing (Tel: 55 3102). (Office hours: 8.00—11.30; 13.30—17.00; closed Sat. pm and Sundays).

In Beijing, as in towns elsewhere in China, the Public Security Bureau (PSB), called *Gong An Ju* in Chinese, is the place to go for applications and extensions for visas and permits. On a transit visa, you may have trouble getting an extension in Beijing (where they go strictly by the book), unless you have a very pressing reason. You may have to continue out to Hong Kong for a new visa or try a much more rural PSB.

Regulations in force in China until Spring 1986, meant that you were entitled by your visa to visit over 100 named places in China. If you wished to visit others, you were required to check if they were 'open' and apply for a separate document, the Alien Travel Permit (*LuXingZheng* in Chinese). Certain areas and places were, and some still are, 'closed' or off-limits to foreigners. However, as part of the development of tourism in China, the Aliens' Travel Permit is now being phased out, and will, disregarding a couple of exceptions, no longer be required as an adjunct to your visa. Your visa will entitle you to travel to those places which are 'open'. The best place to check on the latest open places in a particular province is at the PSB in the capital of that province. A list in the *Appendix* gives an indication of areas currently open to visitors. Unfortunately, news travels in an erratic and distorted fashion to PSB's, so don't expect an up-to-date list of places from a PSB outside the area of interest to you. Some travellers assume that everything is open, unless they meet someone on-site who insists otherwise.

THE TRANS-MONGOLIAN AND TRANS-MANCHURIAN CONNECTION

There are two weekly trains running between Beijing and Moscow: the Trans-Mongolian and the Trans-Manchurian. The cheapest and most convenient travel arrangements are made from Beijing. However, for those with money, time, a taste for complication and tenacity in dealing with bureaucracy, it does not have to be the start or finish of your rail journey. It is also possible, for example, to take the train from or to Harbin in northern China. Another permutation which has only just been announced, without precise details, is the re-introduction of an air service between Beijing and Mongolia (Ulan Bator). For Russians, who prefer the Trans-Manchurian, it is quite usual to buy a ticket with FEC from Beijing to Zabaikalsk on the Sino-Soviet border where they then purchase their ticket to Moscow with roubles during the stop at the station.

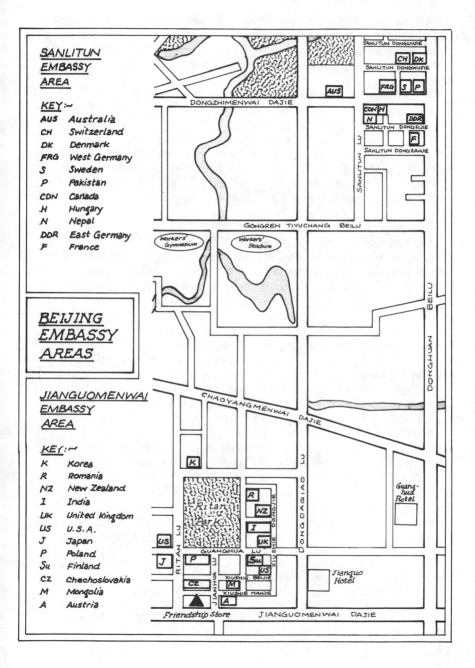

SANLITUN EMBASSY AREA

KEY:~

AUS	Australia
CH	Switzerland
DK	Denmark
FRG	West Germany
S	Sweden
P	Pakistan
CDN	Canada
H	Hungary
N	Nepal
DDR	East Germany
F	France

BEIJING EMBASSY AREAS

JIANGUOMENWAI EMBASSY AREA

KEY:~

K	Korea
R	Romania
NZ	New Zealand
I	India
Uk	United Kingdom
US	U.S.A.
J	Japan
P	Poland
Su	Finland
CZ	Chechoslovakia
M	Mongolia
A	Austria

Incidentally, group travel by rail from Beijing to Pyongyang, the capital of North Korea, is already on offer and individuals, excluding Japanese and American nationals, may soon find it easier. It's expensive, however, and nobody has provided astounding reasons yet to make the effort.

The Trans-Mongolian (Train Nos 3 and 4)

This train runs via Ulan Bator, the Mongolian capital, and is often called the 'Chinese' train because it is served by Chinese Railways. Except for the disadvantage of an extra visa, many travellers prefer the comfort and service on this train which takes 5½ days to cover 7,865km — less than the Trans-Manchurian. Train no 3 leaves Beijing weekly at 7.40 on Wednesday and arrives in Moscow at 15.05 on Monday. Train no 4 leaves Moscow weekly at 9.10 on Tuesday and arrives in Beijing at 15.33 on Monday.

The Trans-Manchurian (Train Nos 19 and 20)

This train, often known as the 'Russian' train because it is served by Soviet State Railways, takes 6 days to cover 9,000km. There is a slight difference in comfort to the Trans-Mongolian, but one major advantage is the chance to meet Russians, who are not segregated from you in your carriage. Train no 19 leaves Beijing weekly at 19.40 on Saturday and arrives in Moscow at 14.55 on Friday. Train no 20 leaves Moscow weekly at 23.50pm on Friday and arrives in Beijing at 6.31 on Friday.

How to pass 'go'

Be prepared for disappointment if you expect to be able to make a fast exit during the peak travel season (June to October) when trains are often booked out for several weeks. Off season, the minimum time required to organise one of these trips, including visas and tickets is a week.

As China becomes more and more popular, forward planning will become essential during the peak season. Some travellers pop into Beijing to book tickets at the start of a long tour of China and reappear there again to obtain visas ten days before their train leaves. Others have been successful in booking Trans-Siberian tickets through CITS (China International Travel Service — address on page 160) in other Chinese cities. An English traveller made arrangements from Kunming:

> I ordered my ticket about 7 weeks prior to my journey in the Kunming Hotel, Kunming. I specified Budapest and had to pay Y17 FEC for the phone call, but was given confirmation of compartment and bed number at once. Although it is, supposedly, possible to pre-book at all major hotels in China, this is not always so. The Kunming Hotel has the reputation of being one of the most reliable places to book.

If you are prepared to switch from one train to the other, the chance of success is higher. CITS has sections dealing with domestic and international air travel, and domestic and international rail trips, and the staff devote attention to the aforesaid matters as well as knitting, learning English, eating and catching up on the latest news.

Try to keep calm during the whole rigmarole which depends on a variety of erratic factors, including embassy office hours and staff. Before setting out to conquer your ticket and visas, phone relevant embassies to doublecheck visa requirements, opening days and hours. Also, make sure you have sufficient passport photos, cash dollars and FEC!

The different steps needed to get your Trans-Siberian ticket should be taken in sequence: first reserve your ticket, then obtain your visas in *reverse* order and, finally, pay for your ticket in full.

Here is a rough itinerary for one of the most involved train routings on the Trans-Mongolian to Europe via Moscow, Poland and East Germany:

Arrive Monday and head for CITS at 8.30am. Book ticket for Trans-Mongolian (No 3 train) leaving on Wednesday of the following week. If the answer is a well-worn negative, examine the status of the seating available and check the idea of taking the Trans-Manchurian instead. A deposit of 40FEC may be required. Make certain you are handed a reservation slip.

Hop on your bike and head for the Polish Embassy before it closes at 11am. Your visa will be ready in an hour.

Take a taxi (try the Friendship Store) or, if you're fit, pedal to the Soviet Embassy (in Chinese *SuLian DaShiGuan*) to apply for your visa before closing time at 1pm. Your passport will not be retained (bring a photocopy). On request, show them your Polish visa and ticket reservation slip. If you wish to arrange stopovers in Siberia or elsewhere in the Soviet Union, the Intourist desk will oblige. You will then be told to come back on Thursday or Friday.

Since the Mongolian Embassy is not open on Thursday, you could pick up the Soviet visa if you happen to be in the area, but it will not speed anything up.

Otherwise, return to the Soviet Embassy on Friday and then hotfoot it to the Mongolian Embassy before it closes at 2pm. With any luck, the Mongolians will provide the visa on the spot; otherwise you'll have to wait until Monday.

Once you are the proud possessor of a Mongolian visa you can traipse back to CITS, lay down the full price and claim your ticket. A point that puzzles me is the price of a ticket from Beijing to Budapest. Although Hungarian Railways give a 50% reduction on rail travel fares between socialist states, including China, it would appear that CITS provides no such reduction from China to Hungary.

You can, however, pay for this ticket in Hungary and just make the reservation in Beijing (see *Hungarian Connection*, page 84).

China International Travel Service (CITS)

Beijing Branch Office, 2 East Qianmen Rd, Beijing. Tel: 75 5272; Telex: 22 350 CITS CN; Telegram: Luxingshe, Beijing. Office hours: weekdays and Sats 8.30—11.00 and 13—16.30; Sun 9.00—11 and 14.00—16.30.

In the *Appendix* there are sample ticket prices in FEC for trains from Beijing to the USSR and Eastern Europe.

Embassies

Apart from the Soviet Embassy, all embassies in Beijing are in one of two special areas, Sanlitun or Jianguomenwai. The flags on the flagpoles in the compounds can provide quick orientation. Beijing is not exactly renowned for fast service, so *don't* leave everything until the last minute, *do* doublecheck opening hours and holidays (unexpected scourge of travellers). Stock up on cash dollars and passport photos. Happy visa hunting!

Mongolian Embassy 2 Xiushui Bei Jie, Jianguomenwai. Tel: 52 1203.

Office hours: Mon. 1pm—2pm; Tues. and Fri. 9am—11am.

Closed: July 11, 12; Nov 7, 8; Dec 31; Jan 1; Mar 8; May 1, 2.

Visas issued within 24 hours; 1 photo; US$18 fee in cash!

Be prepared for the unexpected here — after all, you are probably paying one of the highest transit fees in the world. One foreign couple didn't quite understand the price structure and made a comment about thievery which made the nice man reading Pravda take his legs off the table, scrunch their application forms and comment "no visa!". Only after a soothing phone call from the couple's embassy were ruffled feathers smoothed. Things looked threatening again, for a moment, when the official waved the photos in the air with one hand and said "stick!". But with the other hand he was motioning to a glue pot in the corner.

Hungarian Embassy Dongzhimenwai Dajie No 10, Beijing. Tel. 52 1431.

Transit visa 13Y FEC; Tourist visa 22Y FEC; two photos; helpful staff can also provide tourist brochures.

Hungarian visas are quick (24 hours) to obtain, so, as an exception to the reverse order rule for visas, those in a hurry are occasionally allowed to apply for the Soviet visa first. The Hungarian visa must, of course, be shown when collecting the Soviet visa.

Soviet Embassy 4 Dongzhimen Beizhong Jie. Tel: 52 2051, 52 1381, 52 1267.

Office hours: 9am—1pm, Mon, Thur and Fri *only*.

Built like a cross between a wedding cake and a fortress, this is definitely the largest embassy in town. The consular section is to the left of the main entrance through a small, iron gate. Transit visa available in less than a week for surcharge of 20Y FEC otherwise fee is presumably waived or reduced (do not expect a visa in less than a week). Three photos (identical and clearly showing facial features); CITS reservation slip usually required or, rarely, other confirmation.

Limited tourist information is available, but complete service is supplied by Intourist for transfers and accommodation.

Transit visas are supplied more quickly than tourist visas, and, despite what you may be told, transit passengers do not have to book expensive accommodation in Moscow. Should you be embroiled in an altercation, point out that your train usually arrives in time for you (theoretically) to depart the same day. However, if you miss your connection from Moscow, a viable but uncomfortable sleep is to be had in waiting halls, hotel lobbies etc. and you will have time for some sights.

Since the train leaves Beijing at least a day before you cross the Soviet border, it would appear logical to avoid use of a Soviet visa for travel in China by issuing it for the day *after* departure of the train. This point is worth mentioning (not arguing) since the logic was applied previously, but is less appreciated now.

If you need to obtain your Soviet visa fast, the best route to reserve on is the Trans-Manchurian (no need for a Mongolian visa) and put down your destination as Finland (most major Western countries require no visa). In Moscow you might have a change of heart and ask for a different exit route.

Polish Embassy
Ritan Lu, Jianguomenwai. Tel: 52 1235.
Office hours: Mon, Thur. and Fri. 8.30am—11am.
Transit visa (ready in an hour) for 20Y FEC or 16Y FEC for students; 2 photos.

East German Embassy
3 Sanlitun Dongsi Jie, Sanlitun N. Tel: 52 1631.
Transit visas are issued on the train at the border for DM5.

Preparations for the Trip

For both trains, the Chinese dining-car gives excellent service, but only travels as far as the Soviet or Mongolian border. Thereafter, catering is doomed to Soviet or Mongolian dining cars and grannies at station stalls. It usually isn't quite that bad, but it is still prudent to lug your own stocks of food and drink onto the train. The best place to stock up, before midday preferably, is the Friendship Store which has a mass of goodies including Danish pastries, bread, Heilongjiang cheese, sausage, fruit, instant noodles, peanuts and raisins, instant coffee, thermos flasks, toilet paper, tea bags, foreign cigarettes and spirits. The dreaded Californian (Mediterranean) fruitfly is, reportedly, kept out of Soviet territory by border officials who confiscate fresh fruit. In my own experience, this has led to a prodigious consumption of fruit on the train just before reaching the border, where the surviving apples and mandarins were completely ignored by customs officials.

A shopping expedition in Wangfujing street should yield any other everyday items needed. All the major hotels in Beijing carry international newspapers and magazines, in case you want some reading material. The Friendship Store has a book stall where you can find that colossal epic to suit the distance you are about to cover.

As a result of strict laws on the sale of alcohol in the Soviet Union, the Russian dining-car on the Trans-Siberian section does not carry alcoholic drinks, so the thirsty should stock up in the Chinese dining-car with bottles of beer which can be stached under the seat, and perhaps purchase stronger stuff elsewhere in Beijing. Russians are very keen on foreign cigarettes, Chinese tea, and can dispose of alcohol in any form, just so long as (your) stocks last. Luggage lockers in the Foreigners' International Waiting Room of the station cost Y2 for 24 hours. Large plastic bags with red, blue and white stripes are available from many shops in Beijing and are useful for toting spoils onto the train. Several years ago, an English traveller was so enchanted by the bamboo prams in Beijing, she piled her belongings into one and trundled it onto the train to be used for luggage conveyance all the way to London.

GUANGZHOU (CANTON)

On arriving at Shenzhen by train from Hong Kong, one way to avoid Guangzhou completely is to take the Beijing express (train no 16). A hard sleeper ticket will cost about Y103 FEC. (Hard sleepers are actually quite comfortable — a bunk in a sleeping car). Since you are catching it before Guangzhou, your chances of a hard sleeper berth are good, even if the ticket office is sold out. Just get on the train with a platform ticket (*yuetai piao*) and find the train official in charge (*che zhang*).

Maps are sold in front of the station, at all the major hotels and bookshops.

Places to stay

Shengli Guest House, 54 Shamian St. Tel: 61223.
Bus no 5 from the station.

Guangzhou Youth Hostel

(Formerly Government Service Workers' Hostel.) Shamian Island.
Bus no 5 from the station.

A few metres from the White Swan Hotel, this is the most popular place for budget travellers. Y6 FEC for bed in a packed dormitory. Y8 FEC for bed in a 6-bed room. Noticeboard/mail on the ground floor. Bikes can be hired opposite for YO.90 RMB per hour. The White Swan Hotel, across the road, has useful facilities (gleaming washrooms, post office, film developing, newspapers) and an excellent breakfast (Y11 FEC).

Transport out of Guangzhou

The railway station is a centre of activity and close by are CITS and CAAC. Be especially cautious about your belongings and dealings with hordes of money touts. A taxi ride to the White Swan Hotel costs about Y10 FEC, or take bus no 5.

Useful addresses

CITS
179 Huanshi Lu. Tel: 33454.

CAAC
181 Huanshi Lu. Tel: 662123 (Domestic); 661803 (International).

Public Security
863 Jiefang Bei Lu.
This is usually a well-informed PSB with an up-to-date list of open places.

Hong Kong
Information

Before going to Hong Kong, ask your nearest Hong Kong Tourist Association (HKTA) office for a sample of their comprehensive output of maps and brochures. In Hong Kong itself, two convenient HKTA offices are at Kai Tak Airport (outside the customs hall) open 8am—10.30pm, and The Star Ferry Terminal (Kowloon side) open 8am—6pm weekdays and 8am—6pm Saturdays.

The head office is on the 35th floor of the Connaught Centre (just behind the Star Ferry Terminal — Central side). Open 8am—6pm weekdays and 8am—1pm Saturday. Tel: 5-244191.

There is also a telephone information service (available 8am—6pm weekdays, 8am—1pm Saturday and Sunday) for which you dial 3-7225555.

A service, normally for residents and less for tourists, is provided by the Community Advice Bureau: Tel: 5-245444.

Moneychanging

The airport offices give a lousy rate and the gleaming exchange palaces in Kowloon hide an exorbitant commission rate in small print — don't use them. The Hang Seng Bank has plenty of branches (including one in Ocean Terminal) and offers a competitive exchange rate without commission. Close to Chungking Mansions, at 54 Nathan Road, is Hang Tai Finance Co which offers excellent rates without commission (sometimes roubles, too). The 1986 exchange rate was HK$8 = £1.

Telephone

Local calls are free from private phones. There are three prefixes: 5 — Hong Kong Island; 3 — Kowloon; 0 — New Territories. Do not dial the prefix if you are in the area you are calling. For those without a private phone, overseas calls and telegrams can be organised at Cable & Wireless offices in Ocean Centre and the Connaught Centre (phonecards can also be used for special public phones). Dial 108 for enquiries.

Transport

Taxis These are still a bargain at HK$5 for the first 2km and 70 cents for each extra 0.27km.

Buses Mini-buses run on fixed routes for fixed fares and double-decker buses are useful for longer hauls. Exact change needed so have it ready.

Trams Introduced in 1904, these are leisurely, cheap at 60 cents a ride and enjoyable, provided you keep your head down on the top deck. The Peak Tram climbs from a station opposite the American consulate on Garden Road right up to the Peak for a fine panorama (HK$4, one way).

Ferry Introduced in 1880 and still going strong is the Star Ferry between Kowloon and Hong Kong Island. Certainly one of the world's finest ferry rides. Ride first class for 70 cents or second class below for 50 cents. There are many more ferries criss-crossing the harbour, an interesting way to sightsee. Ask at the HKTA information offices for details of ferries to outlying islands.

MTR The subway is efficient and fast. A tourist ticket for multiple rides is available for HK$15 from ticket offices.

Trains The old Tsimshatsui Railway Station was next to the present Star Ferry pier at Tsimshatsui. All that remains of what was once the terminus of the Orient Express, is the Old Clock Tower. Colonial ladies, wearied
   The new station at Hung Hom (tel: 3-646321) can be reached by bus (Nos 1K, 2K, 5C, 8, 25). From Hong Kong Island all buses with 100-series numbers cross to Kowloon and stop outside the station. A separate Star Ferry service also runs to Hung Hom from Hong Kong Island.

Places to Stay
For the budget traveller there are several possibilities, mostly in Kowloon. The following is a selection:

YMCA
PO Box 95096, Salisbury Road, Tsimshatsui, Kowloon. Tel: 3-692211.
   A location close to the Star Ferry, excellent facilities and relatively modest prices make this a popular choice. Heavy booking is the norm, so reservations are advisable at least a month in advance. For singles expect to pay between HK$140-240; doubles cost HK$160-260; dormitory beds cost HK$50. Even if you are not staying there, the roof-garden cafeteria has a view right across the harbour — recommended before closing time in the early evening. Photo automats at the entrance are useful for all those passport photos for visas. Other facilities include a baggage check (for guests), bookshop, library, hair salon, coffee shop and restaurant.

Chungking Mansions
This rabbit warren of blocks and floors, the 'cheapie centre' of Hong

Kong, contains numerous hotels. Prices are low, but the surroundings are dismal and claustrophobic and you should be on your guard for unsavoury action. An old favourite is The Travellers' Hostel, 16/F Block A (Tel: 3-682505 or 3-687710) which is often packed, always buzzing with the talk of Asian travel. Time Travel Services is on the same floor. Dormitory beds or floor space costs HK$25; doubles with air-con cost from HK$80 upwards. The noticeboard here is full of information about China and the rest of Asia, wants, things for sale, jobs, tickets, travel tips, travel companions, rip-off firms etc. You can find most things here, from hair cuts by itinerant Swiss hairdressers to jobs as film extras, teaching English, 'modelling' (seldom genuine), or waitressing.

There are plenty of other hotels/hostels in A, B and D blocks — just hunt around and bargain.

International Youth Accommodation Centre (IYAC)
6/F, 21A Lock Road. Tel: 3-663419.
Dorm beds for HK$25 and plenty of China information.

Mau Wui Hall (YHA)
Mt. Davis, Hong Kong Island. Tel: 5-875715.
This is a popular Youth Hostel with a spectacular mountain-top location. You have to be out between 10am and 4pm and back by 11pm. If you are not already a member, it costs HK$80 to do so, but the charge per night is only HK$8 for the dormitory. Take bus 5B till the final terminus, then walk back 100m until you see the sign and then trek up-hill for about 20 minutes.

STB Hostel
225—261 Reclamation Street, 2/F Great Eastern Mansion, Kowloon. Tel: 3-321073.
This is a new hostel with 84 beds, common room and travel office. HK$39 per night.

Caritas Bianchi Lodge
4 Cliff Road, Yaumati, Kowloon. Tel: 3-881111.
Singles from HK$190; doubles from HK$250.

Methodist Centre International Hostel
22 Hennessy Road, Wanchai, Hong Kong Island. Tel: 5-272025.
Cabin-singles from HK$55; doubles from HK$100.

Agencies for arranging Trans-Siberian Travel

With the slimmest of shoestring budgets, it is possible to travel by rail with virtually no stopovers from Hong Kong across Siberia to Europe (or vice-versa), for a little under US$500.

However, not everybody wants to expend time and effort on ticket research and visa hunting, especially if schedules are tight. Provided you give agencies up to six weeks, they can handle most of the dirty work in return for fees and a mark-up. For example, if Hong Kong is the first stop on an Asia tour, you could get USSR details sorted out (make sure you give alternative choices/dates) and then continue round Asia (check back occasionally for possible hitches) before returning to Hong Kong and collecting the documents.

Hong Student Travel Bureau (HKSTB) and De Luxe Travel Bureau

8/F Tai Sang Bank Bldg, 130 Des Voeux Rd Central. Tel: 5-414841. Branch office: Rm 1024 10/Fl, Star House, Salisbury Road, Kowloon. Tel: 3-7213269.

This is a large agency with friendly and efficient staff, offering up-market or budget travel, including Trans-Siberian tours arranged via Japan and staff in Beijing. They are agents for the Scandinavian Student Travel Service (SSTS) and can combine their USSR packages with travel arrangements via Japan or China.

Depending on class of accommodation and duration of package, prices range from HK$1,550 to over HK$4,000. Visa charges, handling charges and connecting travel to/from the USSR are extra costs. For an additional service charge, tickets can be booked at the Hong Kong office on the Trans-Mongolian and Trans-Manchurian and will be reserved by their staff in Beijing. Summer is peak season, so book at least six weeks in advance. This is certainly an option worth considering if you are about to spend several months in and around China, have a definite departure date in mind and do not wish to wait around in Beijing to do it yourself.

Wallem Travel

46th Floor, Hopewell Centre, 183 Queen's Rd East, Wanchai. Tel: 5-286514 or 5-283911 Ext. 192/193.

This is the sales agent for Intourist and Fesco. The chief advantage of this agency is that they contact Intourist and Fesco direct in Japan and secure all the necessary ticketing and visas. The disadvantage lies in delays and increased prices. The following is a sample of the itineraries they offer via Japan:

1. Hong Kong (air)— Tokyo (surface) — Yokohama (ship)— Nakhodka (Trans-Siberian) — Moscow (train/air) — Europe.

2. Hong Kong (ship via Yokohama) — Nakhodka (Trans-Siberian) — Moscow (train/air) — Europe. This option is available during the summer for a couple of sailings only.

Wallem can also arrange travel on the Trans-Siberian with a connection via China (Beijing) but they will only arrange the USSR part of your itinerary.

Telex fees, mailing charges and visa handling fees will be added to the cost of your tour (transport, accommodation, transfers, etc.).

Voyages Jules Verne
Travel Promotions Ltd., Office 203/204 2/F Arcade, Lee Gardens Hotel, Hysan Avenue, Causeway Bay. Tel: 5-7953181.

See page 59 for itineraries. Details are available from the address above and the London office.

The China Visa

A visa to China is easily obtained; the price depends on the type required and how soon you want to take it away. If you buy a travel package together with the visa, this will obviously produce extra commission for the travel agency, but it is not compulsory. The agencies normally provide one-month visas, but more varied requests, such as two months, six months or multiple entry can be attempted, providing the cash is up front with two photos, an application form and a passport. A one-month visa can be obtained in three days for approx. HK$70; the same length visa obtained in half a day can cost from HK$140 upwards; a multiple visa was quoted at HK$600. There are plenty of agencies issuing visas, the following is a selection:

China Travel Service
Head Office, China Travel Building, 77 Queens Rd. Central. Tel: 5-236055 or 5-236222

There is also a branch office at 1/Fl, 27-33 Nathan Road, Kowloon. Tel: 3-7219826 or 7211331.

This is one of the official Chinese travel organisations and a useful source of information on visas, tours and tickets. However, at times there are severe pressures and problems in eliciting information or securing travel documentation.

Phoenix Services Agency
Rm 603 Hanford House, 221D Nathan Road, Tsimshatsui, Kowloon. Tel: 3-7227378 or 3-7233006.

Highly recommended by many travellers both for its prices and the attentive service from cheerful staff. Visas, tickets and tours arranged.

Wah Nam Travel
Rm 1003 Eastern Commercial Centre, 397 Hennessey Road, Wanchai.
Tel: 5- 8911161.

Trinity Express
Rm 614 6th Floor, New World Centre, Salisbury Road, Kowloon. Tel: 3-683207.

Crosspoint Tours
Peking Road, Rm 1101 Bank of America Bldg, Kowloon. Tel: 3-7234342.

Time Travel Services
16th Floor, Chungking Mansions, 40 Nathan Rd., Kowloon.
Tel: 3-7239993 or 3-687710.

CONNECTIONS BETWEEN HONG KONG AND CHINA

Times have changed since it was necessary for everyone to trek across the bridge at Lo Wu — there are now numerous connections by air, land and sea. A helicopter link is the latest proposed addition. The following is a brief, but not exhaustive selection of connections.

Air There are daily flights with CAAC from Hong Kong to Beijing; up to three flights daily to Guangzhou (30 min.; HK$297) and other services to Shanghai, Tianjin, Chengdu and Kunming. Prices from Hong Kong are considerably more expensive than those paid within China. Airport departure tax from Hong Kong is now HK$120.

Rail This is the most common route and one of the cheapest. From Hung Hom it's possible to take a direct express which runs non-stop to Guangzhou (3 hours; approx.HK$285) or ride the MTR as far as the border at Lo Wu (HK$12) and then take another train from Shenzhen on the Chinese side to Guangzhou (Y11 FEC). Between Lo Wu and Kowloon, you might still be able to see old KCR (Kowloon-Canton Railway) rolling stock, just outside and to the east of Tai Po railway station. There is a timetable for this service in the *Appendix*.
   It is now possible to purchase rail tickets for China in Hong Kong from China Railway Service (Hong Kong branch) 41, Chatham Road South, Tsimshatsui, Kowloon. Tel: 3-7214543.

Night Ferry One of the least hurried ways to go, is to take this ferry from Hong Kong at 21.00 and arrive in Guangzhou at 7.15 next morning. Book tickets at CTS offices or through travel agents in Hong Kong. Prices start at HK$70 for a seat; HK$140 for a berth in a 4-person cabin. Longer ferry rides connect Hong Kong with Shanghai, Xiamen and Shantou.

Bus Buses run by the Motor Transport Company of Guangdong and Hong Kong Ltd operate between Hong Kong and Guangzhou. A bus service from Hong Kong to Shenzhen is operated by CITYBUS.

Hovercraft Hovercraft run from Hong Kong (Tai Kok Tsui Pier in Kowloon) to Guangzhou (Zhoutouzi Pier) at 8.45, 9.45 and 10.00. Tickets for the 3-hour run cost approx. HK$145.

Miscellaneous notes

Hong Kong is an excellent place for those going into China en route for Siberia to stock up on: film and photo gear; food and drink; clothing; passport photos; items of interest for fund-raising; medicines and, *most* importantly, cash US dollars in small bills. In China, many of these items are unobtainable or have high prices and the situation in the Soviet Union is even less encouraging.

Hong Kong's image as the world's best place for photo and hi-fi purchases is distinctly tarnished now. Take price comparisons from home or ask the HKTA for the phone number of the importing agent who can give you the Recommended Retail Price. Shop prices must be bargained below this price and never buy without trying several shops first. Beware of extraordinarily low prices — the goods may be reconditioned, defective or rejects imported from Japan. Don't pay a deposit (all sorts of tricks are possible) and insist on a worldwide guarantee with the name of the shop stamped next to that of the agent — without this, it is worthless (no matter what slick mouths say). If possible, don't buy in the touristy, southern part of Tsimshatsui but head up towards the northern part of Nathan Road (MTR:Argyle) or try Stanley Street on Hong Kong Island.

Embassy Listing

The Soviet Union and Eastern Bloc countries have no representation, all visa hunting is restricted to travel agencies which, as described above, take several weeks to organise documents by telex or letter via Beijing or Tokyo.

Japanese Consulate

24/Fl Bank of America Tower, 12 Harcourt Road, Central. Tel: 5-221184.
Office hours: 9.30am—12 noon, and 2pm—4pm except Wed and Sat afternoons.

Trans Siberian trips to USSR

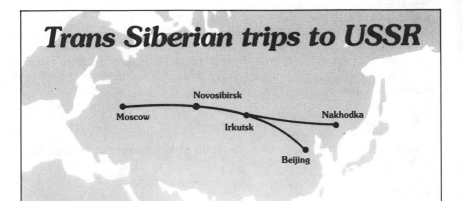

We provide individual and group travel services for USSR visa, train tickets, Soviet hotels and sight-seeing. Visa to other Eastern European countries can also be arranged. Also available are the following individual packages:

Hong Kong — Japan (1) Nakhodka — Moscow 11 days.

Hong Kong — Japan (2) Nakhodka — Leningrad 14 days.

Hong Kong — Beijing (3) Beijing — Moscow 9 days.

Hong Kong — Beijing (4) Beijing — Leningrad 12 days.

Enquiries are most welcome.

Hong Kong Student Travel

Travel Licence No: 350181
Hot Line: 5-8152666
- *8/F Tai Sang Bank Building, 130 Des Voeux Road, C., Hong Kong. Tel: 5-414841 Telex: 66347 HKSTB HX Cable: STBHKG*
- *1021 Star House, Tsimshatsui, Kowloon. Tel: 3-7213269 Telex: 52988 ACSTB HX*
- *1812 Argyle Centre Phase 1, 688 Nathan Road, Kowloon. Tel: 3-900421*

86-AST-06

Japan

Japan is the destination most frequently associated with travelling on the Trans-Siberian. Although many travel out to Japan this way, it's possible, of course, to travel back to Europe from Japan, perhaps as part of a tour of the Far East. Some travellers take advantage of budget flights to Hong Kong from Europe, travel up through China, take a plane or a boat to Japan, and then do the Trans-Siberian routing. Beijing, Shanghai and Hong Kong are all connected by air with Tokyo; ferries link Yokohama with Shanghai and Hong Kong.

This section gives brief guidance to those leaving the Trans-Siberian route or starting it via Japan and concentrates on Yokohama, Niigata and Tokyo as key points.

Information

Nobody can complain about a lack of information material and maps for Japan. Before entering Japan, contact your nearest Japan National Tourist Office (JNTO) and you'll be generously rewarded. They supply masses of material including tourist maps of Japan and Tokyo; *the Japan Travel Manual*; *Your Travelling Companion Japan*; *Budget Travel in Japan* and *Japan Travel Topics: Reasonable Accommodations in Japan*. In Japan itself there is a comprehensive and efficient network of Tourist Information Centres (TIC) bursting with yet more literature.

Japan Travel-Phone This is a nationwide telephone service for tourists (available 7 days a week 9am—5pm). Apart from information on sights, transport, etc., it has also provided language assistance for predicaments such as railway ticket squabbles and dating problems! The procedure to call the Travel Information Centre (TIC) is simple: dial 106 and ask — clearly and slowly — for "Collect call, TIC, please". If you are calling from a public telephone, you will need to insert a 10YEN coin which will be refunded after the call if you are calling from outside Tokyo. In Tokyo call TIC direct on 502-1461.

Money In November 1986, 227 YEN (Y/227) £1.

Railways

If you are a speedster who likes to travel almost as far and fast as a bullet, then you might consider buying a Japan Rail Pass available for between one and three weeks. Apart from the Shinkansen (Bullet Train), you will also be able to use the rest of the Japanese National Railways (JNR) rail, bus and ferry services but not those run privately. Prices for adults start at 27,000YEN. However, you can only buy a purchase order for the pass abroad at one of the many authorised agents. Once you reach Japan, you simply hand over the exchange voucher and receive your pass.

National Holidays
Jan 1, 15; Feb 11; Mar 20; Apr 29; May 3, 5; Sept 15, 23; Oct 10; Nov 3, 23. If any of these fall on a Sunday, the following Monday is taken as part of the holiday.

Warning If you want to avoid monumental crowds and transport jams, try and avoid the peak travel seasons which occur at: Year-end and during the New Year holiday season — December 27 to January 4 and adjacent weekends; 'Golden Week' holiday season — April 29 to May 5 and adjacent weekends; 'Bon' festival season which takes place for a week around August 15.

Accommodation
Up-market accommodation in Japan has a price tag as high as any in the world. For the budget-minded, places such as 'business hotels', *ryokan* (Japanese-style inns) and (youth) hostels have prices varying from moderate (Y/4000) to cheap (Y/1700).

Eating
If you are not careful, eating can be an expensive habit in Japanese cities, but there are plenty of places with acceptable prices. At breakfast time, coffee shops do a 'morning service' which usually consists of coffee, toast and a boiled egg for about Y/350.

At other mealtimes, try the restaurants in the big office buildings (basements are cheap but avoid during peak lunch hour), department stores (open 10am—5.30pm), shopping centres and rail stations for reasonably-priced meals (Y/700—1500).*Teishoku* is a set menu, usually less pricey than special dishes. The ubiquitous fast-food and franchise joints from abroad (Macdonalds, Kentucky Fried Chicken etc.) will also stretch the Yen as will their Japanese counterparts with names like Italian Tomato, Hoka-Hoka Bento and Yoshinoya Gyudon. Ordering can involve pointing to the plastic replica of what you want in the window or paying for a coupon which is then handed to service staff.

YOKOHAMA
Information and maps
When a passenger ship is in port, the information office on the South Pier is normally open. If not try the main offices, just a few minutes away: **Kanagawa Prefectural Tourist Information Centre**, Silk Centre Annex No 1, Yamashita-cho, Naku-ku, Tel: 681-0506, or **Yokohama International Welcome Association**, 1 Fl., Silk Centre Building No 1, 1 Yamashitacho, Naka-ku. Tel: 641-5824 or 651-2668.

These offices provide all the usual services and can arrange a meeting with a Japanese family as part of the Home Visit System.

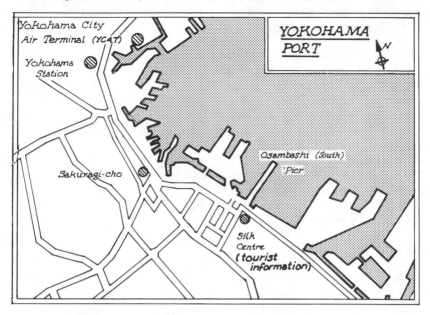

Budget Accommodation
Try the information offices for the latest addresses. There are two hostels: **Yokohama YMCA**, 225 Yamashita-cho, Naka-ku. Tel: 681-2903, and **Kanagawa Youth Hostel**, 1 Momijigaoka, Nishi-ku. Tel: 241-6503.

Transport between Yokohama and Tokyo
From Yokohama If you are arriving by boat in Yokohama, you will normally dock at the South Pier. The easiest method is then to take a taxi either to the closest station, *Kannai Eki*, or to the more distant *Yokohama Eki* (Yokohama Station), and take a train from either of these stations to *Tokyo Eki* (Tokyo Station). Another method is to take bus no 26 from the 'Silk Centre' (tourist information on the 1st floor) to the bus terminal outside the east exit of Yokohama Eki.

The first railway in Japan ran between Yokohama and Tokyo and has become mighty complicated since then.

There are five rail options for the approx. 30 minute run between the two cities: three services run by JNR and two which are privately run (Toyoko and Keihin-Kyuko).

Yokohama station is large and confusing. Buy tickets from automats. If in doubt about the price, which should be about Y/430, buy the cheapest ticket and pay the difference at the Fare Adjustment Office (*Ryokin-seisanjo*) at the other end. Track 2 is for the Keihin-Kyuko (private line) which usually runs to Shinagawa in the south of Tokyo. If you take a JNR train, it's probably best to select one of the faster services: the orange/green Tokaido line on Tracks 7 and 8 or the cream/blue Yokosuka line on Track 10 — both make stops at Kawasaki, Shinagawa and Shimbashi before terminating at Tokyo Eki, in the heart of Tokyo.

From the west exit, you have access to another option: the Toyoko (private line) which operates from Track 2 to Shibuya in the west of Tokyo.

From Tokyo If you go by JNR, take the Yokosuka or Tokaido lines from Tokyo Eki, Shimbashi or Shinagawa stations. If you go on a private line, take the Keihin-Kyuko from Shinagawa or the Toyoko from Shibuya.

Airport transport From Tokyo's major international airport (Narita) there is a special bus to Yokohama City Air Terminal (YCAT). Buses operate between 7am and 11pm; journey time 95 minutes; fare Y/3100.

From YCAT to Yokohama Station (*Yokohama Eki*) take the shuttle bus or walk it in about 10 minutes. Take a train (fare Y/120) to Sakuragi-cho for access to the pier. Expect to pay about Y/430 for a taxi from Sakuragi-cho to the pier.

Remember to allow at least three hours from Narita airport to the South Pier at Yokohama Port.

NIIGATA

Niigata is of special importance to winter-time travellers on the Trans-Siberian because the boat service between Yokohama and Nakhodka does not run in the winter. Instead, there are winter flights between Niigata in Japan and Khabarovsk (USSR) which will make the trip approx. Y/20,000 more expensive than taking the boat from Yokohama.

Apparently this flight connection is highly unprofitable for JAL, but was introduced at the request of the Soviet Union in return for flight rights on the Polar route to Europe via Moscow.

Aeroflot flights operate all year round, but JAL close down their flights between October or November and April.

In the winter, the Aeroflot flight from Khabarovsk to Niigata leaves every Friday at 12.50 and arrives at 14.05; the return flight from Niigata to Khabarovsk leaves every Friday at 15.30 and arrives at 18.50.

Information
Niigata City Tourist Information Office, in front of JNR Niigata Station. Tel: (0252) 41-7914.

Transport between Niigata and Tokyo

Rail The Shinkansen Bullet Train takes just a couple of hours. The Bullet Train terminal for Niigata is at Omiya (a 26 minute ride on the Relay Train from Ueno Station) and there are 21 services daily. The fare is approx. Y/9,200.

The express train Sado takes 5 hours and departs at 7.34 (seasonal), 13.34 and 18.34 from Ueno. The approximate fare Y/6,200.

The express sleeping car train Amanogawa takes 6½ hours, departs at 22.37 from Ueno, and the approximate fare (including berth charge) is Y/11,200.

Airport transport

A bus runs from Niigata Station to Niigata airport (30 min.).

TOKYO

Information

Tourist Information Centre, Kotani Bldg., 1-6-6 Yurakucho, Chiyoda-ku, Tokyo. Tel: 502-1461. Office hours: daily 9am—12 noon and 1pm—5pm; closed Saturday afternoon, Sunday and on national holidays.

This is the place to head for maps, preliminary advice on boat services to and from the USSR, and all imaginable information on Japan, but not for reservations. It's definitely worthwhile asking about the Home Visit Service which arranges an evening visit to an English-speaking Japanese family and tries to match the interests of the visitor with those of the family. Take along a gift of fruit for the family.

Japan National Tourist Organisation (JNTO)

Head Office, 10-1 Yurakucho 2-chome, Chiyoda-ku, Tokyo 100. Tel: 216-1902.

Tele-tourist Service

Around-the-clock taped information on current events in Tokyo. Tel: 503-2911 (English).

Other sources of information to be found at large hotels and travel agencies are free newspapers, such as *Tokyo Tour Companion* and *Tokyo Weekender*.

Places to stay (budget)

Tokyo YWCA Hostel
1-8 Kanda-Surugadai,
Chiyoda-ku
Tel: (03) 293-5421

Tokyo YMCA Hotel
7 Kanda-Mitoshiro-cho,
Chiyoda-ku
Tel: (03) 293-1911

Sawanoya Ryokan
2-3-11 Yanaka, Taito-ku
Tel: (03) 822-2251
Yashima Ryokan
1-15-5 Hyakunin-cho,
Shinjuku-ku
Tel: (03) 364-2534
Okubo House
1-11-32 Hyakunin-cho,
Shinjuku-ku
Tel: (03) 361-2348

Sansuiso Ryokan
2-9-5 Higashi-Gotanda,
Shinagawa-ku
Tel: (03) 441-7475
Mickey House
2-15-1 Nakadai, Itabashi-ku
Tel: (03) 936-8889
Fujikan
4-36-1 Hongo, Bunkyo-ku
Tel: (03) 813-4441

Places to eat (budget)

Shinjuku Area

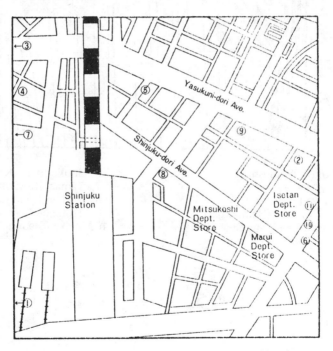

1. Bombay (Indian)
2. Hageten (Tempura)
3. Hashiya (Spaghetti)
4. Meigetsukan (Teppan-yaki)
5. Rengaya (Steak)
6. Spoon House (Grill)
7. Sungary (Russian)
8. Takano World Restaurant
   (Indian, Italian, German, Mexican
   & Scandinavian)

Where to eat (cont.)

Ginza/Yurakucho Area

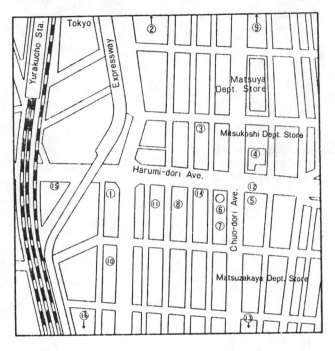

1. Fukusuke (Sushi)
2. Ivy House
3. Kawa (Tonkatsu)
4. McDonald's (Hamburger)
5. Shabusen (Shabu Shabu)
6. Shokudo-en (Korean)
7. Tamazushi (Sushi)
8. Torigin (Yakitori)
9. Tsubame Grill (German)
10. Volks (Steak)

寝かた

*'A piece of music was played over the train system especially for me —
requested by a mystery passenger.' (Barbara Taylor).*

Agencies for arranging Trans-Siberian travel

USSR Government Tourist Information Bureau (Intourist office)
Roppongi Heights 1-16, Roppongi 4-chome, Minato-ku. Tel: 584-6617.
Office hours: 10am—12 noon and 2pm—3pm, except Wed, Sat, Sun and national holidays of the Soviet Union.

Japan-Soviet Travel Bureau Tel: 432-6161.

The following prices (approximate guide only — allow at least US$100 extra for handling costs) are for an itinerary including the boat journey (summer only, see under Niigata for extra cost of winter flights) from Yokohama to Nakhodka and then continuing by rail via Khabarovsk along the Trans-Siberian Railway to Moscow and Europe:
London Y/182,000, Paris Y/177, Vienna Y/137,000, Helsinki Y/130,000.

United Orient Shipping Company 4th Floor, Hazama Bldg., 5-8, 2- Chome, Kita-Aoyama, Minato-ku, Tokyo 107. Tel: 478- 7271.
This company acts as the agent for the Far Eastern Shipping Company (**FESCO**) which runs the boats between Nakhodka, Yokohama and Hong Kong.

Japan-China International Ferry Co. Ltd.
Tel: 078-392 1021.
This agency operates the Nicchu ferry connection between Kobe/Osaka and China (Shanghai). The ferry departs from Kobe or Osaka on alternate Tuesdays at midday annd reaches Shanghai on Thursday morning. The return service leaves Shanghai every Saturday evening to arrive at Kobe or Osaka at midday on alternate Mondays. Economy class costs Y/22,000 including breakfast, but other meals are available from the Chinese restaurant on board.

Transport

Buses These run on routes which are hard to determine and are not recommended unless you have plenty of time to kill when getting lost.

Trains and subways Provide fast reliable transport and run from 5.00 to 24.00. The information offices have maps (Tokyo Railway and Subway). Long-distance tickets are bought at windows, use the automats for other tickets. The rush hours (7.30—9.30 and 17.00—18.00) are to be strenuously avoided unless you like the feeling of being processed in a sardine cannery. When the trains stop after midnight, you are at the mercy of taxis which cruise the streets in search of the highest bidder for their services. All stations have signs above the platforms with Japanese and Roman letters. In big letters in the top centre of the board is the name of the station; the names of the previous station and the next station are written below in smaller letters.

Each of JNR's four commuter train services is painted in a different colour. The Yamanote Loop Line (light green) is an easily-understandable service, circling the heart of Tokyo, and an excellent guide for orientation.

Taxis Tipping is not customary, but the fares aren't cheap either, with a minimum charge of Y/470 for the first 2km and Y/80 for each additional 370 metres plus a time charge if the taxi moves at less than 10km per hour! Between 10pm and 5am there is a 20% surcharge, providing, of course, you can get a taxi to stop for you — by no means easy. Drivers operate best with instructions in Japanese (written preferably) and you should hop out sharply at your destination, otherwise they'll nip you with their rear-door automatic closing apparatus.

Embassy listings

Soviet Embassy
1-1 Azabudai 2-chome, Minato-ku. Tel: 583-4224.

Mongolian Embassy
Shoto Pine Crest Mansion, 21-4, Kamiyama-cho, Shibuya-ku. Tel: 469-2088.

Hungarian Embassy
3-1 Aobadai 2-chome, Meguro-ku. Tel: 476-6061.

Polish Embassy
13-5 Mita 2-chome, Meguro-ku. Tel: 711-5224.

East German Embassy
Akasaka Mansion 5-16, Akasaka 7-chome, Minato-ku. Tel: 585-5404.

British Embassy
1 Ichiban-cho, Chiyoda-ku. Tel: 265-5511.

American Embassy
10-5 Akasaka 1-chome, Minato-ku. Tel: 583-7141.

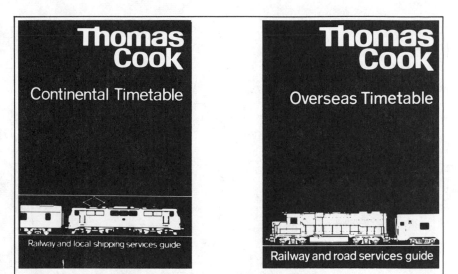

Thomas Cook Publications have a range of timetables and maps to help the Trans–Siberian Traveller. The monthly Continental Timetable takes you from London, Hook of Holland or Ostend to Moscow, the bi-monthly Overseas Timetable gives the train times from Moscow to China and the Pacific coast and the ships to Japan, the Rail Map of Europe helps you to trace the routes to Moscow, and Berlin Transit with its eleven maps and plans explains the special regulations which apply if you are visiting Berlin en route. Ask for them at any Thomas Cook UK travel shop, or buy direct from Thomas Cook Publications, PO Box 36, Peterborough PE3 6SB, England.

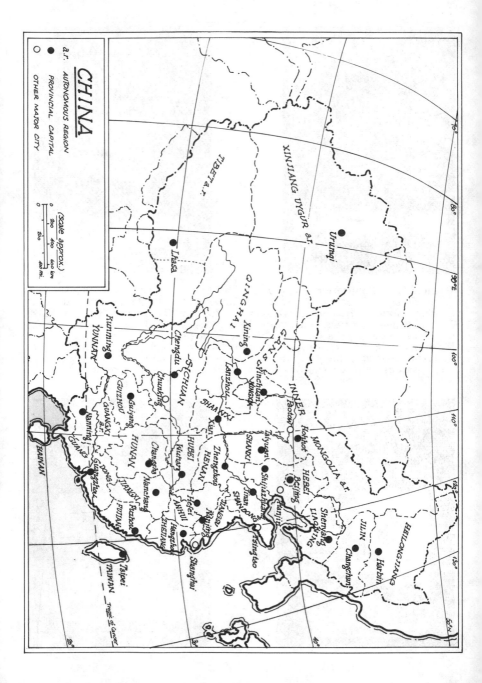

APPENDICES

OPEN PLACES IN CHINA, 1986

The following list is a skeleton outline only. New places are being added continuously, so keep up-to-date at major PSB's (Beijing, Shanghai and Guangzhou) and through other travellers. A: denotes places available on your visa, B: places formerly available on an Aliens' Travel Permit, but now automatically included on a visa. * indicates a provincial capital.

Anhui Province

A: Bengbu*; Hefei; Huangshan county; Jiuhuashan (Qingyang); Tunxi; Wuhu.

B: Anqing; Chaohu; Chuxian; Fengyang county; Huaibei; Huainan; Jingxian county; Ma'anshan; Shexian county; Tongling county; Xiuning county.

A: Beijing municipality.

Fujian Province

A: Chong'an; Fuzhou*; Quanzhou; Zhangzhou; Xiamen.

Gansu Province

A: Lanzhou*.

B: Dunhuang county; Jiayuguan; Jiuquan county; Linxia (Labulong monastery); Tianshui county; Yongjing county; Xiahe (Labrum monastery).

Guandong Province (and Hainan Island)

A: Chaozhou; Foshan; Guangdong (Canton)*; Gaoyao county; Haikou; Huizhou; Jiangmen; Shantou; Shaoguan; Shenzhen; Zhanjiang; Zhaoqing; Zhongshan; Zhuhai.

B: Anding county; Baisha county; Baoting county; Boluo county; Changjiang county; Chengmai county; Danxian county; Dapu county; Deqing county; Ding'an county; Dongguan county; Dongfang county; Fengkai county; Fengshun county; Haifeng county; Heyuan county; Huaiji county; Huidong county; Huiyang county; Ledong county; Lingao county; Lingshui county; Lufeng county; Luoding county; Maoming; Meixian; Nanhai county; Qionghai county; Qiongshan county; Qiongzhong county; Sanya; Shunde county; Sihui county; Tunchang county; Wanning county; Wenchang county; Xingning county; Xinxing county; Yunfu county.

Guangxi Province

A; Beihai; Guilin (and Yangshuo); Liuzhou; Nanning*; Wuzhou.

B: Beilu county; Binyang county; Guiping county; Guixian county; Luchuan county; Rongxian county; Wuming county; Xing'an county.

Guizhou Province

A: Anshun; Guiyang*.

B: Kaili; Liupanshui; Qingzhen county; Shibing county; Huangguoshu Falls (Zhenning autonomous county); Zhenyuan county; Zunyi.

Hebei Province
A: Chengde*; Qinhuangdao (incl. Beidaihe and Shanhaiguan); Shijiazhuang; Zhouxian county.
B: Baoding; Handan; Tangshan; Zunhua county (Dongling tombs).

Heilongjiang Province
A: Daqing; Harbin*; Qiqihar.
B: Hegang; Heihe; Ichun; Jiamusi; Jixi; Mudanjiang; Qitaihe; Suifenhe; Tongjiang; Wudalianchi.

Henan Province.
A: Anyang; Kaifeng; Luoyang (and Longmen caves); Zhengzhou*.
B: Gongxian; Huixian; Linxian; Nanyang; Puyang; Pingdingshan; Sanmenxia; Wenxian county; Xinxiang; Xinyang (Jigong Shan); Yuxian.

Hubei Province
A: Jiangling county; Shashi; Wuhan*; Xiangfan; Yichang.
B: Ezhou; Danjiangkou; Huangshi; Jingmen; Shiyan; Suizhou; Xianning.

Hunan Province
A: Changsha*; Hengyang; Xiangtan; Yueyang.
B: Hengshan county; Xiangtan county (and Shaoshan); Zhuzhou.

Jiangxi Province
A: Jingdezhen; Jiujiang (and Lushan); Nanchang*; Yingtan.
B: Ganzhou; Jinggangshan county; Pengze county (Dragon Palace Cave).

Jilin Province
A: Changchun*; Jilin; Yanji.
B: Antu county (Changbai Shan area); Baicheng; Liaoyuan; Siping; Tonghua.

Liaoning Province
A: Anshan; Dalian; Dandong; Fushun; Jinzhou; Shenyang*; Yingkou.
B: Benxi; Chaoyang; Fuxin; Liaoyang; Tieling.

Nei Menggu (Inner Mongolia) Autonomous Region
A: Baotou; Erenhot; Hohhot*; Manzhouli.
B: Dalad Banner (Xiangshawan); Dongsheng; Hailar; Tongliao; Xilinhot (Abagnar Qi); Zalantun (Butna Qi).

Ningxia Autonomous Region
A: Yinchuan*.
B: Zhongwei county.

Qinghai Province
A: Huangzhong county (and Taersi monastery); Xining*.
B: Golmud; Gonghe county; Ledu; Lenghu; Mangya; Qinghai Lake (restricted access).

Shandong Province
A: Jinan*; Jining (including Qufu and Yanzhou counties); Qingdao: Tai'an (and Taishan); Weifang; Yantai; Zibo.
B: Kenli (Shengli oilfield).

Shangai Municipality

Shanxi Province
A: Taiyuan*.
B: Datong; Fanzhi county; Linfen; Wutai county; Yuncheng.

Sichuan Province
A: Chengdu*; Chongqing; Emei county; Leshan.
B: Dazu county; Fengjie county; Guanxian county; Meishan county; Wanxian county; Wushan county; Xindu county; Yunyang county; Zhongxian county.

Tianjin Municipality

Tibet Autonomous Region
A: Lhasa*

Yunnan Province
A: Kunming*; Shilin (Lunan)
B: Chuxiong; Dali; Jinghong county; Menghai county; Lijiang (Naxi autonomous county); Qujing; Simao county; Tonghai county; Yuxi.

Xinjiang Autonomous Region
A: Urumqi*.
B: Kashgar; Shihezi; Turfan county.

WILL YOU HELP US? We expect this book to go into several editions and want to keep it as up to date as possible. Please send any new information, anecdotes, or general comments to the publisher. Thanks.

CITS (BEIJING) PRICES FOR TRANS-SIBERIAN RAIL TICKETS

Destination	Train no.	De luxe sleeper yuan*	Soft sleeper yuan	Hard sleeper† yuan
Moscow	3	711.80	623.50	445.10
	19	739.20	648.00	462.40
Berlin	3	936.30	848.00	584.40
	19	973.80	882.60	608.40
Irkutsk	3	367.40	322.20	229.90
	19	429.20	376.10	268.40
Ulan Bator	3	220.70	192.60	137.80
	89	same	same	same
Warsaw	3	855.80	767.50	533.10
	19	893.30	802.10	557.10
Budapest	3	908.80	820.50	566.20
	19	951.30	860.10	593.60
Bucharest	3	936.00	847.70	582.50
	19	966.00	874.80	601.40
Prague	3	976.90	888.60	622.80
	19	1014.30	923.10	646.70
Sofia	3	1041.30	953.00	648.10
	19	1071.30	980.10	667.10
Pyongyang (North Korea)	27	174.30	124.20	

*Exchange rate: US$1 Y.3.20. † Hard sleeper on trains within China are, indeed, hard — just benches, whereas on the international trains they are in 4-berth compartments which are perfectly comfortable.

THE GLOBETROTTERS CLUB

An international club which aims to share information on adventurous budget travel through monthly meetings and *Globe* magazine. Published every two months, *Globe* offers a wealth of information, from reports of members' latest adventures to recent travel bargains and tips, plus the invaluable 'Mutual Aid' column where members can swap a house, sell a camper, find a travel companion or offer information on unusual places or hospitality to visiting members.

London meetings are held monthly (Saturdays) and focus on a particular country or continent with illustrated talks.

Enquiries to: The secretary, Globetrotters Club, BCM/Roving, London WC1N 3XX.

AGENCY TARIFFS FOR TRANS-SIBERIAN RAIL TICKETS FROM HONG KONG

Hong Kong to Guangzhou (Canton)	HK$285
Guangzhou to Beijing (1st class)	HK$1,080
Beijing to Moscow (Trans-Mongolian)	
2-berth compartment	HK$2,570
4-berth compartment	HK$2,260
Beijing to Moscow (Trans-Manchurian)	
2-berth compartment	HK$2,650
4-berth compartment	HK$2,350
Moscow to London (2nd class)	HK$1,970
Moscow to Paris (2nd class)	HK$1,810

RAIL CONNECTIONS BETWEEN HONG KONG AND CHINA

Direct Express (Kowloon/Guangzhou)

Guangzhou dep.	Kowloon arr.	Train no.	Kowloon dep.	Guangzhou arr.
8.40	11.31	91/96	8.15	11.50
10.15	13.12	93/92	12.55	15.59
18.39	21.29	95/94	14.35	17.25

Guangzhou/Shenzhen Express

Guangzhou dep.	Shenzhen arr.	Train no.	Shenzhen dep.	Guangzhou arr.
6.25	8.57	105/104	8.10	11.22
6.50	12.10	543/106	10.00	13.13
7.20	9.52	107/108	11.21	14.00
8.10	14.34	501/88	14.08	16.31
10.30	13.05	87/544	13.18	19.04
11.54	14.48	101/102	15.50	18.23
12.50	15.16	197/502	16.30	22.00
16.50	19.50	103/198	17.55	20.23

Purchase rail tickets for China in Hong Kong from China Railway Service (Hong Kong branch) 41, Chatham Road South, Tsimshatsui, Kowloon. Tel: 3-7214543.

Timetables

The following timetables are subject to seasonal and other changes, so cannot be guaranteed to be correct. For the most up-to-date details, consult the latest copy of Cook's Overseas Timetable.

THE TRANS-SIBERIAN

Station name		Departure	Length	Km from
Russian	English	Moscow time	of stop	Moscow
		First day		
Москва	Moscow	14.05 (dep)		
Ярославль	Yaroslavl	17.37	5	282
Данилов	Danilov	18.50	12	357
Буй	Buy	20.02	10	450
		Second day		
Киров	Kirov	03.12	15	957
Пермь	Perm	09.47	12	1437
	Europe/Asia obelisk	14.30 (approx)		1777
Свердловск	Sverdlovsk	15.31	15	1818
Тюмень	Tyumen	19.28	20	2144
Ишим	Ishim	22.43	10	2433
		Third day		
Омск	Omsk	02.26	12	2716
Новосибирск	Novosibirsk	09.56	15	3343
Тайга	Taiga	13.12	10	3571
Ачинск	Achinsk	18.21	3	3920
Красноярск	Krasnoyarsk	21.34	15	4104
		Fourth day		
Тайшет	Tayshet	03.47	7	4522
Иркутск	Irkutsk	15.16	10	5191
Слидуянка	Slyudyanka	17.37	10	5317
Улан Уде	Ulan Ude	22.50	12	5647
		Fifth day		
Чита	Chita	08.27	10	6201
Каримское	Karimskaya	10.13	10	6300
		Sixth day		
Сковородино	Skovorodino	04.15	15	7317
Белогорск	Belogorsk	13.45	20	7873
		Seventh day		
Хабаровск	Khabarovsk	00.38 arr.		8531

Station		Dep.		Km
Boat train		*Eighth day*		
Хабаровск	Khabarovsk	10.30		8531
Спасск Дальний	Spassk Dal'niy	18.57	10	9057
Уссурийск	Ussuriysk	21.17	10	9185
		Ninth day		
	Nakhodka Port			
Тихоокеанская	(Tikhookeanskaya)	02.25		9438

TRANS-MONGOLIAN

Moscow time Arr.	Dep.	Km from Moscow	Station		Local time Arr.	Dep.
	21.10	0	Moscow	Москва		21.10
Wed						
11.20	11.35	957	Kirov	Киров	12.20	12.35
18.25	18.40	1437	Perm	Пермь	20.25	20.40
Thurs						
00.23	00.38	1818	Sverdlovsk	Свердловск	02.23	02.38
12.05	12.20	2716	Omsk	Омск	17.05	17.20
20.20	20.35	3343	Novosibirsk	Новосибирск	00.20	00.35
Fri						
08.25	08.40	4104	Krasnoyarsk	Красноярск	12.25	12.40
15.21	15.28	4522	Tayshet	Тайшет	20.21	20.28
Sat						
02.56	03.08	5191	Irkutsk	Иркутск	07.56	08.08
05.39	05.49	5317	Slyudyanka	Слюдянка	10.39	10.49
11.03	11.20	5647	Ulan Ude	Улан-Удэ	16.03	16.20
	18.20	5902	Naushki	Наушки	21.32	23.20
MONGOLIA						
Ulan Bator Time						
19.00	20.15	5925	Sukhe Bator	Сух-Баатар	24.00	01.15
Sun						
04.00	04.30	6304	Ulan Bator	Улан-Батор	09.00	09.30
16.40	17.48	7013	Dzamyn Ude	Замын Үүд	21.40	22.48
CHINA						
Beijing time						
18.13	20.49	7023	Erlian	二 连	23.13	01.49
Mon						
03.22	03.32		Datong	大 同	08.22	08.32
08.12	08.23		Great Wall		13.12	13.23
10.33		7865	Beijing	北 京	15.33	

THE TRANS-MANCHURIAN

19 到Arr	19 开Dep	自起北京公里 km	车次 T/No	站名 Station	车次 T/No	自起莫斯科公里 km	20 到Arr	20 开Dep
				北京时间 Beijing Time				
	19.40	0		北　京 Beijing		9001	6.31	——
21.18	21.28	137		天　津 Tianjin		8864	4.34	4.44
0.53	1.03	415		山海关 Shanhaiguan		8586	0.58	1.09
3.15	3.25	599		锦　州 Jinzhou		8402	22.39	22.49
6.19	6.34	841		沈　阳 Shenyang		8160	19.42	19.54
8.47	8.55	1030		四　平 Siping		7971	17.20	17.28
10.20	10.32	1146		长　春 Changchun		7855	15.45	15.57
13.30	13.45	1388		哈尔滨 Harbin		7613	12.27	12.42
16.13	16.18	1547		大　庆 Daqing		7454	10.11	10.16
17.46	18.00	1658		昂昂溪 Ang'angxi		7343	8.27	8.41
20.19	20.27	1804		扎兰屯 Zhalantun		7197	6.10	6.18
21.25	21.33	1866		巴　林 Balin		7135	↓	↓
22.37	22.49	1927		博克图 Boketu		7074	4.12	4.24
23.24	23.31	1952		兴安岭 Xing'anling		7049	3.34	3.40
↓	↓	1962		伊列克得 Yiliekede		7039	3.10	3.18
0.34	0.46	2022		免渡河 Mianduhe		6979	2.01	2.09
↓	↓	2062		海　满 Haiman		6939	1.15	1.23
2.26	2.36	2137		海拉尔 Hailar		6864	23.55	0.05
3.56	4.04	2232		赫尔洪得 Hargant		6769	22.27	22.35
5.29	7.01	2323		满洲里 Manzhouli		6678	19.30	21.08
				莫斯科时间 Moscow Time				
3.26夏 2.26冬	6.30	2335		后贝加尔 Zabaikaisk		6666	11.15	15.06夏 14.06冬
15.28	15.48	2797		赤　塔 Chita		6204	0.50	1.10
1.14	1.26	3354		乌兰乌德 Ulan ude		5647	14.57	15.14
8.57	9.12	3810		伊尔库次克 Irkutsk		5191	6.39	6.54
2.59	3.14	4897		克拉斯诺亚尔斯克 Krasnoyarsk		4104	11.46	12.01
15.13	15.28	5658		新西伯利亚 Novo-sibirsk		3343	23.30	23.45
23.04	23.19	6285		鄂木斯克 Omsk		2716	15.08	15.22
10.58	11.18	7183		斯维尔德洛夫斯克 Sverdlovsk		1818	3.19	3.39
16.36	16.51	7564		彼尔姆Ⅱ PermⅡ		1437	21.18	21.34
23.52	0.07	8044		基洛夫 Kirov		957	13.57	14.17
14.55	——	9001		莫斯科 Moscow		0		23.50

Train no 19 from Beijing to Moscow starts from Beijing every Saturday and arrives in Moscow the following Friday. Train no 20 from Moscow to Beijing leaves Moscow every Friday and arrives in Beijing the following Friday.

USEFUL ADDRESSES FOR AMERICAN READERS
Information bureaux and travel agencies

US Department of State
Bureau of Security and Consular Affairs,
Passport Services,
Washington, DC 20524
They provide booklets such as *Tips for Travelers to the USSR* and *Visa Requirements of Foreign Governments.*

Council on International Educational Exchange (CIEE).
205 East 42nd Street, New York, NY 10017.
Tel: (212) 661 1414 or Toll Free: (800) 223 7402.
This organisation which is a prime source of information on budget travel, educational and work opportunities, also has offices in Boston, Providence, Austin, Seattle, Portland, San Francisco, Los Angeles and San Diego. In conjunction with the Scandinavian Student Travel Service (SSTS) it runs various tours for student travel (lower prices than the INTOURIST tours, but more spartan) to the USSR, including travel on the Trans-Siberian.

Adventure Center
5540 College Avenue, Oakland, California 94618.
Tel: (415) 654 1879.
Agents for EXPLORE holdiays on the Trans-Siberian.

Russian Travel Bureau Inc.
20 East 46th Street, New York, N.Y. 10017.
Tel: (212) 986-1500 or Toll Free: (800) 847-1800.
This is a specialist travel bureau which runs both de luxe and economy tours of Russia and Eastern Europe. Special itineraries include travel on the Trans-Siberian and options are available to continue to Mongolia, China or even 'round-the-world' via Hong Kong.

Voyages of Discovery, Inc.
737 Pearl Street, Suite 210, La Jolla, California 92037.
Tel: (619) 459-7250.
This agency runs tours world-wide, including the Trans-Siberian as a separate trip or as part of Russian, round-the-world or Asian tour itineraries.

INTOURIST
630 Fifth Avenue, Suite 868, New York, NY 10011.
This is the official Soviet travel agency which can supply information and a useful booklet called *Visiting the USSR* which lists Intourist-affiliated travel agencies.

Embassy of the USSR
1125 16th Street, N.W., Washington DC 20036.

Consulate General of the USSR.
2790 Green Street, San Francisco, CA 94123.

Hungary
Embassy of the Hungarian People's Republic
3910 Shoemaker Street, N.W., Washington, DC 20008.

IBUSZ Hungarian Travel Bureau
630 Fifth Avenue, New York, NY 10020.

Poland
Embassy of the Polish People's Republic
2640 16th Street, N.W., Washington, DC 20009.

East Germany
Embassy of the German Democratic Republic
1717 Massachusetts Avenue N.W., Washington DC 20036.

China
Embassy of the People's Republic of China
2300 Connecticut Avenue, N.W., Washington, DC 20008.

Consulates are also at the following addresses:
Guest Quarters, Suite 1509, 2929 South Post Oak Road, Houston, TX 77056.

San Francisco Hotel, Rm 1040, Union Square, San Francisco, CA 94119.
520 12th Avenue, New York, NY 10036.

For information on tourism in China:
China International Travel Service
60E, 42nd Street, Suite 465, New York, NY 10165.

US China Travel Service Inc.
500, Sutter Street, Suite 621, San Francisco, CA 94102.

Japan
Embassy of Japan
2520 Massachusetts Avenue, N.W., Washington, DC 20008.

Consulate General of Japan
280 Park Avenue at 48th Street, New York, NY 10017.

Japan Information Center
410 Park Avenue, 18th Floor, New York, NY 10022.

Japan National Tourist Organisation.
630 Fifth Avenue, New York, NY 10111.

Hong Kong
Hong Kong Information
c/o British Embassy
3100 Massachusetts Avenue, N.W., Washington, DC 20008
845 Third Avenue, New York, NY 10022.

Hong Kong Tourist Association (HKTA) addresses:
548 Fifth Avenue, New York, NY 10036.
421 Powell Street, San Francisco, CA 94102.
333 North Michigan Avenue, Chicago, IL 60601.

USEFUL ADDRESSES IN CANADA

INTOURIST
1801 McGill College Ave., Montreal, Quebec H3A 2N4.
Tel: (514) 849-6394.

Canadian Universities Travel Service (Travel CUTS)
44 St George Street, Toronto, Ontario M5S 2E4.
Tel: (416) 979-2406.
   Provides extensive information on budget travel, educational and work opportunities. Other offices in Edmonton, Halifax, Montreal, Ottawa, Saskatoon, Vancouver, Victoria and Winnipeg. They are agents for the Scandinavian Student Travel Service (SSTS) tours to the USSR.

Westcan Treks
10918 88 Avenue, Edmonton, Alberta T6G OZ1.
Tel: (403) 439-0024; (Toll Free) 1 800 661-7265.
Agents for EXPLORE holidays on the Trans-Siberian. Other offices in Toronto, Calgary and Vancouver.

Embassy of the People's Republic of China
411-415 Andrews Street, Ottawa, Ontario KIN 5H3.

USEFUL ADDRESSES IN AUSTRALIA

INTOURIST
37 Pitt Street, Sydney, N.S.W. 2000.
Tel: 277-652

Access Travel
5th Floor, 58 Pitt Street, Sydney.
Tel: 241 1128
  Organise visas and travel on the Trans-Siberian.

Adventure World
11th Floor, 220 George Street, Sydney NSW 2000.
Tel: 27 2159.
  Agents for EXPLORE holidays on the Trans-Siberian. Other offices in Melbourne, Brisbane and Adelaide.

Chinese Embassy
247 Federal Highway, Watson, Canberra, 2602 ACT.

═ РОССИЯ ═

'Before you go, even if you don't learn any Russian, it is extremely useful, especially if you are making independent tracks, to take the brief time necessary to learn the cyrillic alphabet with which Russian is written. This will make it ten times easier for you to find your way around train stations, metro stations, maps, street signs, etc.' (Lucie Lomax and Nancy Webber).

RUSSIAN ALPHABET AND KEY TO PRONUNCIATION

Russian printed alphabet	Russian written alphabet	Approximate English equivalent
Аа	*Аа*	like **a** in father (when accented)
		like **a** in aloud (when unaccented)
Бб	*Бб*	like **b** in box
Вв	*Вв*	like **v** in voice
Гг	*Гг*	like **g** in get
Дд	*Дg*	like **d** in day
Ее	*Ее*	like **ye** in yet
Ёё	*Ёё*	like **yo** in yore
Жж	*Жж*	like **s** in pleasure
Зз	*Зз*	like **z** in zoo
Ии	*Ии*	like **ee** in need
Йй	*Йй*	like **y** in boy
Кк	*Кк*	like **k** in key
Лл	*Лл*	like **l** in love
Мм	*Мм*	like **m** in men
Нн	*Нн*	like **n** in nose
Оо	*Оо*	like **o** in not
Пп	*Пп*	like **p** in put
Рр	*Рр*	like **r** in arrow
Сс	*Сс*	like **s** in miss
Тт	*Тт*	like **t** in take
Уу	*Уу*	like **u** in full
Фф	*Фф*	like **f** in fat
Хх	*Хх*	like **kh** in khan
Цц	*Цц*	like **ts** in its
Чч	*Чч*	like **ch** in chance
Шш	*Шш*	like **sh** in ship
Щщ	*Щщ*	like **shch** in fresh cheese
Ъъ	*ъ*	not pronounced
Ыы	*ы*	like short **i** in bit
Ьь	*ь*	not pronounced;
		softens the preceding consonant
Ээ	*Ээ*	like **e** in end
Юю	*Юю*	like **u** in use; **yu** in yule
Яя	*Яя*	like **ya** in yard

Breaking the ice — useful phrases

By pointing at the appropriate phrase you should manage some basic communication with your Trans-Siberian co-travellers.

RUSSIAN

Hello	Здравствуйте!
Please	Пожалуйста
Thank you	Спасибо
Yes	Да
No	Нет
Sorry	Извините!
Goodbye	До свидания
I don't understand	Не понимаю
What is your name?	Как вас зовут?
My name is...	Меня зовут...
Where are you going?	Куда вы едете?
I am going to...	Я еду в...
I am...	Я –
American*	американец/американка
British	англичанин/англичанка
Australian	австралиец/австралийка
Canadian	канадец/канадка
Where do you live?	Где вы живете?

*Where two words are given the first indicates male, the second female.

I live in...	Я живу
London	- в Лондоне
New York	- в Нью-Йорке
Moscow	- в Москве
Are you married?	Вы женаты/замужем?
Do you have children?	Есть ли у вас дети?
How old are you?	Сколько вам лет?
What is your job?	Кем вы работаете?
I am...	Я -
a student	студент/студентка
an engineer	инженер
a doctor	врач
a nurse	медсестра
a teacher	педагог
a lawyer	адвокат
unemployed	безработный/безработная
I like...	Я люблю
photography	- фотографию
singing	- пение
dancing	- танцы
travelling	- путешествовать
Do you like...?	Вы любите...?

I am...

hungry	Я хочу есть
thirsty	хочу пить
tired	устал/устала

What is this called in Russian? Как это называется по-русски?

How much? Сколько стоит?

Have a good journey! Доброго пути!

The Trans-Siberian Express makes its way around a valley in the taiga. Trains can be as much as half a kilometre long (eighteen carriages) — this photo was taken from the same train's window!

CHINESE

Hello	你好
Please	请
Thank you	谢谢你
Yes	对
No	不对
Sorry	对不起
Goodbye	再见
I don't understand	我不明白
What is your name?	你叫什么名字？
My name is...	我的名字叫......
Where are you going?	你到哪儿去？
I am going to...	我去......
I am...	我是
American	美国人
British	英国人
Australian	澳洲人
Canadian	加拿大人
Where do you live?	你住在什么地方？
I live in...	我住在
London	伦敦
New York	纽约

Are you married? 你结婚了没有？

Do you have children? 你有孩子吗？

How old are you? 你的年纪多大？

What is your job? 你干什么工作？

I am... 我是一个

a student 学生

an engineer 工程师

a doctor 医生

a nurse 护士

a teacher 教师

a lawyer 律师

unemployed 待业者

I like... 我喜欢

photography 摄影

singing 唱歌

dancing 跳舞

travelling 旅游

Do you like...? 你喜欢不喜欢……？

I am... 我

hungry 饿了

thirsty 渴了

tired 累了

What is this called in Chinese?　用　怎么说 ?

How much?　多少钱 ?

Have a good journey!　祝 你 旅 途 愉快

One	一	Eleven	十一	Thirty	三十
Two	二	Twelve	十二	Forty	四十
Three	三	Thirteen	十三	Fifty	五十
Four	四	Fourteen	十四	Sixty	六十
Five	五	Fifteen	十五	Seventy	七十
Six	六	Sixteen	十六	Eighty	八十
Seven	七	Seventeen	十七	Ninety	九十
Eight	八	Eighteen	十八	One hundred	一百
Nine	九	Nineteen	十九	One thousand	一千
Ten	十	Twenty	二十	One million	一百万

JAPANESE

Good morning	おはようございます
Good afternoon	こんにちは
Good evening	こんばんわ
Please	どうぞ
Thank you	ありがとう
Yes	はい
No	いいえ
Sorry	失礼
Goodbye	さようなら
I don't understand	わかりません
What is your name?	お名前は
My name is...	．．．．．です
Where are you going?	どちらへ 行かれますか
I am going to...	私は ... へ 行きます
I am...	
American	私は アメリカ人 です
British	〃 イギリス人 〃
Australian	〃 オーストラリア人 〃
Canadian	〃 カナダ人 〃
Where do you live?	どちらへ お住まいですか

I live in...

London 私は ロンドンに 住んでいます

New York 〃 ニューヨークに 〃

Are you married? 結婚していますか

Do you have children? お子さんは いらっしゃいますか

How old are you? おいくつですか

What is your job? お仕事は何ですか

I am... 私は ・・・ です

a student 学生

an engineer 技師

a doctor 医者

a nurse 看護婦

a teacher 教師

a lawyer 法律家

unemployed 無職

I like... 私は ・・・ が好きです

photography 写真

singing 歌を歌うの

dancing 踊り

travelling 旅行

Do you like...? あなたは ・・・ が好きですか

I am...

hungry	私は 空腹です
thirsty	喉が かわきました
tired	疲れました
What is this called in Japanese?	日本語 で何と言いますか
How much?	いくらですか
Have a good journey!	良い 御旅行を

NOTE: Japanese numerals are very similar to Chinese, so are not repeated here.

言語の教授

CALENDERS FOR TRIP PLANNING

1987

	January			
Su.	..	4	11	18	25
M.	..	5	12	19	26
Tu.	..	6	13	20	27
W.	..	7	14	21	28
Th.	.. 1	8	15	22	29
F.	.. 2	9	16	23	30
S.	.. 3	10	17	24	31

	May			
Su.	3	10	17	24	31
M.	4	11	18	25
Tu.	5	12	19	26
W.	6	13	20	27
Th.	7	14	21	28
F.	1	8	15	22	29
S.	2	9	16	23	30

	September			
Su.	6	13	20	27
M.	7	14	21	28
Tu.	1	8	15	22	29
W.	2	9	16	23	30
Th.	3	10	17	24
F.	4	11	18	25
S.	5	12	19	26

	February			
Su.	1	8	15	22
M.	2	9	16	23	30
Tu.	3	10	17	24
W.	4	11	18	25
Th.	5	12	19	26
F.	6	13	20	27
S.	7	14	21	28

	June			
Su.	7	14	21	28
M.	1	8	15	22	29
Tu.	2	9	16	23	30
W.	3	10	17	24
Th.	4	11	18	25
F.	5	12	19	26
S.	6	13	20	27

	October			
Su.	4	11	18	25
M.	5	12	19	26
Tu.	6	13	20	27
W.	7	14	21	28
Th.	1	8	15	22	29
F.	2	9	16	23	30
S.	3	10	17	24	31

	March			
Su.	1	8	15	22	29
M.	2	9	16	23	30
Tu.	3	10	17	24	31
W.	4	11	18	25
Th.	5	12	19	26
F.	6	13	20	27
S.	7	14	21	28

	July			
Su.	5	12	19	26
M.	6	13	20	27
Tu.	7	14	21	28
W.	1	8	15	22	29
Th.	2	9	16	23	30
F.	3	10	17	24	31
S.	4	11	18	25

	November			
Su.	1	8	15	22	29
M.	2	9	16	23	30
Tu.	3	10	17	24
W.	4	11	18	25
Th.	5	12	19	26
F.	6	13	20	27
S.	7	14	21	28

	April			
Su.	5	12	19	26
M.	6	13	20	27
Tu.	7	14	21	28
W.	1	8	15	22	29
Th.	2	9	16	23	30
F.	3	10	17	24
S.	4	11	18	25

	August			
Su.	2	9	16	23	30
M.	3	10	17	24	31
Tu.	4	11	18	25
W.	5	12	19	26
Th.	6	13	20	27
F.	7	14	21	28
S.	1	8	15	22	29

	December			
Su.	6	13	20	27
M.	7	14	21	28
Tu.	1	8	15	22	29
W.	2	9	16	23	30
Th.	3	10	17	24	31
F.	4	11	18	25
S.	5	12	19	26

1988

	January			
Su.	.. 3	10	17	24	31
M.	.. 4	11	18	25
Tu.	.. 5	12	19	26
W.	.. 6	13	20	27
Th.	.. 7	14	21	28
F.	1	8	15	22	29
S.	2	9	16	23	30

	May			
Su.	1	8	15	22	29
M.	2	9	16	23	30
Tu.	3	10	17	24	31
W.	4	11	18	25
Th.	5	12	19	26
F.	6	13	20	27
S.	7	14	21	28

	September			
Su.	4	11	18	25
M.	5	12	19	26
Tu.	6	13	20	27
W.	7	14	21	28
Th.	1	8	15	22	29
F.	2	9	16	23	30
S.	3	10	17	24

	February			
Su.	7	14	21	28
M.	1	8	15	22	29
Tu.	2	9	16	23
W.	3	10	17	24
Th.	4	11	18	25
F.	5	12	19	26
S.	6	13	20	27

	June			
Su.	5	12	19	26
M.	6	13	20	27
Tu.	7	14	21	28
W.	1	8	15	22	29
Th.	2	9	16	23	30
F.	3	10	17	24
S.	4	11	18	25

	October			
Su.	2	9	16	23	30
M.	3	10	17	24	31
Tu.	4	11	18	25
W.	5	12	19	26
Th.	6	13	20	27
F.	7	14	21	28
S.	1	8	15	22	29

	March			
Su.	6	13	20	27
M.	7	14	21	28
Tu.	1	8	15	22	29
W.	2	9	16	23	30
Th.	3	10	17	24	31
F.	4	11	18	25
S.	5	12	19	26

	July			
Su.	3	10	17	24	31
M.	4	11	18	25
Tu.	5	12	19	26
W.	6	13	20	27
Th.	7	14	21	28
F.	1	8	15	22	29
S.	2	9	16	23	30

	November			
Su.	6	13	20	27
M.	7	14	21	28
Tu.	1	8	15	22	29
W.	2	9	16	23	30
Th.	3	10	17	24
F.	4	11	18	25
S.	5	12	19	26

	April			
Su.	3	10	17	24
M.	4	11	18	25
Tu.	5	12	19	26
W.	6	13	20	27
Th.	7	14	21	28
F.	1	8	15	22	29
S.	2	9	16	23	30

	August			
Su.	7	14	21	28
M.	1	8	15	22	29
Tu.	2	9	16	23	30
W.	3	10	17	24	31
Th.	4	11	18	25
F.	5	12	19	26
S.	6	13	20	27

	December			
Su.	4	11	18	25
M.	5	12	19	26
Tu.	6	13	20	27
W.	7	14	21	28
Th.	1	8	15	22	29
F.	2	9	16	23	30
S.	3	10	17	24	31

Bibliography

The Trans-Siberian Railway and Siberia.

Guides and background literature
Guide to the Great Siberian Railway.
This was first published in 1900 in St Petersburg. A reprint of the English translation (Newton Abbot 1971) is now out of print.

To the Great Ocean. Siberia and the Trans-Siberian Railway by Tupper Harmon. (London, 1965). Fascinating account and recommended reading if you can find it. Out of print.

Modern travelogues
Trans-Siberia by Rail and a Month in Japan by Barbara Lamplugh (Roger Lascelles 1979). This is a personal narrative, half of which is devoted to the Trans-Siberian and the rest to Japan.

The Big Red Train Ride by Eric Newby (Weidenfeld & Nicolson 1978. Penguin 1980). Reportedly subject to spasmodic confiscation by Soviet customs, this is a lengthy account with some amusing anecdotes.

The Great Railway Adventure by Christopher Portway (Oxford Illustrated Press, 1983). A chapter on the Trans-Siberian includes an account of Portway's 'escapade' to Vladivostok in 1971.

The Great Railway Bazaar by Paul Theroux (Hamish Hamilton, 1975). The Trans-Siberian chapter seems to reflect Theroux's fatigue after a mammoth dose of train journeys.

Books on the Soviet Union
The Complete Guide to the Soviet Union by V. and J. Lewis (Michael Joseph, 1980).

Next time you go to Russia by Charles Ward (John Murray, 1980). Detailed coverage of architecture in main tourist cities.

Holy Russia by Fitzroy Maclean (Weidenfeld & Nicholson, 1978).

Russian language
Russian — Language and People by Terry Culhane (BBC Publications, 1980). An excellent short course, intended to help visitors understand enough to 'survive'.

Berlitz Russian Phrasebook. Useful pocket phrasebook.

Addenda–1988

ENGLAND

p57   The INTOURIST office in London now advises booking travel to Beijing at least three months (preferably much longer) in advance. During the peak period April–October they will only make reservations for package deals (hotel accommodation in Moscow; full board; sightseeing tours; transfer by coach; rail ticket and meals on the train as far as the Soviet border). Prices for this type of package now start at Pound Sterling 230. In Feb 1988, the London office was only able to offer tickets on the Trans-Manchurian or Trans-Mongolian routes between October and December. Prices have increased by 20% on the Japan route.

p58   Yorkshire Tours is no longer operating. The directors, Ida and Laurie Shaw, have finally retired at the age of 80!

EAST & WEST BERLIN

p77   Apparently some trains DO go direct to West Berlin (Bahnhof Zoo) – check and see if the destination on your ticket reads 'Berlin Zoo Station' or ask a bright-looking train official. If it reads simply 'Berlin', you will arrive in East Berlin (Ostbahnhof); take the S-Bahn in the direction of Alexanderplatz and ride four stops to Berlin-FRIEDRICHSTRASSE where you leave the station and follow the signs for 'Grenzuebergangsstelle'.

Once you've gone through passport control, take the S-Bahn again to Berlin-Zoo station which is in the centre of West Berlin.

A "Geldwechsel" (Bureau de Change) in the station has a 24-hour, automatic teller which accepts Eurocheque cards and dispenses German Marks.

On the Kurfurstendamm, close to the station, are several late-night cafes. Cheap accommodations at Bahnhofsmission (turn right from the Zoo station, 200 metres down a side street under the railway arches). Also, Jugendgästehaus am Zoo (4th floor of Bote und Boch building, Hardenberg Strasse 9a).

INTOURIST
153A Friedrichstr., 1080 Berlin, E. Germany
Tel 229-19-48

INTOURIST
Kurfurstendamm, 1000 Berlin 15, W. Germany
Tel 88-00-77

SCANDINAVIA

p87   FINLAND
INTOURIST
Etela Esplanaadi 14, 00130 Helsinki 13, Finland
Tel 63-18-75

DENMARK
INTOURIST
Vester Farimagsgade 6, 1606 Copenhagen V
Tel (01) 11-25-27

SWEDEN
INTOURIST
Sergelgatan 21, 11157 Stockholm
Tel 21-59-34

USSR

p103 The Bolshoi Theatre building is closing for major structural repairs which are expected to take three years.

p106 Telephone number for the Mongolian embassy: 241 10 46. Open from 9am to 6pm, Monday to Friday; closes between 1pm and 2pm.

p107 For foreign visitors, the Poste Restante address in Moscow is:
c/o Intourist, Moscow K600.
This is the address of the post office for foreign visitors which is in the Intourist Hotel, 3-5 Gorky St. Some mail makes it, some doesn't.

MONGOLIA

p140 Diplomatic relations between Mongolia and the USA were resumed in February, 1987.

CHINA

p153 Travelers report that another section of the Beijing subway has just been opened (see map). The Soviet embassy is very close to 'Dongzhimen' subway station which is only three stops from the 'Jianguomen' subway station, a short walk from the Mongolian and Polish embassies.

p155 The noticeboard at the Qiaoyuan hotel sometimes has inspiring news for buyers of last-minute Hungarian Trans-Sib tickets, but check that the expiration date doesn't fall before your date of travel.

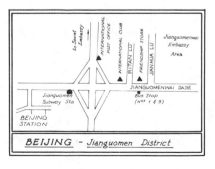

BEIJING - Jianguomen District

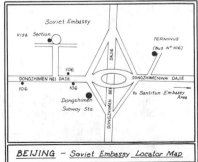

BEIJING - Soviet Embassy Locator Map

p158   Apart from using the newly opened top loop of the Beijing subway (see note for p153 and locator maps) there are now several more ways to get to embassy areas from the Qiao Yuan Hotel or from the CITS office.

From CITS:
For the Mongolian and Polish embassies, take bus No 1 or 4 one block north of CITS and travel east to the Friendship Store. For the Soviet embassy, take trolley bus No. 106 which stops across the road from CITS and goes north. Get off one stop before the terminus.

From the QIAO YUAN HOTEL:
For the Mongolian and Polish embassies, take trolley bus 106 and get off at the CITS stop before taking bus No 1 or 4 going east. For the Soviet embassy, take trolley bus 106 and get off one stop before the terminus.

p161   Soviet Embassy. Does not open on Thurs, but on Wed from 9am–1pm. Transit visas available in 4 days for Y4OFEC or in 10 days for Y5FEC.
Polish transit visas now cost Y26FEC. All trains pass through Poland within one day, so make sure you write "one day" under "length of stay". If you don't, you'll be given a tourist visa (Y52FEC) which also requires US$15 to be changed for each day of your stay.

p162   Luggage lockers no longer available.

p163   Guangzhou (Canton). Bikes can be hired for YO.90RMB per hour, NOT Y90RMB!

p160   Mongolian Embassy. Opening hours are 8am–10am on Mon, Tues and Fri. Transit visas available same day for US$24 (pick up at 3pm) or the following day for US$16 (pick up during office hours). They don't often have change, so take the exact amount in CASH. A stopover in Mongolia requires an entry visa (4 photos; US$18) and permission, obtained via telex (232U-BT TLX) or letter, from ZHUULCHIN (the State Travel Bureau) in Ulan Bator. When purchasing tickets from China Railway Service, you usually have to book seven days in advance.

p164   Hong Kong. Taxis are now HK$5.50 for the first 2 km. Moneychanging: the exchange rate for sterling is HK$14; the rate against the US$ is fixed at HK$7.80.

p167   **Hong Kong Student Travel Bureau** have moved their customer departments which are now close to the Star Ferry Terminal on Kowloon side:

833-835 Star House, Tsimshatsui, Kowloon
(Tel 3-696323).
1021 Star House, Tsimshatsui, Kowloon
(Tel 3-7213269 or 3-693804).

In room 1023A, there's a "Traveller's Corner" with a collection of guide books available for reading on the spot.

Wallem Travel, the local agents for AEROFLOT and INTOURIST, have set up a separate "Russia desk". Since this desk is about to move, it may be best to check with the Hong Kong Tourist Authority (HKTA) who will be able to provide the new address.

The current address is:
WALLEM Travel Ltd.
Suite 202, D'Aguilar Place, 7, D'Aguilar Street.
Tel: 5-221 144

Vanbond is a new company, run by Joseph Lo,specialising in travel to the USSR including Trans-Siberian options. Tel 5-410 700. Check address details with HKTA.

JAPAN

p179   The full address for the Japan-Soviet Travel Bureau is:
Kamiyacho Bldg., Annex, 2-4-1 Hamamatsucho, Minato-ku
Tokyo 105. Tel (03)432-6161

Their updated prices for 2nd class tickets are:

Nakhodka–Khabarovsk	Y/8,000
Khabarovsk–Moscow	Y/30,000

Moscow to:

Berlin	Y/16,000
Budapest	Y/14,000
Paris	Y/55,000
London (via Oostende)	Y/60,000
Helsinki	Y/13,000

These prices are due to be increased by 20% in 1988.

China National Tourist Office:
1-27-13 Hammatsu-cho, 6th Fl, Minato-ku, Tokyo
Tel 03-433-1461

p180   Chinese Embassy
Moto-Azabu 3-4—33, Minato-ku, Tokyo
Tel 403-3383

APPENDICES

p183-5   In 1987, the number of places automatically open to foreigners bearing a valid visa was increased to 430.

p186   By late 1987, CITS had raised the prices for Trans-Siberian tickets by 43%. However, devaluation of the Chinese Yuan means that the price can still seem favourable if considered in a hard currency such as US dollars. CITS plans no further price raises in 1988.

SINGAPORE

For USSR and Trans-Siberian reservations contact: Sinair Travel Agency, 5 Fl,527 Orchard Towers, Orchard Road, Singapore 9. Flights to Beijing o/w are about US$500.

THAILAND
Most of the travel agencies in S-E Asia have found it quick and convenient to use the USSR embassy in Bangkok rather than its counterpart in Tokyo. The local agency for Trans-Siberian Travel is:
Global Union Express, 21/4 Thai Wah Tower, 3rd Floor,
Sathorn Road, Bangkok 10120.
Flights to Beijing o/w are about S$387.

AUSTRALIA
Trans-Sib trips are becoming popular with Aussie travellers as an alternative Asian overland route. Prices start around A$4000 for a journey all the way to London.

The following agencies offer Trans-Siberian trips with a variety of Chinese, Mongolian or Japanese combinations:
Access Travel
5th Fl, 58 Pitt St, Sidney NSW 2000
Tel (02) 241 1128

INTOURIST
Underwood House,37-49 Pitt Street, Sydney NSW 2000
Tel (02) 277652

Sundowners Travel Centre
10th Fl, 66 King St, Sydney NSW 2000
Tel (02) 29 1511
Also has offices in Melbourne, Adelaide, Brisbane and Perth.

STA, 220 Faraday St, Carlton, Melbourne, Victoria
Tel (03) 347 6911

Eastern Europe Travel Bureau
Tel (02) 262 1144

For general information on China try:
China National Tourist Office
Floor 11, 55 Clarence Street, Sydney NSW 2000
Tel (02) 29 4057

HONG KONG
p187   Good news! The agency tariffs have been reduced on some routes by over 20%.

USA/CANADA
p191   The following agencies can arrange travel to the USSR:
CALIFORNIA
Amity Tours
  1735 East Bayshore Rd., #29B, Redwood City, CA 94063........(415) 364-5930 800-523-8406
ANI Travel Service
  447 North Azusa Ave., West Covina, CA 91791... (818) 915-5811
Beverly International Travel, Inc.
  9465 Wilshire Blvd., #431 Beverly Hills, CA 90212........................... (213) 271-4116,272-3011

Inter-Tours Corp.
164 S. Edinburgh Ave., Los Angeles, CA 90048......................... (213) 933-7153 800-421-4690
Love Holidays, Inc.
15315 Magnolia Blvd. #110 Sherman Oaks, CA 91403.............. (213) 873-7991 800-423-5458
Margo's International Travel Service
1812 Irving Street, San Francisco, CA 94122........................... (415)665-4330,800-33 MARGO
Russart Travel Service
291 Geary St., #511, San Francisco, CA 94102.. (415) 781-6655
Sidon Travel & Tourism, Inc.
5825 Sunset Blvd., #217, Los Angeles, CA 90028....................... (213) 466-9161 800-826 7960
TRAVCOA (Travel Corporation of America)
4000 MacArthur Blvd., #650E., Newport Beach, CA 92660....... (714) 476-2800 800-992-2003
Vart Travel Agency
5300 Santa Monica Blvd., #207, Los Angeles, CA 90029................................. (213) 465-4926
Visas International,Inc.
3169 Barbara Court, #F, Los Angeles, CA 90068........................ (213) 850-1192 800-638-1517
Voyages of Discovery
1298 Prospect, Suite 2G, La Jolla, CA 92037............................. (619) 459-6160 800 453 0123

DISTRICT OF COLUMBIA
Tour Designs, Inc.
510 H St., S.W. Washington, D.C. 20024.................................... (202) 554-5820 800-432-8687
Travel Advisors of America
1413 K St., N.W., #800, Washington, D.C. 20005.. (202) 371-1440

FLORIDA
Cosmos International Tours, Inc.
12 South Dixie Highway, Lake Worth FL 33460.................... (305) 585-5187 800-556-5305

ILLINOIS
American Travel Service Bureau
9727 South Western Avenue, Chicago, IL 60643.. (312) 238-9787
Citi Travel, Inc.
500 Skokie Blvd., Northbrook, IL 60062 ....(312) 564-8240
Gordon Travel Service, Inc.
Prudential Plaza, Chicago, IL 60601.. (312) 644-3003
TRAVCOA (Travel Corporation of America)
875 North Michigan Avenue, #3732, Chicago, IL 60611........ (312) 951 2900 800-992-2005
Vega International Travel Service, Inc.
201 North Wells St., #430, Chicago, IL 60606... (312) 332-7211

KANSAS
Maupintour, Inc.
1515 St.Andrews Dr.,Lawrence,KS 66046(and branch offices)(913)843-1211 800-255-4266

MASSACHUSETTS
Crimson Travel Service
39 JFK Street, Cambridge, MA 02138... (617) 868-2600
Coloyan Travel Service
379 Trapelo Road, Belmont, MA 02178... (617) 489-1860
Garber Travel Service Inc.
1406 Beacon St., Brookline, MA 02146............................... (617) 566-2100 800-225-4570
Harvard Travel Service, Inc.
1356 Massachusetts Ave., Cambridge, MA 02138... (617) 868-8080
Trans-Atlantic Travel Service, Inc.
393 West Broadway, P.O. Box 116, So. Boston, MA 02127... (617) 268-8764 800-722-1300

University Travel Company, Inc.
129 Mt. Auburn St., Cambridge, MA 02138.. (617) 864-7800
Wegiel Tours, Inc.
1985 Main Street, Springfield, MA 01103 ....(413) 734-8223

NEW JERSEY
Scope Travel
845 Sanford Ave., Newark, N.J. 07106 ....(201) 371-4004 800-242-7267
Sunny Land Tours, Inc.
166 Main Street, Hackensack, N.J. 07601............................... (201) 487-2150 800-631-1992

NEW YORK
Allied Travel, Inc.
11 East 44 St., New York, NY 10017... (212) 661-7200
American Express Co.
All branch Offices in the USA 800-241-1700
American Travel Abroad, Inc.
250 West 57 St., #1120 New York, NY 10107......................... (212)586-5230 800-228-0877
Anniversary Tours, Inc.
250 West 57 St., #1428, New York, NY 10107......................... (212) 245-7501 800 223-1336
Bennet Tours, Inc.
270 Madison Ave., New York, NY 10016............................... (212) 532-5060 800-221-2420
Cosmos Travel, Inc.
40 E. 49 St., New York, NY 10017................................... (212) 832-7550
Extra Value Travel, Inc.
437 Madison Ave., 26th Floor, New York, NY 10022.............. (212) 750-8800 800-223-1980
Five Star Touring Inc.
60 East 42 St., #1733, New York, NY 10165...................... (212) 818-9140/41 800-792 7827
General Tours, Inc.
770 Broadway, 10th Floor, New York, NY 10003
(& branch offices)... (212) 598-1800 800-221-2216
International Cruise Center, Inc.
185 Willis Ave., Mineola, NY 11501..................................... (516) 747-8880 800-221-3254
ITG Russia Tours, Inc.
175 Fifth Ave., #211, New York, NY 10010........................... (212) 474-7773 800-327-3765
Inter-Pacific Tours International
485 Fifth Ave., 2nd Floor, New York, NY 10017................... (212) 953-6010 800-221-3594
Kobasniuk Travel, Inc.
157 Second Ave., New York, NY 10003 .... (212) 254-8779
Orbis Polish Travel Bureau, Inc.
500 Fifth Avenue, #1428, NY 10110............................... (212) 391-0844
Russian Travel Bureau, Inc.
20 East 46 St., New York, NY 10017 (& branch offices)........ (212) 986-1500 800-847-1800
Robert J. Ellyn Travel, Inc.
501 Fifth Ave., #1605, New York, NY 10017......................... (212) 972-0200 800-935-6688
Simiro International Travel, Inc.
424 Madison Ave., #707, New York, NY 10017 ....(212) 838-2490
The Cortell Group, Inc.
3 East 54th St., New York, NY 10022 ....(212) 751-3250 800-223-6626
UAS Travel, Inc.
767 Third Avenue, New York, NY 10017............................... (212) 371-0088 800-223-5633
Union Tours,Inc.
79 Madison Avenue, Suite 1104, New York, NY 10016............................... (212) 683-9500

OHIO
Shipka Travel Agency, Inc.
5434 State Rd., Cleveland, OH 44134.. (216) 351-1700

PENNSYLVANIA
Travel Anywhere
Society Hill Towers Plaza, Philadelphia, PA 19106............... (215) 923-4300 800-523-1650

TEXAS
Atlas Travel, Inc.
3411 Montrose Blvd., Houston, TX 77006...................................... (713) 527-4555
Percival Tours, Inc.
One Tandy Center Plaza, #400, Fort Worth, TX 76102........... (817) 870-0030 800-433-5656

WASHINGTON
Bendel Tours, Inc.
12057 15th Ave., N.E. Seattle, WA 98125 ....(206) 362-5930
Klineburger Worldwide Travel
3627 First Ave., South, Seattle, WA 98134 ....(206) 343-9699
Eastern Europe Tours
1402 3rd Ave., #1127, Seattle, WA 98101............................... (206) 682-8911 800-641-3456
University Travel Service, Inc.
4534 11th Avenue N.E., Seattle, WA 98105........................... (206) 527-6544 800-426-6602

ALBERTA
East-West Travel
10553A-97th St., Edmonton T5H 2L4... (403) 424-8284
P. Lawson Travel Ltd.
705-5 St., S.W., Calgary, T2P 1V8.. (403) 263-4810
P. Lawson Travel Ltd.
Ap. 1806 Principal Plaza 10303, Edmonton T5J 3N6.................................... (403) 428-1422

BRITISH COLUMBIA
Globe Tours
2679 E. Hasting St., Vancouver V5K 1Z5.. (604) 253-1221
P. Lawson Travel Ltd.
150-409 Granville St., Vancouver V6C 1T4...................................... (604) 682-4272
Intra- Hagan's Travel Service Ltd.
5915 West Boulevard, Vancouver V6M 3X1...................................... (604) 263-1951

MANITOBA
Globe Tours, 613 Selkirk Ave., Winnipeg R2W 2N2 .... (204) 586-8371
P. Lawson Travel Ltd.
444 St. Mary Ave., Winnipeg R3C 3T1... (204) 944-9900

NOVA SCOTIA
P. Lawson Travel Ltd.
Suite 400, 5991 Spring Garden Rd., Halifax B3H 1Y6................................... (902) 429-3100

ONTARIO
Allan's Travel Service Ltd.
30 Metcalfe St., Suite 606, Ottowa K1P 5L4 ....(613) 237-0400
Canadian Travel Abroad Ltd.
80 Richmond St., West, Suite 1202, Toronto M5H 2A4................................. (416) 364-2738
Cansov Travel Ltd.
280 Queen St., West Toronto M5W 2A1... (416) 977-5819
Globe Tours
962 Bloor St., West, Toronto M6H 1L6 ....(416) 531-3593

Kentours
  294 Queens St., West, Toronto M5V 2A1 .... (416) 593-0837
P. Lawson Travel Ltd.
  Suite 1817, 2 Carlton St., Toronto M5B 1K2.. (416) 977-7581
Intours Corporation
  1013, Bloor St., West, Toronto M6H 1M1.. (416) 537-2168
Super Tours
  2461 Bloor St., West, Suite 6, Toronto M6S 1P7... (416) 762-7803

QUEBEC
Exotik Tours
  1117, St. Catherine St., West, Suite 905, Montreal H3B 1H9......................... (514) 284 3324
La Societé Culturelle Québec-URSS Voyages Inc.
  4570 Rue St. Denis, Montréal H2J 2L3 ....(514) 845-5778
Voyages Globe Tour
  4570 Rue St. Denis, Montréal H2J 2L3 ....(514) 845-5481

NEW ZEALAND
Sun Travel
120 Great South Road, Newmarket, Auckland
Tel 543 389
Arranges Trans-Siberian itineraries

RECENT NEWS–SOVIET FAR EAST & NORTH EASTERN CHINA

Of interest to Trans-Siberian travelers is the recent news that China and the USSR have reached agreement on thier border along the Amur river.

INTOURIST and CITS are finalising details for river trips along the Amur. Visitors will be able to travel between Heihe in China and Khabarovsk in the USSR, possibly with a stop-over in Blagoveshchensk.

There are also plans for direct flights between Harbin (China) and Khabarovsk; flights already operate within China between Harbin and Heihe.

Despite catastophic forest fires on both sides of the border, particularly in the Dahinggan region, tourism officials expect to be able to continue with their projects.

TRAVELER'S TIPS AND COMMENTS
CHINA

"The radio announced our impending approach to BADALING. The Great Wall (Chinese: Wan Li Chang Cheng). We had pre-arranged a trip to the Great Wall once we'd arrived in Beijing so this stop en route (Trans-Mongolian) was a bonus. With 15 minutes or so on the platform we had time to marvel at one of the wonders of the world..."
(David and Pat Evans, England)

"More than four weeks in advance, I went to CITS in Shanghai. I left Y20 with them for a phone call which they made whilst I was away. When I came back–Shanghai CITS had done the paperwork in the meantime–I bought my ticket to Berlin."
(Almuth Higler, W. Germany)

MONGOLIA

"The paranoia about film and photography has subsided somewhat. After winding film back and stashing irreplaceable exposed rolls down underpants (quite painful, this), our entire compliment of passengers passed through both border posts unmolested. Even more surprisingly, at Ulan Bator I (almost) detected smiles on the official's faces as mass photography took place on the platform during our 30-minute stop. However, it still helps to have innocent glossy magazines to break the ice with customs officials. One young guard spent half an hour in our compartment engrossed in an article about marine life. His enthusiasm was understandable when you consider that he had never seen the sea." (John Pilkington, England)

WEST GERMANY

"There are several 'Mitfahrzentrale' in Berlin. They are listed in the phone book. Ring them up, leave your address and pay a small insurance fee (about DM10). A lift to Cologne costs about DM50." (Almuth Higler, W. Germany)

Author's note: the lift-sharing idea is now more widespread in Europe where the biggest organisations operate under the name INTERSTEP. In England, the place to contact is Liftoff CarSharing Service, PO Box 1000, London, SE17 2UA.

Index
See Table of Contents for other subjects.

"In Siberia a hundred kilometres is not a distance, ten degrees is not a frost, a double vodka is not a drink and 40 years is not a woman".
(Siberian proverb).

SOME OTHER TRAVEL BOOKS FROM BRADT PUBLICATIONS

In Malaysia by Denis Walls and Stella Martin.
An anecdotal and personal account of the traditions, beliefs, festivals and wildlife of the Malay Peninsular. Includes a guide to lesser known places.

The Two Year Mountain by Phil Deutschle.
Two stories are interwoven here: the author's account of life and events in an isolated Himalayan village where he taught science for two years as a Peace Corps volunteer, and his solo expedition to climb 20,000 foot peaks in the Everest region.

Up the Creek by John Harrison.
An exciting account of a canoe trip up one of Brazil's least explored rivers — the Jari

Backpacker's Africa by Hilary Bradt.
A very popular guide to east, central and southern Africa, mainly for walkers and overlanders.

Backpacking and Trekking in Peru and Bolivia by Hilary Bradt.
The fourth edition, published in 1987, of this 'bible' for Andean explorers. Numerous treks and walks, plus information and travel tips on all aspects of the two countries

Backpacking in Mexico and Central America by Hilary Bradt and Rob Rachowiecki.
Second edition. The first book to cover the countryside of Central America in detail, with a particular emphasis on Costa Rica and its excellent national parks. Also information on climbing Mexico's volcanoes.

This is just a selection of the books and maps for adventurous travellers that we stock. Send for our latest catalogue.

Bradt Publications, 41 Nortoft Rd, Chalfont St Peter, Bucks SL9 0LA, England

Some of the above books are available from Hunter Publishing, USA. See page iv for address.